Wisdom from Reb Zalman
Embracing the Jewish Spirit

WISDOM FROM REB ZALMAN

Embracing the Jewish Spirit

Edited by

Goldie Milgram and Shohama Wiener
with Carola de Vries Robles
and Robert Esformes

Introduction by Rodger Kamenetz

Reclaiming Judaism Press

First Edition

Published by Reclaiming Judaism Press
A Division of Reclaiming Judaism
17 Rodman Oval, New Rochelle, NY 10805
www.ReclaimingJudaism.org

Permission forms for reprints and citations are downloadable at
www.ReclaimingJudaism.org.
Information: rebgoldie@gmail.com or (+1) 914-500-5696.

A CIP catalogue record for this book has been requested through the
Library of Congress

ISBN-13: 978-0-9915489-3-4

Reclaiming Judaism Press
A Division of Reclaiming Judaism
17 Rodman Oval
New Rochelle, NY 10805
Manufactured in the United States of America
10 9 8 7 6 5 4 3 2 1

In Memoriam

"Reb Zalman"
Rabbi Zalman Schachter-Shalomi
August 28, 1924 - July 3, 2014

I went up to Reb Zalman and said,
"Reb Zalman, you're a rock star!"

He smiled and replied,
"No, I'm a jazz singer."

— Vignette provided by Jack (Ya'akov) Gabriel [0.1]

TABLE OF CONTENTS

Reb Zalman at Lama Foundation, 1988
Photo Credit: David Pascale

The Tale of the Ear
By Howard Schwartz

It had rained all day and night in Zolkiev, and a few drops fell into Reb Hayim Elya's study. When he went there in the morning, he saw something strange outside the door—it looked like an ear! Bending closer, he saw that it was a flesh-colored mushroom, looking exactly like an ear. It had appeared overnight, and there it was, a mushroom in the shape of an ear, at the entrance of his study.

Hayim Elya knew the mushroom must be a sign, but of what? Now normally, when perplexed, Hayim Elya would seek out Reb Zalman. He would no doubt know whether it was a good sign or a bad one, and what it meant. But now Reb Zalman had taken leave of this world and was no longer among them. So Hayim Elya asked himself, "What would Reb Zalman say?" Hayim Elya meditated on this question all day.

Night fell, and this time the sky was clear, and the stars could be seen. As he stood there, peering into the stars, Hayim Elya tried again to think of what Reb Zalman would tell him, and at that instant he heard Reb Zalman's voice saying, "Listen!"

Foreword

Welcome. Our goal in this volume is to deliver diverse replicable examples of Reb Zalman's radically innovative, illuminating, and often healing approaches to relational spirituality, i.e., experiences that arise within, between, and Beyond. We hope that you can then benefit from applying these examples in your own life and work.

These over 250 vignettes and small stories from 118 contributing authors have been carefully edited to reveal only what Reb Zalman said and did that changed their Jewish and/or personal journeys, so that you, the reader, are given space to have your own thoughts, feelings, and interpretations of what he said and did — to have your own experience of his approaches to restoring spirituality and spiritual intimacy to Judaism.

We decided to remove or minimize any accolades, or subsequent feelings and thoughts on the part of the contributing authors — his beloved students and colleagues — in order to provide a word portrait of Reb Zalman. Hundreds of stories and vignettes arrived in incredibly diverse formats, and distilling them down to the essence you find here was a deeply challenging creative task for editors and contributing authors.

While there are many published books of Reb Zalman's own writings, many published analyses of his role in Jewish religious history and philosophy, and a number of festschrifts (collections) dedicated to him, this book is something new and different — it is a learning tool that we pray you will bring to discuss, debate, implement, and adapt some of Reb Zalman's approaches with your friends, families, students, and communities. His dream was to co-create a healthy and holy Jewish future with you, and to empower us all going forward to evolve Judaism as a world wisdom tradition for the good of All That Is and Will Be.

Acknowledgements

As co-editors and innovators in the field of Jewish spiritual education and guidance, we are profoundly thankful for the investment of wisdom, time, attention to detail, and editing flexibility of the contributing authors—Rodger Kamenetz for the Introduction, Howard Schwartz for the two tales, Robert Esformes and Steve Schwartz for copy editing, Reuben and Yehudit Goldfarb for proofreading, Carola de Vries Robles for chapter advising, James Royce Young for the cover photo, David Pascale and Justin Freed for the inside photos, Kayla Niles for the glossary, and Karen Farkas for administrative support, and, as is our policy, to the ever-unnamed full array of jurors.

Reb Zalman had a way of saying goodbye that Carola de Vries Robles sent in, "Each time I see you, I love you more." And, as she sent to us, "Reb Zalman, each time I think of you, I love you more." And so do we. Participation in this volume reflects the gratitude of all contributing authors for the love and support Reb Zalman so generously gave us, and to so many the world over.

Transliteration, Translation, and Formatting Notes
The translation of a word appears at its first occurrence in the text, and can also be found in the glossary. Transliterations show the sound for pronunciation, rather than nuanced correlation with specific Hebrew letters. Most non-English terms are translated at their first appearance within the text and, if they recur, can be found in the glossary. Contributing authors' preferences as to terming the phenomenon Reb Zalman set in motion as Jewish Renewal or Jewish renewal are honored herein.

With blessings upon your lives and pathways,
Goldie Milgram and Shohama Wiener

Introduction
By Rodger Kamenetz

Reb Zalman began life as a German-speaking Viennese Jew with a Galician-Polish background. He became a *Hassid*, a devotee of Chabad, in the early forties, at the time of his arrival in America, but by the late fifties was already venturing into wider contexts of psychology and comparative religion. In the 1960s, Reb Zalman plunged chin deep into the American counterculture, learning from and teaching to a new generation. With chutzpah and joy, he burst through the narrow barriers of denominationalism and factionalism, gradually establishing an entirely post-denominational approach—known now as Jewish renewal. Like a modern day North American Baal Shem Tov, he turned attention back to the power of prayer, ecstasy, and joy in Jewish life, creating a model for a vibrant, renewed, enthusiastic, inclusive, active living Judaism.

One great achievement: Reb Zalman brought God back into serious consideration. Fancy talk about God was never as important, Reb Zalman taught, as experiencing the presence of God in this very moment. It was Reb Zalman who first insisted that God is a verb—not a noun—that any God we can name is already inadequate to our experience and the mystery of creation. And he insisted that such experience was possible, now, right here, because he knew the many phases of his own life presented many faces of God, each one appearing convincing and real, yet soon replaced by another, also convincing and real.

Reb Zalman spoke of God in an unembarrassed and unembarrassing language which the postwar generation of Jews could absorb. He incorporated humanistic and Gestalt psychology, Freud and Jung, and contemporary science in his discourse. He intuitively understood that the word God and other Hebrew terms needed to be made more user-friendly. So he would say, *Yah*, as in *hallelu-Yah*—praise God, or *Shechinah*, pronounced in his warm Yiddishstyle as *Sh'chinna*—God as the experience of divine Presence in nature and in prayer. He warmed up the traditional *Ribono shel Olam*, Master of All Worlds, with the Yiddish inflection *"Riboino Sheleilem."* He would encourage us to spell God not as G-d but as G!d.

Reb Zalman was a living emissary from the old Jewish world to the new, and he carried all of its traumas. He'd fled the Nazis with his family through Belgium, to an internment camp in France, to North Africa, to the Caribbean, finally landing in New York City in 1941. Along the way he met Rabbi Menachem Mendel Schneersohn (later to become the seventh Chabad Rebbe) in Marseilles and was deeply impressed by his mystical teachings. In New York he received ordination from the Lubavitcher Yeshiva. His talents for outreach were recognized by the sixth Rebbe, Yosef Yitzchak Schneersohn, who sent him as an emissary to college campuses. Reb Zalman especially loved speaking with young Jews drawn to other spiritual traditions.

Reb Zalman's own natural curiosity eventually led him into academic realms. He took a Master of Arts degree in the Psychology of Religion in pastoral counseling at Boston University, studying with Howard Thurman (who was also Martin Luther King's teacher). He later earned a Doctor of Hebrew Letters from Hebrew Union College. He taught in the Department of Religion at the University of Manitoba, and at Temple University. His last academic position was as the first holder of the World Wisdom Chair at Naropa University in Boulder.

Reb Zalman found God in the heavens and holy sanctuaries, the charts and letters of the Jewish mystics, in the music and dancing of group prayer, in solitary meditation, and in the face of the person praying in front of him. Applying the language of Kabbalah, with its ten *sefirot*, divine attributes, and Four Worlds— physical, emotional, intellectual and spiritual—he gave people a sophisticated reality map for their inner experiences, and helped them outgrow the constrictions of pediatric Judaism. He insisted on a Judaism that could be experienced and not just verbalized.

Reb Zalman understood the need for a renewed Jewish language in the post-*Shoah* (Holocaust) era. Back in the sixties, when death of God theology became re-popularized, he responded that the issue was really the death of God's old name. To "update the Jewish software," he brought Hassidic teachings into the computer and Internet age, embracing the vocabulary of contemporary technology as yet another storehouse of metaphors to describe the unnameable and ineffable. He introduced the Talmud to chaos theory, Kabbalah to laser beams. His theology sounded at times like spiritual science fiction as he speculated about *Shabbos* on the moon, the consciousness of an entire planet, and how meditation reformats the layers of the brain.

Reb Zalman was also a tremendous social innovator. He made Jewish renewal open, porous, and available across the spectrum of Jewish life. He welcomed the intermarried and the hyphenated into the great dance of the Sabbath bride. As a teacher and prayer leader, he stimulated the mysteries of individual attunement to the magisterial radio of the group mind. Zalman also combined forces with Jewish social change agents, anti-war protesters, passionate environmentalists, and Israeli peace activists.

A proponent of what he named "deep ecumenism," Reb Zalman dialogued with Catholic monks, imams, Native American shamans, and religious and secular healers from cultures worldwide. He danced with Muslims at Joseph's tomb, becoming an ordained Sufi sheik in the order of Pir Vilayat Khan, taught with Buddhist monks, and met the Dalai Lama on solid ground, even while invoking angels. He came to terms with emerging feminism and did *teshuva* (admission of the need for adjustment) for the patriarchal mindset of his early education, moving his reverent focus over the decades from Kabbalah's distant and infinite uttermost *Ein Sof* (ineffable eternity) to a warm female presence, *Shekhinah*, friendly to the body and embodied most dearly in the natural beauties of mother Earth.

By combining Hassidism with social conscience, Reb Zalman revived something like the brief flowering of urban Hassidism that arose in Vienna, Warsaw, Leipzig, and Berlin between the wars—the Hassidism of Hillel Zeitlin and the socialist Chabadniks of Antwerp—and brought it to bloom in its American setting. In many ways, he put into actual practice the more literary and theoretical neo-Hassidism of his two great predecessors, Martin Buber and Rabbi Abraham Joshua Heschel. They wrote of imagined and remembered rebbes, whereas Reb Zalman remembered and imagined that rebbes could be any one of us, gay, trans, or lesbian, and certainly female. In other ways, he complemented the outreach work of Chabad Hassidism, his original spiritual home in America. Reb Zalman was like some deep undercover agent of the Rebbe himself, sent to open the hearts and minds of those Chabad could never hope to reach.

Of course he did none of this alone; he did it in the company of colleagues and students, lovers and friends, wives and children. Many of his students and colleagues in Jewish renewal became strong and independent figures in the Jewish landscape. Always, Reb Zalman was thinking ahead of the tasks he wished to complete, the work he still had to do. If two words could define him, "thinking ahead" would be good candidates. And that was one of the paradoxes of his life: that a born futurologist had spent most of his life wrestling with, cajoling, pushing, "agenting" change for one of the most ancient religious traditions on the planet. His organization to advance the return of the Jewish spirit after the Holocaust, ALEPH: Alliance for Jewish Renewal, grew out of the B'nai Or Religious Fellowship, which he had founded in 1962.

Reb Zalman was an innately, deeply curious experimentalist, with a true scientific bent, who also engaged himself with the tradition of rabbinic rules and God-given eternal laws. This pragmatic mystic used his platforms to help healing happen by insisting that the most ineffable spiritual experiences were discussible, mappable and replicable, that there was an assignable value to "socialized meditation," that the findings of prayer were no less verifiable than the findings of the laboratory. He integrated difficult opposites: future and past, the particular and universal, the pragmatic and the mystical.

In doing so, Reb Zalman widened the expression of Judaism and opened up the gates of a renewed Jewish connection to an often alienated generation. He created a meeting ground for such disparate forces as Kabbalah and feminism, political activism and Torah, deep ecumenism and Jewish particularism, Gaian ecology and his renewed approach to *halachah* (Jewish law), first called *psycho-halachah* and later called "Integral Halachah." This approach took into account the human experience, and ways to compassionately texture and evolve Jewish ethics. For this process-based approach and all of his innovations, Reb Zalman loved to invoke Rav Kook: "What is old becomes new and what is new becomes holy."

Reb Zalman began privately ordaining rabbis in 1974, but did not give *smicha* (ordination) to a woman until 1981. Ten years later, when I first encountered Jewish renewal, the presence and energy of women teachers was powerful. Since 2003 the process of ordination has evolved and been formalized into the first hybrid distance learning and residential Jewish seminary, the ALEPH Ordination Program, which has become a substantial and influential body in Jewish life.

Reb Zalman's teaching helped found the now rapidly developing field of Eco-Kosher living. He emphasized sensitivity to support-ing Gaia, the earth's need for human support through careful attention to recycling, free-range farming of animals, proper and timely compensation and care for workers, and a wide range of environmental precepts.

Around age 60, after a forty-day retreat at the Lama Foundation, Reb Zalman became concerned about the problems of despair and depression that so often troubled older people. He began developing what he called "conscious aging," how a contemplative view of one's own aging process could lead one to harvest the wisdom of a lifetime in order to serve as a "spiritual elder." This became the Spiritual Eldering Institute, a program that continues to be developed and offered by founders and graduates.

By 1999, Reb Zalman had given over the leadership of ALEPH. He felt that as he aged, the organization needed a more vigorous direction from younger people. To mark this transition, he created instructive events, including his seventy-fifth birthday, where the achievements of the past were acknowledged and recognized and the new leadership installed with his blessings.

Toward the end of his life, Reb Zalman entered what he called the "December Years." This too, became a project, which included teaching, writing, and talking honestly about body changes, pain, and how personal foci shift toward simplicity, completions, joy, love, and a fearlessness born of the sense that "something continues." He sought and offered spiritual tasks, tools, and coping strategies for this season of life, as he had in his writings and teachings for each of life's seasons.

Reb Zalman left behind a number of books for guidance, including *The First Step* which became widely distributed as an appendix of the *First Jewish Catalog*. His book *Spiritual Intimacy* is a scholarly study of Hassidic counseling (1991). Among many important works are *Paradigm Shift* (1995), *Jewish with Feeling* (2005), *A Heart Afire: Stories and Teachings of the Early Hassidic Masters* (2009), *Sh'ma: A Concise Weekday Siddur for Praying in English* (2010), *Gate to the Heart: A Manual of Contemplative Jewish Practice* (2013), and *The December Project* (2014).

Reb Zalman taught one last class over Shavuot in 2014. He gave his blessings to new teachers, he conscientiously said his personal farewells to long-time friends, and even left behind personal messages. I received one through Goldie [Milgram]—that I will never forget. He told me, "I will do my best to stay in touch."

I knew what he meant—we had worked together with his dreams. He has come to me many times that way since with words of encouragement and always pointing to the light. While he has stayed in touch with me personally in dreams, he's really in touch with all of us who have read his words, seen his videos, known his blessings, learned his teachings and carried them on.

Through his students, and the students of his students, as this volume so vividly illustrates, Reb Zalman has touched us all.

1

Naming and Reframing

Reb Zalman expanded upon Jewish naming
traditions in ways that equalized social
hierarchies and advanced the possibilities
for awareness and healing in many lives.

I first met Rabbi Zalman Schachter-Shalomi in 1990 in the JFK airport. We were on our way to India — and the Dalai Lama. I reached down to shake his hand — his back was propped against a column, his long legs stretched out on the gray carpet. He wore a soft gray sweater and had a gray beard and impish eyes. With his blue beret, he looked like a veteran jazz musician.

He invited me to join him. I stretched my legs alongside his. I said, "Rabbi Schachter." He said, very friendly, "Call me Reb Zalman." Holding a small red book in the palm of his left hand, he scribbled in a notebook. He was translating the *Dhammapadda*, a book of Buddhist wisdom poems — into Hebrew.
— *Rodger Kamenetz [1.1]*

While contemplating whether to accept the use of "Reb" for myself as a form of address, I inquired, "Reb Zalman, why are you addressed as 'Reb' by so many and not 'Rabbi' or 'Doctor'?"

Reb Zalman replied, "I request and prefer it because traditionally 'Reb' means 'mister.' Not rabbi, not rebbe, just mister. This way no one is given more status than another just because of attaining a professional title. It's about humility. I see that some of the women among us are adopting 'Reb,' as well. While that's taking some getting used to, I like it, because it creates a shared form of every-day address that can function as a social equalizer."
— *Goldie Milgram [1.2]*

"God's name is ineffable," Reb Zalman taught, "A name that can only be pronounced by breath — by living fully alive, by paying attention to our breath, to the expansion and contraction of our chests, to the give and take, to the rush of the waves approaching and receding from the shore, to the *ratzo* and *shov*, the attraction and repulsion as we encounter the *kedushat HaShem* — that awesome and awful sensation of the Great Silence, the silence of the One."
— *Moshe Waldoks [1.3]*

As I was not given a Hebrew name at birth, Reb Zalman invited me to find my Hebrew name. He also suggested the practice, perhaps each year, perhaps also at moments of transition, of taking an extra name for "additional inner guidance and to sustain a new phase of spiritual development. And, it becomes even more powerful announcing it in community with the Torah as witness."

He also modeled and encouraged us to be consciously working with the many different names of God in order to draw down different types of blessings for our lives and world.
— *Carola de Vries Robles [1.4]*

It was January 1980. "So, *nu*? What's on your mind?" Reb Zalman inquired and paused. It turned out there were three things that arose in that safe space of real listening. And they were all related to returning Home at some level or another.

"For years I have been searching inwardly for a name that would reflect my inner being with my outer changes," I told him.

Reb Zalman said the name would emerge at the perfect moment.

Taking a deep meditative moment, I then shared the Holy Goddess name that had emerged earlier in response to my inner question.

The next day at the Gainesville Florida Hillel, there was an extra *aliya*, opportunity to witness and bless for the chanting of the Torah.

I nudged my sweetheart for him to accept the honor. "*Nu*," he said, "why don't you accept it?"

The idea had not occurred to me.

Okay. I was next. Reb Zalman whispered, "Do you want to take a new Hebrew name, now?"

Startled, I answered firmly, "Yes."

"So, *nu*, what do you want to be called?" he asked.

How startling to be caught again in a patriarchal expectation, that he would name me.

Meditating, I opened to my connection with the Source of Life, and on the exhale I breathed out the word "light."

Reb Zalman continued breathing, inhaled deeply, and breathed out "*Bahira,*" adding the translation "effulgence."

And then, with his inimitable twinkle and good sense Reb Zalman suggested, "Well, meditate with it for a while. See how it fits, we can always do a new one!"

And so I was called to the Torah by my new name. And, as this experience continued, we moved into Reb Zalman's *I Ching* ritual. The way this works is that while up at the Torah one asks an internal, personally specific or general question and understands that the place where one stops the pointer is a Holy Profound response to one's question.

The answer to my question of the ongoing holy moment was a sentence from Genesis, "And he sustained them." As Reb Zalman chanted it in Hebrew and English, he put this in context—it was about Joseph who sustained his family during the time of famine after the experience of having felt cast out.

Whew! Layers upon layers of meaning. Reb Zalman was gently touching my back behind my heart, and giving me space and time before I would chant the blessings after the Torah reading.
— *Bahira Sugarman [1.5]*

During a retreat, I asked a friend to deliver a *kvitel* to Reb Zalman. A *kvitel* is a brief, folded, petitionary note, like the ones people put into the cracks of the Western Wall in Jerusalem. In the note, I asked for *yechidus*, a deep and loving private audience a rebbe shares with his student, to help me get through a problem. In *yechidus*, I could talk about matters close to my heart.

After greetings, Reb Zalman asked me what I needed. "Oy! I'm having big problems. I can't finish projects anymore. There is no shortage of great things for me to work on. I start out fine and half way through get discouraged, and start something else. It's making me crazy. What should I do?"

Reb Zalman closed his eyes for a minute or two, then opened them and smiled as he took my hands. "You need more closing energy. You don't have to get frustrated, or *chas v'chaleela* (God forbid), get angry at yourself. Here's what we'll do. I want to add a new name to yours: *Moshe* (Moe-sheh, Moses). *Moshe* was a good closer. You need more *Moshe* energy."

Reb Zalman called all the rabbis on the retreat together. "Let's do a naming ceremony for our friend. With your help, the *kavanah* (intention), is to tie his heart to the soul of the original *Mosheh*, Moses."

I trembled when he said that, as if to a baby boy at a *bris* (covenantal ritual). He then renamed me:

> *V'y'kareh sh'mo b'Yisroel, may he be known among his Jewish brothers and sisters as HaRav Ya'acov Moshe Ben Tzion HaLevi ben Dovid v'Mataleh, Rabbi Jack Moses Ben Zion of the tribe of Levi, son of David and Mathilde.*

The rabbis sang *Siman Tov u'Mazel Tov*, a familiar celebratory song, as we shared small cups of grape juice and wine. Reb Zalman then stood up, hugged me and whispered in my ear, "It's gonna be okay."
— *Jack (Ya'acov) Gabriel [1.6]*

At a rabbinical and cantorial student meeting, Reb Zalman told us that he wanted us to call him *zayde*, Yiddish for grandfather. More importantly, he imparted that he saw himself as *zayde* to all of us.
— *Edwin Harris [1.7]*

I approached Reb Zalman at the end of a meal and asked what he thought of "X" name for me. With great enthusiasm, he went into details of why it was the most accurate name — from its ancient Ugaritic sources and its meaning in the *sefirot*, etc. I was overjoyed and able to have a naming at my synagogue shortly after.

Some years later, I was at the Elat Chayyim Retreat Center for a *shabbaton* (twenty-four-hour Shabbat celebration), and I was unaccountably drawn to follow the Torah procession, which was something I had never done. As I reached the outskirts of the tent, Reb Zalman reached out his hand and stopped me. He said, "Do you have a middle name to go with X?"

I replied that I had recently completed work with our matriarch Rachel, and did he have something in mind?

He stepped back, looked into me and said, "*Tamar!*" He saw my startled expression and said I didn't need to take it. I asked Reb Zalman to give me a minute, went "inside" and immediately felt stronger, taller and straighter like a date palm.

In the next moment, I felt more forthright and courageous, like Tamar, the Biblical character, and I said, "YES."

During the Torah service Reb Zalman called me up to the Torah by my new name, affixing it in the traditional manner.

Much personal growth came from this.
— *Ellen Weaver [1.8]*

We were in an elevator with Reb Zalman and, as his floor came and he was leaving the elevator, my friend said, "Z, have a great day!

Reb Zalman whirled around, stopped the elevator with his hand and sternly said, "Never call me Z. Never deny a person their name; a name is a precious garment of the soul."

He turned and left. The next minute he was his normal sweet self.

I never saw him hold a grudge.
— *Goldie Milgram [1.9]*

I was standing nearby Reb Zalman, observing how present he was to all who were bringing personal questions to him. Witnessing this, waves of emotion arose within me, leading to cascades of tears.

Upon opening my eyes, there was Reb Zalman standing right in front of me with a warm smile. He asked, "*Maidele* (young woman) why are you crying? Why didn't you come over to talk to me? What is going on for you?"

As the tears continued to flow, Reb Zalman said, "Let's hug." He hugged me and held me close. His kindness was gentle, safe, and delicious. He then stepped back, looked at me and asked for my name. When I responded, he clarified," Your Hebrew name."

"My Jewish name is in Yiddish, Suri Kressel."

"Do you like your name?" he asked.

"I don't really use it. It doesn't mean much to me."

Reb Zalman then said, "Maybe it is time for a new name. I will give you a new name. You don't have to take it if you don't like it. But, if you do like it, tomorrow is Rosh Chodesh, the celebration of the New Moon. Go to the *Shacharit*, the morning service, and ask for a *mishebeirach*, a personal blessing. Your new name will then become official." Once more he pulled me close, and he wrapped his arms around me. As I lay my head upon his heart, he breathed and hummed a tune softly.

Soon, Reb Zalman opened his eyes and offered me a new name, *Yocheved*. The name was unfamiliar and I did not know what to do with it.

The next day I attended the morning service, and with the Torah scroll open, the name suggested by Reb Zalman became mine. That afternoon, I attended a *mishpacha* group, a small process group for conferees.

When my turn to speak came, the tears returned. The participants asked what was going on for me. I explained that my mother had Alzheimer's. She needed more care and support to keep her safe and so needed to move out of her house to a more supportive environment. Helping her to understand and accept this was an ongoing struggle that had become painful for both of us.

After listening respectfully, my peers then asked, in order to pray for me, "What is your mother's name?"

"Magda."

"No." they said. "What is her Hebrew name?"

"*Miriam*," I replied.

Everyone was smiling at me as soon as I said my mother's Hebrew name. And in that moment I realized that I, the new renamed daughter, *Yocheved* (Moses' sister who watched over him in the river and brought their mother to care for him), had become the mother of my mother, *Miriam*.
— *Aggie Goldenholz [1.10]*

2

Spiritual Guidance

Reb Zalman practiced unique ways of guiding
souls on their Jewish and personal journeys
in response to questions, during spontaneous
encounters, and scheduled one-to-one sessions.

Reb Zalman loved the story, which I heard from him more than once, of the rebbe, a spiritual teacher and leader, who inherited that role from his father. Some of the older *Hassidim* came to him to say, "You're not rebbe-ing the way your papa did."

And his son, the new rebbe responded, "I am. He didn't do it the way his papa did it, and I don't do it the way my papa did it."
— *Shaya Isenberg [2.1]*

"Reb Zalman," I said into the phone, "They offered me the presidency of my professional organization. What do you think, should I take it?"

"Do you want to?" he asked.

"Yes." I said.

"Then yes, you will do a good job. Take it."

"But isn't it just ego?"

"Everything is ego, until it is not." Reb Zalman said.
— *Laurie Sanford [2.2]*

Until setting an appointment to meet, my time with Rabbi Zalman was spent as one would with a friend. We'd discuss school, books, and life in general. But, when my stepfather committed suicide, I needed him for something more—I needed him as a rabbi in the role of counselor.

Rabbi Zalman knew why I was coming. He employed his usual method of never giving a direct answer to my questions, and guided me deeper into my emotional state.

As we volleyed back and forth about the big questions that arise when we lose someone we love, he inquired, "Do you keep a journal?" When I told him I didn't, he encouraged me to take on the challenge. "The soul doesn't like to repeat itself," he said.

As we discussed the merits of writing a journal, we moved on to consider origins of spirituality and their relationship to consciousness. Rabbi Zalman then asked, "Do you have dreams when you sleep? Anything not of this world is worth documenting."
— *Rodney Weiss [2.3]*

Reb Zalman told me the story about the rabbi who, before every speaking engagement, would reach into his pocket, pull out a small note, meditate on it for a moment, and put it back in his pocket. Then he would pull out a small note from the other pocket, stare at it, and put it back in his pocket.

One day a congregant asked, "Rabbi, for all these years you consistently begin every talk with reviewing those two notes. What are they? Prayers?"

To which the rabbi replied, "I suppose you could say that. The first note says: 'It's not about you,' and the second: 'Just tell them what God wants them to hear.'"
— *Ira Wiesner [2.4]*

Two of our grandchildren went with their father to visit Reb Zalman shortly before his death. They knew it was an important opportunity to ask him questions. One was even thinking about what he should ask a few nights before their trip. He didn't have to worry, though, for as soon as they were at his bedside one looked directly at Reb Zalman and asked, "What makes you so smart?"

Reb Zalman chuckled. "I'm not proud of being smart," he said, "That didn't come from me. What I'm proud of is being wise."

Without skipping a beat, the child continued, "Well then, what makes you so wise?"

"Oh," Reb Zalman replied, "what makes me wise is that I've learned from my mistakes."

And then he laughed and laughed. "And," he continued, "if you don't believe me, ask your *sabba* (grandfather) and *savta* (grandmother), they'll tell you, they were there!"
— *Neal Rose [2.5]*

After leaving the yeshiva world in Jerusalem and returning to Toronto, I felt all alone and disenfranchised from the Jewish world. Randy Robinson, a Hillel programmer at York University in Toronto, brought Reb Zalman in as a guest for a *shabbaton*. She said, "You are looking for guidance; you must come and meet the very most far-out rebbe alive today." That was enough to sign me up immediately!

After checking into the retreat center, I was running a little late for the *Kabbalat Shabbat* service to welcome the Sabbath. Looking down from the balcony, I could see the service which had strobe lights flashing, music playing, and a large, overtly happy Hassidic rebbe dressed in a traditional black *kapoteh* (long coat) and *shtreimel* (fur-trimmed Hassidic hat) dancing and singing with the *minyan* (ten or more praying), "Put your right foot in, take your right foot out, sing *Gut Shabbos*, and you do the hokey-pokey and you turn yourself about; that's what it's all about." I went into shock and froze on the spot.

Reb Zalman stopped the service, looked up at me and said, "If you are not going to join us, then you can't watch us." Slowly I began descending the staircase; my heart pounding as I joined the *minyan*.

Later that night, Reb Zalman said he would hand out "bakery numbers" if we wished to have fifteen minutes of private time with him on Shabbat afternoon. I grabbed a number and prayed. I can still feel his big smile and his warm welcome as I entered the room for the *yechidus*.

Once I began, it was very easy to talk to him about my *frum* (religious) yeshiva background and my efforts to integrate the pieces of my life into a happy, holy and meaningful spiritual path.

I was studying *Hassidus* and Kabbalah at night while going to art college by day—painting nudes. My life felt full of contradictions. I cried as I poured my *kishkes* (guts) out to him.

I must have spent at least one and a half hours with Reb Zalman, despite the allocated fifteen-minute "bakery card time." Reb Zalman's advice was for me to go to the Aquarian Minyan in Berkeley, where I would find my soul's *chevra* (community) and not feel lonely anymore. There, I would learn how to blend the tradition with creative and experiential prayers and rituals. There, I would meet other former Orthodox yeshiva *chevra*, even some rabbis.

"Don't worry," Reb Zalman said in a reassuring tone of voice. "I visit Berkeley often and I will stay in close touch with you."

I wanted to take Reb Zalman's advice even though I was totally financially broke. Making my way across Canada for free in a "drive away" car that I dropped off in Victoria, I stopped in Vancouver for Shabbat and Simchat Torah at Or Shalom, the first Jewish renewal congregation in Canada. After a few weeks, I arrived in Berkeley and was warmly welcomed to the Aquarian Minyan. My Jewish spiritual life went very quickly from black and white to Technicolor!
— *Sarah Leah Grafstein [2.6]*

I once heard Reb Zalman exclaim, "The path to spirituality is through joy!"
— *Sharon Alexander [2.7]*

The year our son came with us to a Shavuot retreat with Reb Zalman, he had recently completed his Master's Degree in Violin Performance. He was living with us at the time while working as a private violin teacher, playing the odd concert, and auditioning. It wasn't an easy time for him. He was also struggling with the deeply conflicting issues of Judaism and a music career. Reb Zalman had counseled our son in prior years concerning issues related to music performance and Jewish observance, and that had been very helpful.

Our son was present during Reb Zalman's teaching on the final day of the retreat. When the lesson was concluded and people were milling about, Reb Zalman again spoke with him. This time, Reb Zalman asked if he'd brought his instrument with him to the retreat center. He had. Reb Zalman further inquired if he would be willing to play the *Schindler's List* theme in relation to a dramatization planned for the evening. Reb Zalman and Eve would be imagining aloud having been two of the souls standing at Sinai. And play, he did.

This experience taught our son so such about performance as a spiritual practice.
— *Bob Weissberg [2.8]*

As a long-time student of Reb Zalman living in the Netherlands, I often went for weeks of retreats at Elat Chayyim. I would bring some Dutch cheese and farmer's rye bread which he loved. He spoke a bit of the Dutch language, and he wanted to be updated on Jewish life, the people he knew there, and our organizational platform for Jewish renewal.

One such day, hearing me speak and cry, sharing the burden of not being seen and feeling so alone, his voice was so loving, and he moved me into a radical insight when he simply said, "You have a tendency for melancholy."
— *Carola de Vries Robles [2.9]*

Reb Zalman would say, "When you arrive somewhere, see where you are being deployed by God."
— *Jack (Ya'akov) Gabriel [2.10]*

Inspired by Reb Zalman, I got a shofar and, becoming passionate about the mitzvah of blowing it, began to write a book on the topic. He would often inquire, "So, Michael, how's the book coming? What questions do you have?"

One year, on the second day of Rosh Hashanah, my mind kept wandering and I could not muster the *kavanah* required to sound shofar with meaning. I sounded the horn, but did not release the voice of shofar.

Reb Zalman called me to his seat on the *bima* (stage) and said softly, "Sometimes, when someone blows a long *tekiah gedolah* (the final blast), the shofar blower's ego starts thinking, 'Wow, I'm good. This is a really long blast. I hope everybody is noticing me.'

"So there is a way when, just before falling asleep at night, that we visualize we are giving our breath back to God. Doing this helps us prepare for when we die and get to give our last breath to God. This is a good *kavanah* for the shofar blower. When you do it this way, the shofar blasts carry our prayers straight to God."
— *Michael Chusid [2.11]*

Reb Zalman led a workshop and he paired us each with people we didn't know. He began the session by asking everyone to look closely into the eyes of the person across from them who was to be their partner in the exercise. Reb Zalman asked us to figure out who this person reminded us of. He explained that you can't really know someone and learn from them, if you don't see them without the extra baggage of stuff that you put on them, because they might remind you of someone else.
— *Cherie Koller-Fox [2.12]*

Reb Zalman told me he was like a spider, drawn to exploring dark corners.
— *Howard Schwartz [2.13]*

Reb Zalman told me the story of Jack, who was a student who had come to the Lubavitcher Yeshiva in 1941 or 42 from Harrisburg, Pennsylvania. He came from an observant background. His father was a *shochet* (kosher slaughterer).

Jack had won a blue ribbon award in high school for his being a fast typist. He had brought his typewriter to the yeshiva (orthodox

Jewish day school) and he would always do notes in English at the *shiurim* (learning sessions).

At midday, he and a few others and I, instead of standing in line to wait for the dishing out of lunch, would pass a ball or play "punch ball" because bats we didn't have, and sticks we didn't use. So we did "punch ball" in the yard downstairs.

One of the *Rosh Yeshivas* (head principals) didn't like the fact that *bocharim* (young men) from the *bes midresh* (area for study) were playing ball downstairs even though it wasn't during a *shiur* (class).

Instead of waiting in line we played ball, then we came in fifteen minutes later, having run around a little bit. The *Rosh Yeshiva* had come down, taken a scissors and cut up the ball that we were playing with, and thrown the pieces away. He'd said, "shame on you, *bocharim* from the *bes midresh* playing ball!" Having achieved great satisfaction with what he considered a righteous deed, he went away.

Jack wasn't at lunch but after, he comes waving before us a carbon copy of a note he had written to the Rebbe.

> Dear Lubavitcha Rebbe, *Shlita* [an acronym of honor],
> I'd like to know what kind of yeshiva you run here. It says in *Shulchan Aruch* (book of traditional guidelines for living) that before you eat you should warm up your stomach and should move around, and instead of waiting around in line for the food like everybody else, we took the 15 minutes to do just that, to warm up.
> And I need to know: Was this on your say-so that the Rosh Yeshiva said that we couldn't play ball? Or because it was his own thing? Because if he did this because you wanted him to, I don't want to study in this yeshiva.
> Sincerely yours,
> *Yakov Ben Etel*

We ask, "Has this gone to the Rebbe yet?"

He says, "Yes, I didn't go for lunch today. I typed it, then I gave it to the Rebbe's secretary, and I saw him take it up about 10 minutes ago."

We say, "Oy, Yankle, it's going to be terrible. You're going to be sent home! What did you do that for? The Rebbe can't make him wrong!"

He said, "I don't care. I want to know."

In those days we were provided with milk, little six-ounce milk bottles that came in cases. Three cases were stacked one on top of the other, and I'm doing push-ups with those cases, lifting with my arms up-down-up…and the *chevra* are counting, 21, 22, 23, so that's what we were doing instead of playing ball. Meanwhile, the *Rosh Yeshiva* is lurking upstairs to see what's happening.

Then, the little door opens up on the balcony, and the Rebbe gets wheeled out in his wheelchair by the Rebbe's secretary. I'm standing up there pushing the cases up and down and everybody freezes and stops counting. I'm looking up from underneath the milk cases and see that the Rebbe had been wheeled out. He turned his face away so I could put the *peckel* (package) down.

Then the Rebbe's secretary hands the Rebbe a box on his lap and takes off the lid from the box. The Rebbe takes the box and over the railing tosses down a dozen tennis balls to us.

It was wonderful, that scene, him tossing the balls over.

The payoff is that the *Rosh Yeshiva* comes running out, swanting to have one of the Rebbe's balls for a memento.

And the *Rosh Yeshivah* never bothered us again.
— *Ruth Hirsch. This is Ruth's transcription of a tape of Reb Zalman telling this story to her. [2.14]*

A particular story Reb Zalman loved to tell was about two competitive young sons of a legendary rabbi. While playing together, one said to the other, "I have a new game. Let's pretend we're *Tateh* (Daddy) and see who can copy being him the best."

"I can do it better than you," one brother said smugly.

"No you can't," replied the other brother.

"I can, but I'll let you go first."

So his brother kissed the *sefer* (the holy book) he was studying on the table, like his father would. Next, he poured himself some hot water for tea from the silver samovar. He motioned to some imaginary people in the room to be seated. And then he began *laizen un taitchen*, reading and translating the text in a sing-song way.

"Pretty good," said his brother. "Now it's my turn. I'm going to show how *Tateh* does *yechidus*." First, he gets up from his chair, reads a small folded up note given him by the *Hassid* who came, and puts his hand on his *Hassid*'s shoulder. Then *Tateh* says, "I will give you a *bracha*, a blessing."

He looks at his brother with a gloating smile and says, "There, just like *Tateh*."

"No that wasn't!" the other brother retorts.

"It was too!"

"No…it wasn't. When *Tateh* reads a *kvitel*, he always sighs before looking at the *Hassid*."
— *Jack (Ya'acov) Gabriel [2.15]*

Once, when I was desperate and crying out, "What is the truth in all of this?" Reb Zalman invited me "to stand in my truth" in order to better listen for guidance. He guided me in standing, as in the

Amida prayers — silent, taking the letter *Aleph* up above my crown; placing my full body presence, especially the heart/belly, in the letter *Mem* circling around me; and putting the *Tav* under my feet. Standing vertically and wide-around with *Aleph, Mem, Tav — EMeT*, Truth.
— *Carola de Vries Robles [2.16]*

In the early seventies I had the honor and pleasure to live with and work beside Reb Zalman.

He gave me his four-string guitar and the key of D minor.

During that time, he saw my fascination with the Hebrew letter symbols. So, he drew and gave me the following beautiful *Aleph*, [hand-painted in yellow, red, green, and blue].

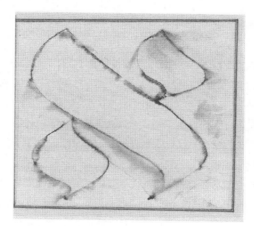

A year or so later he mailed me the *Sefer Yetzirah* (Book of Creation) in three scripts, English, Hebrew, and King David script, with a note that read, "Ancient Hebrew runes, very good for visualizations and meditations."
— *Prahaladan (Philip) Mandelkorn [2.17]*

Upon receiving clearance to fly after hospitalization for a stroke, I packed a blood pressure cuff in a carry-on bag along with *tallit* (prayer shawl, e.g., *tallis*) and *tefillin* (sacred meditation tools), and headed to a rabbinic gathering in Colorado. On the very last day of the conference, I saw Reb Zalman walking toward me with a colleague. She was aware of my health situation, and so paused and asked him to bless me.

"Rachel, *leibn* (heart friend)," he said. His eyes were gentle and his gaze direct. "I hear you were in the hospital. Tell me what happened."

After I did, he held my hands in his and thought for a moment, to all appearances going inside to some interior place of guidance. His hands were surprisingly warm despite the January chill.

"Physically," Reb Zalman said, "consider craniosacral therapy. Do you know it?"

I told him that I didn't, but that I would look it up when I got home. He nodded in approval.

"Spiritually," he said, "you might wish to spend some time with a psalm. How old are you?"

When I told him thirty-one, he brightened. "Psalm 31. It's a good psalm of comfort. '*B'yado afkid ruchi* — Into Your hands I place my spirit,' like in *Adon Olam*. *Daven* (pray) that every day."

I thanked him, fervently. And then he blessed me that my healing should be complete, smiled, and went on his way.
— *Rachel Barenblat [2.18]*

Several days after my friend told me he was facing an operation for stage four pancreatic cancer, and that he believed he was one of the *Lamed-Vavnikim* (thirty-six righteous people for whom the world is sustained), I emailed Reb Zalman to ask what to do with my friend's disclosure.

My friend told me he is addicted to helping others. "I suffer when I see injustice. I can get physically ill. This is how I know," he shared.

I queried Reb Zalman, "Do I validate him as a *Lamed-Vavnik*? Or, tuck his secret away as a keepsake that should never be found?" Shortly after sending the message, the phone rang.

"Tamara, this is Reb Zalman. I just received your email and I thought it best if we discussed this over the phone. Yes?"

"Yes."

Reb Zalman said, "If one believes that he is Moses, then he is Moses. If your friend believes that he is one of the thirty-six, then that is who he is being in the world. His purpose is bound up with his role as a *Lamed-Vavnik*. He is kind. He is generous. He takes on the pain of the world. And he is suffering for all of us."

Then Reb Zalman asked me to take out my *ArtScroll Prayer Book*. "Find the *Seder Hatarat Nedarim*, the ritual for the releasing of vows," he said. "Your friend has made a vow to himself that he would suffer for the sake of others. We don't know why he made this vow, or when he made it, but in order to avert his suffering, and possibly prevent his untimely death, he must renounce this vow in front of a *Beit Din* (a rabbinical court of three colleagues). Do you think he would agree to do this?"

The text reads:

> Any utterance that escaped my mouth, or that I vowed
> in my heart to perform, any of the various optional good
> deeds, or good practices, or any good thing that I have
> performed three times but without specifying that the
> practice does not have the force of a vow…regarding all
> of them I regret retroactively…therefore I request
> annulment for them all.
> [*The Complete ArtScroll Siddur, p. 762*]

My friend did not answer the phone again. He died shortly after the surgery.

Reb Zalman offered guidance: "Your friend's suffering will not pass into the next life. He has quietly completed his holy tasks, and his life has been a blessing. Now, he will appear before the ultimate *Beit Din*. Accept the wisdom he has bequeathed you, and use it to quietly make your life a blessing, too."
— *Tamara Miller [2.19]*

I heard someone ask Reb Zalman if he was a theoretical Kabbalist, or a practical Kabbalist and he answered, "A practical Kabbalist." And then he added, "I only mean the opposite of impractical Kabbalist."
— *Rodger Kamenetz [2.20]*

During Reb Zalman's Mystery School, he dedicated one complete weekend to expressing our anger at God. He said, "How can you ever come to love *HaShem*, if you don't have the kind of honest relationship where you can let *HaShem* know how angry you are that S/He allowed six million innocent people to be murdered without intervening?" He used all the expressive therapy techniques he knew that weekend like primal scream. And, he demonstrated with his own screaming at God.
— *Sharon Alexander [2.21]*

"Reb Zalman," I said on the phone, "I need help. I am angry."

"What are you angry about?" he said.

"It doesn't matter what I am angry about," I said. "I don't want to be angry. It's not very spiritual."

"Ah," he responded. "Sometimes there is a good reason to be angry and anger is the right response. And the right response is spiritual."
— *Laurie Sanford [2.22]*

Once Reb Zalman approached me to inquire why I didn't call him more often. I sheepishly admitted to him that I actually felt intimidated. He smiled that sweet smile of his, and said, "Yocheved, *leibn*, teach me something."

"*Gevalt*, wow," I thought. "What could I teach this Rabbi of Rabbis?" Blanching, I stammered out the traditional phrase, "*Ivdu et HaShem b'simcha*—Serve God in joy."

Reb Zalman laughed and said, "Good. Now we can talk."
— *Yocheved Mintz [2.23]*

Reb Zalman was never one for small talk. I remember him asking me, on at least a couple of occasions, as I sat in the passenger seat of his car, accompanying him on one of his errands, his famous query, "So, what is your question?"
— *Sharon Alexander [2.24]*

Addressing the full Ohalah conference, Reb Zalman said, "I want each of you to work with a spiritual mentor for the rest of your life—whether this be a soul friend or a *mashpia* (spiritual director). We all have blind spots and need someone else to help us see what God is asking of us."
— *Shohama Wiener [2.25]*

One day, while walking and gazing down at the sidewalk carefully, I saw that Reb Zalman had spotted a centipede. Bending down, he gently scooped the centipede up and placed it on his arm.

As the centipede undulated up and down his arm, Reb Zalman spoke quietly, "*Baruch HaShem* (May God be Blessed), given that we can gain such wisdom from this little creature! Look at its many legs. You know, we are like the centipede. We each walk on hundreds of feet and somewhere along our lives' journeys, we discover our genuine two feet. All the others feel inauthentic, unreal, like marshmallows, like pillows. We don't really feel anything beneath our feet and we aren't really connected to the vitality of the earth beneath them.

"And, it is when we discover our *real* feet, we begin to feel deeply connected to holy ground, just as *Moshe Rabbeinu* (Moses our teacher) felt before the burning bush. With our real feet, we feel heat and cold. We feel joy and pain. We feel softness and harshness, and sharpness—we feel Life! Make sure, *leibn*, that you find your authentic feet and walk honestly upon them."

Years later, I reminded Reb Zalman of his words about the centipede. He smiled and simply asked me, "So, *nu*, have you found your feet yet?" When I answered that I thought so, Reb Zalman laughed and said, "*Baruch HaShem.*"
— *Leila Gal Berner* [2.26]

Arriving for the first time at Reb Zalman's home in Philadelphia on Emlen Street, I'm surprised to see an abundance of computers. On one side of the room is something like an IBM 5150, on the other what appears to be an early Sinclair, possibly the ZX-81; and here's also a Commodore computer of some sort.

Reb Zalman's first words were, "Good, you made it. I appreciate you volunteering to do some editing. You can use the IBM. Oh, and did you walk or bring your car?"

"Car. We had to put chains on the snow tires to get here because it's still rough out there given last night's ice storm. Plows seem to come through this part of Mt. Airy last. Why do you ask?"

"There's something I forgot to do, and I'd like you to drive me there first."

Reb Zalman coughs deeply as he wraps a plaid scarf around his throat. He'd mentioned in class that he'd sustained a lung injury while imprisoned in a camp under the Vichy French and that he can get quite ill from something others of us might shake off easily. Given the below freezing weather, I ask, "Could I do the errand for you, so you won't have to go out in this weather?"

"It would be too hard to explain. Are you hungry? I made vegetable soup. Would you like to warm up first?"

"Thank you. We're both dressed for the outdoors already, so how about we both warm up with soup when we get back?" Outside, the sun-melted streets are freezing up again under newly arrived cloud cover. Reb Zalman directs each turn from memory. "Now, stop at that house with the tilted porch....Good. No, don't get out. I'll just take a shovel from the trunk and will do my errand and be right back."

The house Reb Zalman has brought us to looks abandoned. Some windows are broken and patched with cardboard. The siding and steps are rotting and need painting. Instead of going in, Reb Zalman inches his way across the still mostly frozen lawn toward the side of the house. He shovels out a hole next to the crawl space and pulls a shovel out from under there. Cautiously sliding along the wall, he begins digging snow away from the side of the house. Finally, he reaches into the space, turns something, takes the stick puts it into the space, pulls it out, and appears to be reading it like a giant dipstick. He nods. Reaches back into the hole to apparently turn something. Restores the stick to the crawl space and begins his return trip on the ice to the car.

Back at the car, I turn to see Reb Zalman returning the shovel to the trunk and as he slams the trunk — *kerplop!* He slips, flips, and hits the ice hard.

Dashing from the car I find him grinning sheepishly and then he pushes himself toward me on his bottom like a human sled saying, "Goldie, *leibn*, go back into the warm car. I'm fine, I don't break so easily." At the curb Reb Zalman stands, gets into the car, and sinks into his seat without complaint.

While I drive, Reb Zalman is talking to himself: "Not good. She'll never get through the day. The tank is almost empty."

I realize he's talking to God and praying, as he continues, *"Ribono shel Olam*, I need a little inspiration here."

"Reb Zalman, you said 'she'. Who is she? How did you know to come here? How come you didn't knock and let her know we're here? What now? How is prayer going to help put oil in a tank?" "Don't you ever pray for inspiration?" asks Reb Zalman and continued, "Such prayers are often answered. Now, however, we make a different kind of call."

Rubbing his elbow, Reb Zalman grins, a Cheshire cat I've-got-something-surprising kind of grin. He reaches behind the seat and drags his carry bag forward, pulling out a black plastic case with old-fashioned luggage-like clasps on each side and opens it...."

"Reb Zalman...is that a...phone?"

"It's called a cellphone. A fellow lent me this one to try. Never mind about it. We can't waste time. She needs the oil. I hope we can get it to her today."

Plugging the phone monstrosity into the cigarette lighter, Reb Zalman dials a number from memory and asks of the person he reaches, "If I give you an address, would you call my heating oil company and use your credit card to make a payment for a poor neighbor I recently met? Could you keep her on your card until my people get her into public housing? If you have any contact with her just say it's a public service; don't give my name. The street address is...and the number for the oil company is...."

Reb Zalman pulls a napkin with the number out of his glove and starts to read aloud: "2-1-5-4" until suddenly exclaiming, "Oy! There's no signal."

Reb Zalman tugged on his beard thoughtfully. "Let's head back; we can use the phone at the house. Meanwhile, I'll keep trying to get this machine to work. Such an exciting development! Oh, and I

meant to ask you, do you like science fiction? We could trade paperbacks you know."
– *Goldie Milgram [2.27]*

In the winter of 2003, Elat Chayyim, a Jewish renewal retreat center then in Accord, New York was looking for a new Executive Director. I applied for the position and received a call offering me the position. Simultaneously, another offer came in from a different organization. I accepted the latter.

The next summer I signed up to take courses at Elat Chayyim, including with Reb Zalman. Upon arrival, unbeknownst to me earlier, I was a day early for the start of classes. Walking up the deserted front steps of the main building I was met by the shining countenance of Reb Zalman. "Where have you been?" he inquired looking me unnervingly and mischievously in the eye as I came to the top of the steps. Before I could reply he said, "Nachum, we've been waiting for YOU," and put an arm around my shoulder and led me into the building. Inside sitting in a semicircle were a group of eight others.

Reb Zalman turned to me again and said, "Nachum, we couldn't start the *davenen* till YOU arrived! YOU needed to be the tenth person to complete our *minyan* today."

We walked forward and Reb Zalman announced, "Ahhhh, he's here—Nachum! Now we can begin our special *Shachris minyan* and welcome the new director!"

I was a little flummoxed at this point, but quickly realized that I had stumbled into the welcoming *minyan* for the new Elat Chayyim Executive Director…the position that I'd been offered and much to my consternation, and deep regret, had turned down.

Needless to say, we davened. Reb Zalman offered blessings and a special *kavanah* for the new director. At the conclusion of the service, Reb Zalman came over to me and again put his arm around my shoulder and said quietly, "So, Nachum, see how we needed you today." He then looked me in the eye again and said, "You know, Nachumele, you had another role to play; it's very hard sometimes to know which role we are deployed here to play."

With emphasis and finality, Reb Zalman added, "Now let go and be where you need to be. I'll see you at class tomorrow." And with that he walked away...and never during the class the following week, nor ever after, did he mention the episode again.
— *Neil Markowitz [2.28]*

Reb Zalman had offered to lead a Lama Foundation group in some kind of movement exercise. I responded to the experience with uncontrollable inner chuckles, and despite trying hard to contain them, they became audible. Reb Zalman turned around to see the source of the sound. He looked at me, and said warmly, "I am so happy you are enjoying yourself."
— *Neshama (Rose) Lipari [2.29]*

At my first face-to-face meeting with Reb Zalman, he greeted me on the way to dinner after a *Kabbalat Shabbat* with a hug, took a step back, then touched the magenta birthmark in the center of my forehead, saying, "You know how to dance with Divine Providence!"

Six months after receiving this message via Reb Zalman, I asked him why he had said that to me. He replied that he didn't know, that sometimes he was impelled to transmit something, and he had learned to do so without massaging the transmission into something that made sense to him.

"So," he said, "perhaps you might seek the counsel of Chana Rochel Werbermacher of Ludomir, a woman called by her community to serve as their rebbe, even though such a thing was 'unacceptable' two hundred years ago in nineteenth-century Ukraine."
— *Raachel Jurovics [2.30]*

Reb Zalman once confronted me out on the porch of a rustic mountain cabin; the two of us sitting in our respective rocking chairs, half facing one another. "You need to work on your gratitude," he said.
— *Sharon Alexander [2.31]*

We were young students and struggling financially. Upon learning of this, Reb Zalman insisted on helping with the rent, and then took me out for a walk to help me calm down. It was a gentle walk along Riverside Drive in New York City to Grant's Tomb.

All of a sudden Reb Zalman stopped walking. He was pointing his finger at something. "Do you see that?" he asked excitedly. I looked down at the ground and said, "A dandelion, is that what you're pointing at?"

"Yes," Reb Zalman said. "Do you see its determination? Such a strong desire to survive, even through concrete; ...such a strong desire to live!"
— *Carol Rose [2.32]*

I asked Reb Zalman what I could do as an olive branch for the only congregation on my island and for its new rabbi. Reb Zalman said, "It will be Shavuot soon. Give them a *Megillat Rut* (Book of Ruth, in scroll form)."

So I had a *sofer* (scribe) write a *Megillat Rut*, and donated it to the congregation. The new rabbi used it that one Shavuot and never again.

Reb Zalman said, "Just because you give a congregation *Megillat Rut* does not mean they will no longer be ruthless."
— *Arthur Segal [2.33]*

During one of our meetings and also in class, Reb Zalman and I had a huge argument about the feminine principle, female roles, rights, and ways of thinking. As I can be fierce and "stiff-necked," at a certain point Reb Zalman cut through the argument to say, "You are really concerned about *Bina*."

"*Bina*?! Can I embody *Bina* when I have no sense of the presence of the Divine Mother that *Bina* represents?"

Reb Zalman explained *Bina* is in the top triangle of the Kabbalists' "Tree of Life" as a "Mother/Womb of Knowing and Holding"; and that *Bina* is a safe place beyond the intellectual meaning of "understanding."

He invited me to go into the deep "standing-under" quality of grounding and a "being held" in unconditional Love. "*Bina* is the place where *teshuva* lives," he said. By connecting with *Bina*, the redemptive power of rebirth, being forgiven and restored in and through a Great Embracing, Love can happen.

I was led into experiencing this Wombing Power, coming from what Reb Zalman called, "God Godding us from the Field of All Possibility."
— *Carola de Vries Robles [2.34]*

"On the last morning of the conference I was the only person on the elevator….The elevator stopped on the fourth [floor] and Reb Zalman got on….He looked at me for a moment without saying a word. Then he said, 'Y'know, Aryeh, *leibn*, we haven't had much time to connect over these few days.'

"'But I've been looking at you, and….' He paused. Often, in the past, he had told me something about where I was falling short and what I needed to do in order to do better. These reflections have always been painful, but…motivated me to make necessary improvements….

"'And I see,' Reb Zalman continued, 'in your eyes, how you've really been coming to terms with life, and I just want to say *kol ha-kavod* (all power/respect to you).'"
— *by Aryeh Hirschfield, of blessed memory; from Beth Hirschfield [2.35]*

"Do you know the laws about shaving with a razor? If you do, I won't repeat them."

"No. Please tell me."

In fact, I knew these laws quite well and had struggled with the meaning and purpose of what ultimately appeared to be a barber's questions.

It was the winter of 1960. Reb Zalman was our scholar-in-residence at the Jewish Theological Seminary. He regaled me with all the details of the intricacies of shaving and not shaving with an electric razor.

Several hours later he came to my dormitory door. Rabbi Schachter carried a handful of mimeographed sheets; among them was a first edition of his now quite well-known guide to returning to Jewish practice, *The First Step*.
— *Neal Rose [2.36]*

Reb Zalman taught: "Reb Nachman said that you can't have a spiritual experience without telling your body about it."
— *Julie Leavitt [2.37]*

At our last encounter, I was sitting next to Reb Zalman awaiting a presentation by a colleague at a conference in Colorado. As the room began to fill up, Reb Zalman told me, and the others in the row with him, to go sit up front, "to show her the honor her teachings merit."

Reluctant to move, I leaned into Reb Zalman and said, "Oh, I'd rather sit here and bask in your aura."

To which he replied, "Rochel, *leibn*, my aura reaches to Raleigh."

Raleigh is where I live.
— *Raachel Jurovics [2.38]*

"At the beginning of Reb Zalman's teaching session on the last day of the Ohalah gathering he said, 'So, for the few hours we are together…it is important not to flee the dark….Follow the way a root seeks to go down into the dark, and the power a root has to even split boulders. So we have to become experts…Like the Eskimos have so many words for snow…we have to have more words for what happens in the dark. Most of us want to seek enlightenment. Matthew Fox says we need a little *endarkenment*. That place of germination.'"
— *by Aryeh Hirschfield, of blessed memory, from Beth Hirschfield [2.39]*

I was honored to be an advance reader of Reb Zalman's biography called *My Life in Jewish Renewal*. When I told him I felt that his life partners deserved more space in the biography, such as recognition for tending to home and children during the years he was out meeting interesting people, he told me in no uncertain terms that he would not do it. He was, however, pleasant and calm in his response, and shared some of his thinking with me as to why doing so was not a viable option.

I also urged him to rename the book *My Life Before Jewish Renewal*, because so much of it took place before the development of ALEPH and his ordination of so many amazing rabbis.

Again, he listened to the feedback and never became annoyed or confrontational.
— *Leah Novick [2.40]*

Reb Zalman liked to use the word "marinating" and expressed the importance for us to speak and act from an inner, reflective place. He encouraged us to "marinate everything in God's Presence." And he suggested that we become aware of how we were marinated by our life issues.

Reb Zalman told us, "Use my words as signposts."

Reb Zalman also guided us to place our issues upon our hearts, to meditate upon them, be with them, and to explore "innerly toward self-realization."

Other examples of "Reb Zalman expressions" that I have witnessed are:

• Go up the electronic High Way, bring it to *HaShem*.

• Leave out "but," in order to respect others, and when you have something to add, say "and." He said the essence of Jewish meditation is to meditate together, and that we were to use this "and-and" approach.

• Once experienced, spoken, or an action taken, nothing is outside "there" anymore; everything is inside "here" (he'd be pointing at his heart while saying this). He also applied this to matters of "God" and "the Other."

• Reb Zalman taught: "We are here to co-create the Godfield."
— *Carola de Vries Robles [2.41]*

In 1961, when Reb Zalman knew me as a seventeen-year-old sophomore at UC Berkeley named Judy Lowenthal, I sent him a hand-drawn Rosh HaShannah (Jewish New Year) greeting card and received this response:

Dear Judy,
    Your picture is up in my vacation corner in the office. I have a little corner where I take five-minute vacations. Whenever I am tired of the routine, I read some poems some people have sent me, look at pictures and generally have a ball recognizing that on the whole life is not bad at all. So that is where you are.
    Your card is very lovely, but you are worse than an optimist. In your dream congregation, the one you wish to join, you want Max Helfman as Cantor, Rabbi Gordis as a Rabbi, and me for a *shames*, and that kind of congregation

does not happen until *meshiach* (the messiah) comes. But by all means don't be satisfied with less.

I would appreciate your reaction to the two Buber books you read and I am sending you with this letter *The First Step* and *Meshivath Nephesh*. Again your reaction with these will be appreciated. I promise to answer every time you write.

Shalom, Zalman [handwritten in Hebrew]
— *Yehudit Goldfarb [2.42]*

I was living deep in the mountains of Colorado back then (1984), working on the Double-K Ranch (the Triple-K wouldn't have me). And I figured the only way to get a guy off my back was to break down and call him. So I drove into town and found a reasonably clean phone booth decorated with chewing gum and spilled soda.

"Yes, operator," came a friendly female voice on the other end. "We will accept the charges. Thank you…. Good afternoon, B'nai Or Fellowship, this is Leah. Is this Rabbi Winkler?"

"Rabbi Who?" I asked. I had escaped the rabbi scene years ago, and being called "Rabbi" was like calling me Henrietta.

"Is this Gershon Winkler?"

"Uh…yeah. I…"

"Wait…hold on! Omigosh. Just a moment. Reb Zalman wants to…." And off she went somewhere.

I waited. What a waste of time. I just want to be left alone. This guy's been bugging me with these one-sentence letters now for about a month: "Gersh, call me." "Gersh, call collect." "Gersh, we need to talk." "Gersh, please get in touch…."

I mean, I don't even know the guy.

"Gersh?" It was him, that strange rabbi guy. I'd met him only once, way back when I was Orthodox and attending one of them Jewish campus conference things. I was working then for a yeshiva based in Israel. They had sent me to the conference to find unsuspecting seekers of the absolute truth and talk them into studying in their yeshiva. I wasn't very persuasive.

So I meandered about hither and thither and peeked into this room and that room to see what other people were doing in the *Yiddishkeit* (Jewishness) business. That's when I first encountered the Zal Man. And at the time, it traumatized me. There he was, holding hands with women!! And in a circle of both men and women all holding hands!!! And of all the sacrilegious things to do, he was davening with them. Unbelievable!!!

Years had passed since then. I had become far more sacrilegious than Reb Zalman and Spinoza together.

"Gersh?" it was him. "Gersh, listen. I am glad you called. I thought it would take the Jaws of Life to get you to return my call. Listen. You and I, we have to talk. I assume you visit your family in New York from time to time, so I need you to stop by in Philadelphia the next time you're east. Actually—listen to what I tell you—I am going to send you a plane ticket. Come early next week. We need to talk. This is very important."
Click.

"Rabbi Scha...? Hello? Hello?"

Dial tone.

I hung up the phone feeling like some kind of secret agent who'd just received word about his next assignment. I stood there for a moment waiting for the phone to explode. My head was spinning. What had I done? What was I getting myself into?

A week and a half later, I found myself on the platform of a train station in Germantown, a suburb of Philadelphia. It was close to ten at night and there wasn't a soul in sight other than this older bearded dude in a well-worn beret pacing nervously up and down the platform. I looked around, wondering where the heck are the disciples of this supposed guru? Aren't they coming to pick me up?

"Reb Gershon?"

"Reb Zalman?"

We shook hands. Two rabbis, neither of whom was dressed anything like one, each looking for someone who might look somewhat like someone who might be something like a rabbi.

He escorted me downstairs from the platform to a tiny illegally parked Fiat so faded I couldn't make out its color even under the flickering lamppost. I got in beside him amid a rubble of papers, cassettes, brochures, pencils, paperclips, and books. Names of God were flying all about the windshield, suspended from the rear-view mirror by crystal-woven strings. The traditional prayer for journeying was pasted crooked on the dashboard, half-covered by coffee stains painted by sudden stops.

"What's all this?" I asked him, pointing at the dancing names of God.

"That's in case, you know, that God Forbid there's a fatal accident, I would want to go out with the name of the *Riboyno shel Oylam* on my lips…."

"You mean as opposed to Goddamit! Shit! Fuck!!?"

Reb Zalman laughed so hard we almost collided with a trolley.

"Not now, Gersh," he begged. "Not now."

We arrived at a big house resembling the set from the movie "The Addams Family," and even though he turned off the ignition, the engine kept running for a while, coughing, rumbling, sputtering, and then kaput.

"Does your car always sound-off the God Names before shutting down?" I joked.

He laughed while searching for his house keys. "Not now, Gersh. Not now."

Turned out Reb Zalman enjoyed my humor a great deal, only not just now. It was never the right time. Too much to talk about. Too much to get done.

Life was short. The world was standing on the verge of a major paradigm shift and I was cracking jokes.

Inside Reb Zalman's deeply lived-in living room, he bid me to find a comfortable spot to sit, which took me a while as most of the sitting spaces were layered with thousands of years of ancient Hebraic and Aramaic source texts. He disappeared into the kitchen while I sank deeply into a vacant spot on a sofa probably built long before the advent of springs. From the kitchen he called to me, asking if I was hungry. I was about to say "Yes" when he yelled something about making me eggs.

"Gersh?"

"Yeah!"

"Would you like your eggs scrambled, or over-easy?"

I hadn't a clue what "over-easy" meant. Five years was hardly enough time to acculturate a bona fide yeshiva boy in the ways of the nations and their strange culinary dialect.

"Scrambled is fine!" I yelled back. God, how I missed my cabin in the Rockies.

"Gersh!"

"Yeah!"

"Do you smoke?"

"No!"

"You know which 'smoke' I'm talking about?"

"The kind that comes out of a cigarette?"

"Never mind. Do you want some juice?"

"Sure! Thanks!"

"We have apple, cranberry and orange!"

"Orange!"

I couldn't believe it. It was eleven o'clock in the evening and I was being served breakfast by a master elder with no servants at his beckoning, no disciples in waiting.

The eggs were badly charred but tasted fair with a lot of ketchup and orange juice. I assumed the master would join me, but instead he slipped on his jacket, grabbed his car keys, and headed for the door.

"Gersh! I'll be right back. Do you mind babysitting *a shtikel*? (a bit)?"

"You have a baby?"

He laughed. "Not now, Gersh. Not now."

"Oh, so when is it due?"

He laughed harder. "Please, Gersh, not now. There are three kids sleeping upstairs. I'll be right back." And off he went into the mystery of night, leaving me in complete perplexity.

The following morning, I found myself seated alongside Reb Zalman in his Fiat again as we drove all over the city on a wide variety of errands. First, we dropped-off his youngest, Yotam, at a preschool place. Then we sped out to the countryside to pick up a bathing suit that his daughter Shalvi had forgotten at Day Camp. Then we headed back to the business section of town so Reb Zalman could "up" his optical prescription by one point to ease his work in front of the computer screen.

As he drove frantically through the maze of city streets and traffic, he slapped a clipboard on my lap and had me take notes as he distilled thousands of years of Kabbalistic wisdom into a fresh bottle of *Sefirot* (qualities on the Kabbalists' Tree of Life). I had no idea what he was talking about.

Careening around the corner of every known street in Philadelphia, we stopped at virtually every optical store, double-parking or parking in front of fire hydrants and driveways—whatever it took. My job was to sit in the car and look out for the police while he would rush inside to try and convince the opticians to upgrade his lenses by a single point. I couldn't figure out why he kept coming back to the car frustrated each time, and why we were hopping from one store to the other. When we eventually came upon a legal parking space, I followed him inside.

"I need these lenses moved up a point."

"Do you have a prescription for your request, sir?"

"No, I don't. But I know exactly what I need, just one point stronger."

"I am truly sorry, sir, but we need a doctor's prescription to do that."

"Listen, I don't have time to sit in a doctor's office right now, couldn't you just give me lenses with one point stronger than these? I know what I need."

"Again, sir, we cannot do this without a prescription."

"I will take full responsibility. Just one point."

"Sorry, sir. Can't do."

"Can I talk to the manager?"

"I am the manager."

As we got back into the car, he restored the clipboard to my lap and continued discussing the contemporary applications of the shattered vessels, which emerged from the implosion of Genesis.

"What's a paradigm shift?" I finally asked him as he pulled out of the latest parking spot.

Reb Zalman laughed. "Not now, Gersh. Not now."

One day, under the ruse of serving as his suitcase-shlepper (carrier) on one of his lecture tours, he suddenly rose up out of his teaching chair at Chicago's Oasis Center one afternoon, dropped Rebbe Nachman of Breslav's magnum opus on my lap, and whispered, "I have to go to the bathroom—you take over" and vanished, forcing me to translate and teach from the complex wisdom of Rebbe Nachman's multilayered commentaries, a body of wisdom I'd never thought of exploring.

Needless to say, his "visit to the bathroom" lasted well over an hour. How in the Four Worlds could Reb Zalman have known who I was, let alone whether or not I was worth the trouble of restoring?!
— *Gershon Winkler [2.43]*

I first heard the words "paradigm shift" from Reb Zalman when he was teaching for our community: "We made the transition from King to Father, from the offering of gifts to words of praise and petition. Now we're leaving behind the Father and moving to…."

So I inquired, "What is our relationship with the Divine in this emerging paradigm? *Haver* (friend)? After all, we're called a *havurah*."

"Not *haver*," he responded quickly. "Not *haver*, not friend. At its root the meaning of *haver* is 'joining.' A joining with the Holy One might draw you out of the world. Gather the *havurah*. I'll tell a story."

We gathered, perhaps eighty souls in the great room, to *nosh* (snack) on the remnants of the *cholent* (Sabbath stew), and to listen to Reb Zalman's story. It was of a bartender who was angry by nature, who took the Holy One to be his partner in business. Because the Holy One was his partner, the bartender developed the ability to pronounce blessings to great effect.
— *Mitchell Chefitz [2:44]*

When I was seventeen years old, I met Reb Zalman who shared his teachings of *Hassidut* and Kabbalah with me, along with his versions of the Nachman tales. I particularly recall him offering spiritual guidance through a Reb Nachman story about a wood cutter who finds a precious jewel that gets lost. The story's refrain was, "Never give up, never lose faith, always believe that things will unfold as they are intended to."
— *Carol Rose [2.45]*

When doing private retreats at the Lama Foundation, typically food was left for me to do my own cooking at the base of the mountain. The hermitage huts were up above. One morning I heard a huffing and puffing coming my way. Looking to see what it was, I opened the door and there was Reb Zalman schlepping a tray full of breakfast. He said, "I thought you should have something to eat."
— *Neshama (Rose) Lipari [2.46]*

When Reb Zalman was a visitor for a day at Camp Ramah, I was a counselor for the oldest youth, the Machon group. I invited him to talk to my campers who were mostly rowdy thirteen year-olds who always resisted going to sleep.

That night Reb Zalman visited, he mesmerized them. His presence itself brought a calm and curiosity. He taught the campers about *Kriat Shema al ha-Meeta*, the traditional bedtime prayer practice. He covered his eyes at the beginning, after explaining that the tradition to do so was to teach that God should not be identified with any existing element of the created world—that was idolatry.

God, Reb Zalman taught, was the creator of all and yet transcended all.
— *Michael Lerner [2.47]*

The last time we met, I performed for Reb Zalman with a group of musicians. After the performance he embraced me in the middle of the room and did the *yechidus* that he had written about in his book *Spiritual Intimacy*. He whispered a blessing in my ear. It was serious, took a few minutes, and we were alone even though we were in the middle of a room full of people. He spoke my purpose.
— *James Stone Goodman [2.48]*

Reb Zalman at the Lama Foundation, 1988
Photo Credit: David Pascale

3

Davenology

Reb Zalman introduced and modeled
davenen — heartfelt, connected prayer — using
traditional and innovative approaches drawn from
the human potential movement, contemplative and
mystical traditions, and unique takes of his own and
his students' translations, melodies, and lyrics.

Shabbat

In 1994 I was sixty-one years old and had not been to a *shul* since my Bar Mitzvah. One *Shabbos* I decided to try P'nai Or, a Jewish Renewal Congregation founded by Rabbi Zalman Schachter-Shalomi.

I was on the way in when I encountered Reb Zalman, himself, also about to enter. Never having met him formally, I wasn't sure what to say or even how to address him. So, I blurted out, "Rabbi, this is my first time at services in forty-eight years."

Expecting a perfunctory acknowledgement, I was taken aback when he stopped, caught my eye, and recited, as I later learned, the traditional Jewish blessing upon hearing good news!

I have been an active member ever since.
— Melvin Metelits [3.1]

Having come from an Orthodox yeshiva background, I was blown away by Reb Zalman's translation of *Yedid Nefesh,* which could be sung in English. It was a revelation that one could *daven* in English and forego responsive readings.
— Moshe Waldoks [3.2]

In the 1970s and '80s Reb Zalman was doing "gigs" at synagogues and he would talk to me on the way about trying to create an alternative to what he called "seat belt Judaism." When we went to do a service in New Jersey one time I understood what he meant. It was like pulling teeth to get the congregants to sing, participate, do anything other than be passive and listen.

A teaching of his of that time that sticks in my memory is that "Each *Shabbos* is a pearl, and we carefully string them together on a necklace." And indeed, for the most part, all of the *Shabbos* moments with friends and family blend together as one beautiful string of pearls, an array of memories, visions, and candlelit moments.

One family teaching of Reb Zalman's that I recall is the "five *minuteses*" that he shared as a pre-*Shabbos* practice. Everyone in the family gets to say what makes them joyous or feel "*shabbosdik*" (in a Sabbath mood) and then leads something, while everyone does it along with them. The example he gave was how his young son suggested everyone jump up and down for joy! And they all did!
— *Ahouva Steinhaus [3.3]*

Our prayer circle filled the room on the day Reb Zalman led Shabbat morning services. We began quietly, and as the energy grew, all of the inviting instruments from the basket in the center of the room were put into use—finger cymbals, bongos, rattles, and tambourines.

When we came to the psalms, Reb Zalman said, "These are the Psalms of King David. What are your psalms?"

He guided us in turning toward our neighbor and sharing our own feeling-filled psalms. He said, "When you look upon your neighbor, know that the *Shechinah* is present. You are gazing upon the face of God."
— *David Arfa [3.4]*

Reb Zalman said, "So, tonight through our davening and singing, let us reach a high so that Shabbat dwells in us, and we luxuriate in Shabbat."
— *Hal Miller-Jacobs [3.5]*

While sitting at dinner with Reb Zalman at the beginning of a twenty-four-hour *shabbaton* in Ashland, Oregon, I was starting to eat a delicious dessert and offered to get some for him. As Reb Zalman was in a period of time when he was being careful about his weight, he said, "No, you eat and I'll taste over here."
— *Yitz Husbands-Hankin [3.6]*

As a regular *davenen* leader at Kehillah Ahavat Hesed in Toronto in 1990, I was excited to lead during a Shabbat when Reb Zalman was in town, having met him in the mid-1980s, and to learn that he would be praying with us. I shared the first liturgical melody I had ever composed, which was inspired by a book of Reverend Howard Thurman's writings I came upon in the Martin Luther King Jr. Center Bookstore in Atlanta, Georgia.

As I began to chant "Open unto me light for my darkness, Open unto me courage for my fear…," out of the corner of my eye I saw Reb Zalman begin pacing in the back of the room. When the service finished he rushed up to me, his face beaming in delight and eyes sparkling. "That's my African-American Rebbe," he proclaimed. "Where did you find these words?!"
— *Shawn Israel Zevit [3.7]*

I was in the tenth grade in the fall of 1969 and my brother brought me to a *shabbaton* at Rutgers Hillel. The leader, Reb Zalman, was until then unknown to me. He shared that except on *Shabbos,* when he had the time and presence-of-mind-heart-and-soul to appreciate the animal that gave its life for food, he ate a vegetarian diet. And at *Shabbos* lunch he had us feed each other!
— *Rita Hindin [3.8]*

I first met Reb Zalman as a summer camper in the Torah session for high school students at the Reform Movement's Olin-Sang Union Institute in Oconomowoc, Wisconsin, in August, 1966. I was seventeen, just about to begin my senior year in high school, so Reb Zalman must have been about to turn forty-two, the same age as my mother.

He had been invited to spend Shabbat with us by some of the Reform rabbis who taught at the camp who were part of a group known as the Covenant Theologians who met regularly to talk theology and share their papers with one another. I'll never forget the figure Reb Zalman cut, a tall and dynamic all-black-clad emissary, wearing his long Shabbat *kapoteh,* fur-trimmed *shtreimel,* and soft slippers.

I can almost hear him now, speak-singing in his melodic way, as he swayed and fairly danced between our Shabbat tables, set up in the open air, teaching us the fine points of things like how not to put *pareve* (non-dairy) margarine on the table with our Shabbat chicken dinner, even though it was kosher, because it looked wrong—the principle of *marit ayin* (creating the appearance of doing something not within traditional Jewish practice).

He also taught us how, to our sages, appearances mattered—not in the way they mattered to suburban teenage kids, but in the way that a person's behavior, even "permitted" behavior, might express or in some way betray the intent of the soul.
— *Diane Elliot [3.9]*

In 1985, as we were planning the first Kallah, a straight, young couple requested to have their wedding during this national gathering. The request sparked a passionate debate. How could we place a celebration of heterosexual love at the Kallah, when sanctification of love between gay and lesbian folk was impermissible within all of the established Jewish movements?

Reb Zalman listened and, once we had decided not to approve the couple's request, he declared with evident delight: "Birth pangs of the *Shechinah!*" And, at the Shabbat Torah service in 1985, Reb Zalman opened the space for an *aliya* to become a coming out ritual for gay, lesbian, and transgender folks.
— *Barbara (Bobbi) Breitman [3.10]*

In Reb Zalman's tradition, a group of those present comes up for an aliya, to witness the Torah reading and be blessed with a chosen theme that fits with the verses being chanted. One *aliya* on the verses in *Parshat Bo* includes where Moses declares to Pharaoh in God's Name [Exodus 10:3]: "*Ad matai me'anta l'anot mi'panai?* — How long will you refuse to humble yourself to answer Me?" and "*Shalach ami v'ya'avduni*—Let My people go that they may serve Me."

This was my first time interpreting and chanting Torah before seminary classmates and faculty members. My plan was to try on Reb Zalman's psycho-spiritual approach to connecting people's lives to the Torah verses, after teaching about the Torah portion. When the time came, I called up those who would be witnessing the reading: "*Ya'amdu* — rise and come forward, anyone seeking courage to release something — an idea, habit, or view of self — whose time has come for release, so the humility of letting go can create a new spaciousness for inner freedom and holy service."

Immediately Reb Zalman leapt out of his seat exclaiming, "Make room. This *aliya* is for me!"

A wave of laughter washed over the prayer space. With Reb Zalman to my left, a substantial group soon assembled around us to receive the chanted words of Torah.
— *David Evan Markus [3.11]*

Reb Zalman taught that we are to lift a light into the house we have inherited, remembering that in the building of the Biblical Israelites' wilderness tabernacle, we were instructed to lift up a light [Numbers 8:1]. So he taught that the light will need a little lift.
— *James Stone Goodman [3.12]*

Holidays

One year, Reb Zalman asked the congregation to allow him a *shofar* (ram's horn blown on the High Holy Days) solo. This is how I remember his explanation:

"It was 1941. I was in a Vichy prison camp in German-occupied France, waiting for documents so I could leave Europe and come to America. Rosh Hashanah was coming, and we didn't have a *shofar*. So I escaped from camp and went to the nearest village and entered a butcher shop. The butcher could see that I was a Jew and that I was terrified—what if the Germans saw me in his shop! He said I should take what I wanted and leave. We were hungry, but all I took was a horn from a butchered sheep.

"I had to sneak back into the camp, if you can imagine. Working in secret, I made a *shofar*. Then, on Rosh HaShannah morning, all the prisoners were lined up at sunrise for inspection. That's when I blew the *shofar*.

"Well, the commandant of the camp came running out, with his uniform, his boots, a pistol in one hand and a whip in the other. 'Who blew that?' he shouted. I stepped forward and said, 'I did.'

"The commandant laughed and said, 'Well, blow it again, Jew. Your emigration papers have just arrived.'

"This is the *shofar* I blew in the camp. So when I blow it today, I blow it for all the souls that did not survive the camps, that they should find peace."
— *Michael Chusid [3.13]*

Reb Zalman said the most important thing he learned from "the Rebbe" was to "Live in Jewish Time."
— *Carola de Vries Robles [3.14]*

The sages say hearing the *shofar* awakens the soul. My awakening was on Rosh Hashanah 5754 (1993) when Reb Zalman was leading the davening at a synagogue in Los Angeles. That year, and for many years after, at least part of the High Holy Days was with Reb Zalman. Instead of shushing people, he started our services by inviting us to turn to those around us and speak together about what we wanted to leave behind in the year that ended and what we wanted to make room for in the new year.

Throughout the day, he would stop the inexorable flow of liturgy to ask, "Where are you?" and to respond to questions from congregants. He invited us to say the *Shema*, a central prayer, using one's own name, "*Shema* (listen) Michael," in my case. He got us all out of our chairs to sing and dance in joy and prayer.
— *Michael Chusid [3.15]*

The first time I experienced Reb Zalman was at Rosh Hashanah services at UCLA in 1996. There were over 1000 people gathered engaged in prayer. He smiled widely and spoke in a kind, open, and inviting manner.

Reb Zalman dressed like a rebbe, behaved and moved like a rebbe. There, I noticed that he did two things unheard of in the part of the Orthodox world that had educated me Jewishly. Reb Zalman shifted a word in the Friday night Shabbat liturgy, a word that had long kept me distanced from traditional Jewish prayer. He modified the phrase "*bahar banu mi-kol ha'amim* — [God Who] chose us **from** all the nations" to "*bahar banu eem kol ha'amim* — Who chose us **with** all the nations."

Reb Zalman had added one single letter and changed an entire prayer. Another astounding thing that happened at that service was that he invited us to express the personal longings of our hearts to God!
— *T'mimah Audrey Ickovits [3.16]*

Reb Zalman's approach to *shofar* was different from the prevalent staid rituals. He explained the mitzvah is not to blow, but to hear — to hear with your entire being and in all the worlds. The blasts are a two-way spiritual technology that contains messages to those who listen, and carries our prayers that cannot put into words. The sound is not from the one standing blowing the *shofar* on the *bima*, but the very breath of creation.

The sequence of *shofar* blasts, Reb Zalman explained, are the steps of *teshuva*, sometimes translated as repentance, but also signifying a return to our true self.

"Imagine," Reb Zalman said, "that all the habits that are not serving you are an enormous boulder, too big for you to move. You would take the biggest sledge you could find, raise it over your head, and swing it with all your might—whack! to crack the boulder into chunks—that's the *shofar* blast of *tekiah*.

"Next, you would take a smaller hammer that you could swing faster—bang bang bang—and break the chunks into pieces: that's *shevarim*. Then, you would take a small mallet and pulverize the pieces into dust with quick ta-ta-ta-ta-ta-ta-ta-ta strokes—that's *teruah*.

"Then what?" He asked and answered, "You have a pile of dust, and your bad characteristics are still polluting your life and the world."

Reb Zalman often used metaphors from science and technology. "Take the dust," he advised, "and shape it into something positive. In manufacturing there is this technique where small particles are consolidated, sintered, by striking them with great intensity. That's the *tekiah gedolah*, a powerful blow to set your intentions for the New Year."
— *Michael Chusid [3.17]*

For several years, Reb Zalman led High Holiday Services at a traditional conservative congregation in Cambridge, Massachusetts. Most of the people were elderly, some survivors and a few hippies from Cambridge. He wanted people to participate in the service, so he used melodies that he knew they would know about. I remember one was a popular commercial and another was "We shall overcome."

On Yom Kippur, all of a sudden the lights in the synagogue sputtered and then went out. Only the small lights around the *bima* remained. Reb Zalman said to the congregation, "Don't worry, I have my prayerbook and I can see, just follow along with me." People sat there in the dark and continued to pray with him.

Suddenly, all the lights went out and Reb Zalman said, "Don't worry, I know these prayers by heart. I don't need the book. Just follow along with me." And the people sat there, in the complete darkness, not moving, and continued to pray with him.

Then it was time to open the ark for the Torah service. As soon as Reb Zalman went up to the ark and pulled on the string, all the lights went on. And Reb Zalman said, "I should have thought to do that sooner!" And without missing a beat or a holy moment, he continued the service.
— *Cherie Koller-Fox [3.18]*

I attended my first Yom Kippur service with Reb Zalman at Fellowship Farm outside of Philadelphia in around the early eighties. It was a Yom Kippur like nothing I had ever experienced before.

Although we used the black Silverman *machzorim* (High Holiday prayer books) and the liturgy was very traditional, Reb Zalman had many new approaches and spiritual interpretations for us. For example, he pulled the *aron kodesh* (holy ark) away from the wall, so that anyone at anytime could go behind it to be close to the Torah scrolls, be part of the group, and yet have privacy in which to offer their deepest prayers.

Reb Zalman accompanied the prayers on a zither. And, at the end of the *Neila* service as Yom Kippur concludes, Reb Zalman made *Havdalah* with sparklers!
— *Latifa Berry Kropf [3.19]*

Instead of a single shofar blower for the congregation—a Talmudic tradition—Reb Zalman invited everyone with a shofar to blow. One year he would have the shofarists blow in unison, another he would line us up to sound one after the other. Sometimes from the *bima*, other times from our seat in the sanctuary.
— *Michael Chusid [3.20]*

During the 1970s amazing retreats were held at Fellowship House Farm where, among many other things, for Simchat Torah we first developed the dances of the *sefirot* for each of the *hakafot* (circlings) that are traditionally done while holding the Torah. Reb Zalman divided us into groups and then we were instructed and inspired to dance into our vision of the realm of consciousness that we had chosen through the Tree of Life practices of the Kabbalists.
— *Ahouva Steinhaus [3.21]*

Before Pesach (Passover) in 2013, I asked Reb Zalman to share his practices for the Passover Seder. He said that the essential spiritual orientation of the seder is flowing down from the highest places and that this is the meaning of Pesach as *"itaruta d'l'eila"* awakening from above.

Before beginning the seder he asks each participant what they need to get from the seder. This is his application of the *Tannaitic* rule "The Paschal sacrifice may only be eaten by those who have signed on to it." [*Mishna, Zevahim* 5:8]

Kadesh. He lays out the various foods on the Seder Plate only after making *Kiddush* "so that the children ask" and the details become a topic of conversation.

Karpas. He puts out many varieties of *karpas*, greens, so that people will not be hungry during the *Maggid* section of the seder.

Karpas. He mixes vinegar into the salt water to evoke the experience of "sweat and tears."

Yahatz. The matzah broken for the *Yahatz* section of the *seder* is the matzah that corresponds to the *Sefira* of *Bina*. This is because the *Sefira* of *Bina* is where absolute Divine unity is broken and hints of multiplicity begin to make their appearance.

Maggid. Of the text of the *Maggid* section, he makes sure to say the order itself (*Kadesh, U'rhatz,* etc.) and the three teachings of Rabbi Yishmael in the Haggadah (*Pesach, Matzah* and *Maror*).

Maggid. Regarding the response to the question of the second son, Reb Zalman said that it is generally not useful to break the teeth of a person who considers themself to be evil.

Matzah. On the first night of Pesach, before eating matzah he would ask what each person needed to sustain their faith so they would be open to receiving that from the matzah, which is referred to as "faith food." On the second night he would ask what each person needed to sustain their health so they would be open to receiving that from the matzah, which is referred to as "healing food." [Both terms are based on *Zohar* 2:183b]

Maror. It is good for the *maror* to be grown locally. Reb Zalman told me that when he lived in Philadelphia he would go before Pesach and pick dandelion greens growing in the cracks of the sidewalks and use them for *maror.*

Korech. He puts the middle matzah between two damp towels so that it softens and can actually be used as a wrap, *Korech.*

Tzafun. The practice of eating matzah at the end of the seder (*afikoman*) is deeper than the eating of matzah at the beginning of the meal. It reflects the understanding that follows the experience. The first time we eat matzah it is like explaining birth to a woman who has never given birth before. But the matzah we eat at the end of the meal is like the understanding of the woman after she has given birth.

Elijah's Cup. Because of the Talmudic tradition that Elijah will resolve all questions and difficulties (*teiku*) Reb Zalman asks participants what each one would like to ask Elijah. After Elijah had been invited in, each person would pour a bit from Elijah's cup into her own cup and share what she had received from Elijah.

Hallel. In the Great *Hallel* (*Tehillim*, Psalm 136) each participant says something they are grateful for, and the others all respond, "*ki l'olam hasdo* — God's grace is eternal."
— *Ebn Leader [3.22]*

During the May 2014 Shavuot retreat at Isabella Freedman Retreat Center, at the last session, Reb Zalman spoke about davening — authentic, heartfelt prayer. He showed erudition, humor, sensitivity, and drive in how he was able to speak, even with tubes feeding oxygen in through his nose. Then, at the very end, he removed the oxygen, stood up, came down off the stage, and stood before us. Reb Zalman's davenology instructions to the two hundred-some people present were brief: "Just stand up, put your *tallis* over your head, and speak to God out loud from your heart."

I positioned myself near him, and covered my head with a *tallis* for the first time. No words came…too self-conscious.

Reb Zalman was praying, in a combination of Yiddish, English, and Hebrew. Hearing him, I began to cry and call out to God from the place of my deepest yearning.
— *Meira Bracha Sumka [3.23]*

On Shabbat morning of the 2005 Shavuot retreat at the original Elat Chayyim, Reb Zalman led services. It was my first experience of him. The service was thoughtful, joyous, and filled with group energy.

At some point, perhaps during the morning service *Amida* — a silent, standing, personal prayer time — I stood and stretched upwards toward the heavens. A hand reaching out for the Holy

One of Blessing. A quiver went running through my body. In a flash it was over.

After Shabbat, emerging from the bookstore, there was Reb Zalman. When our eyes met, he crooked his finger, signaling that I should approach.

"Something happened to you this morning?" Reb Zalman half questioned, half observed.

"Yes. Something did," I responded.

My burning desire had been noticed by the matchmaker.
— Audrey Seidman [3.24]

One year Reb Zalman came to the Aquarian Minyan's Shavuot retreat. He stayed up all night and taught non-stop and in the morning we davened. When we came to the *Hallel* service of Psalms, he asked us all to go on the stage where the amphitheater was so that we could "perform the *Hallel* for God."

Also on a Shavuot retreat, Reb Zalman did "Torah oracle" readings at the Aquarian Minyan; usually we saw this done on Simchat Torah. He invited those who wanted to participate to roll the Torah, stop, and point to a random verse and so receive our message from Above. At the time, a friend had serious skin issues all over her body. When she rolled the scroll, she stopped and pointed to a verse: it was about *tza'ra'at* — a skin discoloring derived from the Prophetess Miriam's emotional distress.
— Sarah Leah Grafstein [3.25]

Gan Eden, paradise was our local Thursday nights and *Shabbos* mornings in Boulder, Colorado, learning *Hassidut* with Reb Zalman. We sometimes also celebrated holidays together, including the Fourth of July and Thanksgiving.

Reb Zalman delighted in teaching the *Tanya* (a Hassidic text), including where it is written: "a righteous person lives by his faith, his awe, and by the flashes of fire of the flame of his love [of God]...." He exemplified this during a quiet Thanksgiving where Eve and a few friends were present in the last year of his life.

Reb Zalman was quite weak, but ever the rebbe. Knowing that most people there knew each other, he asked each to take turns going around sharing something they especially valued about everyone present.
— *Yehudis Fishman [3.26]*

Daily Prayer

"Reb Zalman said, 'What I think is me, is the Creator playing Zalman. So all I can do is offer my will to give God a good ride every day.'"
— *Written by Aryeh Hirschfield, of blessed memory; from Beth Hirschfield [3.27]*

In the 1980s in Philadelphia when Reb Zalman was sharing custody of his two youngest sons, both boys stayed with him for a number of days each week. Reb Zalman and I would *daven Shacharit* together early each morning. We both held *siddurim* (prayer books), but since Reb Zalman knew the entire service by heart, we each proceeded at our own pace.

Often one of the children would wake up and need a diaper change. Without stopping his prayers, Reb Zalman would take off the arm piece of his *tefillin*, leaving the headpiece in place. He'd then go get his son and carry him into the kitchen. He'd change the diaper at the sink wearing his head *tefillin*, praying quietly and serenely while performing the other "required task."

Then he'd bring his son back to bed, put his hand *tefillin* back on, and complete the morning prayers.
— *Andrew Gold [3.28]*

I'd been davening three times a day for a decade and had stopped feeling the words. Soon I was sitting across from Reb Zalman outside the main building of Elat Chayyim. "I am bored with prayer," I explained. "But I don't want to stop praying. What should I do?"

Reb Zalman's first question was whether I knew another language, besides English and Hebrew. "Yes, I speak French," I told him, puzzled by his question.

"Get a French prayer book. Pray in French," Reb Zalman said, adding that solitary prayer was best, and recommending that I not go to the morning *minyan* the next day, and rather pray in the garden.

I told Reb Zalman one of my problems with prayer was that I couldn't let go of my ego while davening. My conscious mind kept yapping at me. He told me, "If someone tells you to let go of your ego, watch your wallet." He continued, explaining that the ego is like a dog. It barks because it's supposed to. It's not doing anything wrong, just what it was designed to do. So, when it barks, just say, "Good doggie. Come along with me now."

As an afterthought, Reb Zalman asked about my next steps. I told him I was going to rabbinical school in the autumn. He warned me that the seminary I had chosen could sometimes be dry. "I bless you," he said, "that rabbinical school should not harm you in any way."

Being quite accustomed to disregarding the advice of elders, and wanting to go to morning *minyan*, I did. Reb Zalman saw me and frowned, and that mattered somehow. So the next morning I went to pray in the garden.
— *Jill Hammer [3.29]*

Living in post-Holocaust Judaism in the Netherlands, being a Jew meant being traumatized, victimized, and caught in this physical reality of being a leftover Jew. Reb Zalman showed me how to use the *siddur*, to speak some Hebrew, to try on *tefillin*, and to call the angels and masters of wisdom in.
— *Carola de Vries Robles [3.30]*

I remember the first time Reb Zalman taught us to chant the *Shema*, not just once, but rather three times — once for ourselves, once for a person or a place that needed it, and once for ourselves in the future. The latter for deposit in our "*Shema* bank account." This was done both alone and during *minyan*.
— *Sarah Leah Grafstein [3.31]*

Reb Zalman would teach, "We are all familiar with the *Shema*, that outcry into the world to see the interdependence of all things: *Shema Yisrael Havaya Eloheinu Yah Echad.*"

Then he would have us turn to the one next to us, uttering the *Shema* silently with that person's name in lieu of *Yisrael* flowing in a ribbon across the room. And he would have us say it to ourselves, inserting our own name:

Shema Moshe Adonai Eloheinu Yah Echad

Reb Zalman would explain, "Listen, be awake, and open yourself to the voice of the Other." And he would teach that the *Shema* calls out to us as individuals, as a *ben/bat Yisrael* (son or daughter of Israel).

"And so while we are part of a collective, we are also individually called to fulfill our capacity of being transformed into *Yisrael*, one who wrestles with God; one who is *Yashar-El*, one who is straight with God; one who is *Shir-El*, one who sings God's song."
— *Moshe Waldoks [3.32]*

Reb Zalman was teaching with Roshi Bernie Glassman during the second year of Elat Chayyim. We were settling into class after lunch and with a twinkle in his eye, Reb Zalman said, "Let's play a trick on Bernie. When he comes in, let's all be saying the *Shema* together, stretching out each word with a full breath, like a full, long *Om*." We were eager to give it a try and worked on suppressing our giggles.

When Roshi Bernie came in, he didn't flinch, blink, or show any sign of surprise. Instead, he reverently began to sit. When we were done, the humor had turned to hushed awe. We asked Roshi Bernie if he realized we were joking. He just said, "Joke? It felt like you were all praying from your depths."

A new tradition was born.
— *David Arfa [3.33]*

When Reb Zalman was speaking of love, *ahavah*, at P'nai Or, Philadelphia, many decades ago, he pointed out that the *bracha* before reciting the *Shema* prayer, when chanted during the evening service, opens with "*Ahavat olam ahavtanu* — with eternal love You have loved us." But during the morning service, the same prayer opens with "*Ahavah rabbah ahavtanu* — with great love You have loved...."

"So, why the difference?" Reb Zalman asked rhetorically. "Because," he answered, "there is love that rises to the heights, consumes one's being, burns bright, and, yes, inevitably, over time, fades away. And there is also love that is deep, quiet, steady, and enduring. Forever love." [*Tosafot* on *Talmud Berakhot* 11b]

And then he continued, "In the evening we acknowledge the quiet love, while in the morning the passionate love, because we need both."
— *Reuben Modek [3.34]*

On a balcony overlooking the Kangra Valley in Dharamsala, during a 1990 trip to India, while davening *b'yechidus* (individually, but in a group, as we didn't have a *minyan*), Reb Zalman snuck up on each of us at the end of the *Shema* and whispered, "*Adonai eloheichem emet* — *your God is truth.*" This phrase, so often said by rote, brought tears.
— *Moshe Waldoks [3.35]*

Reb Zalman would also give assignments. For instance, he asked me in the beginning to commit a whole year round to study the *parshiot*, the weekly Torah portions. To live to be a Jew, Reb Zalman explained, means "learning by doing."

He even assigned me to do "the Rabbi-ing" as a lay leader. He called upon me and many others worldwide to study, teach, lead, and learn. He spoke of this as "delving in and actualizing this Torah we were given before we were born."
— *Carola de Vries Robles [3.36]*

When Reb Zalman would come to visit the Bay Area, he was at the beginning of developing "davenology" and tried out many of his innovations on us. I remember him teaching us how to *daven* in dyads and triads without a *minyan*.

For example, I remember sitting on the floor across from Reb Zalman as he read me the English and Hebrew of a psalm in the opening psalms of the morning service. I had my eyes closed and received their beauty and power visually for the first time. Then he had me read them to him, having his own experience. Sometimes we would alternate reading verses to each other, the receivers sharing how the verse touched them.
— *Sarah Leah Grafstein [3.37]*

During the 1970s, Reb Zalman introduced the custom of unrolling the entire Torah scroll, outside, as we gathered in a circle according to our birthdays. He would look at where we stood and read a *pasuk*, (a verse) to us from that *parsha*, Torah portion, as a "reading" or individual inspiration for the coming year.
— *Ahouva Steinhaus [3.38]*

Reb Zalman encouraged us to "Work with a *pasuk*, a phrase, one line, a letter, or letters, and to "turn challenges and tragedies into blessings." For instance, he modeled this by having us in a circle, each person holding an upper edge of the Torah scroll until it was completely revealed. And he'd search for a verse for us to have for contemplation at the place where each of us was standing.

He would give people a verse from Torah or a prayer as a mantra to help with the core issues of our lives. He showed me how to place myself into the hands of God and not be afraid. From the *Adon Olam* prayer he taught me the verses *"b'yado afkid ruchee —* into Your hands I give notice of my spirit" and *"Adonai li v'lo ira —* You are *Adonai* (God) for me and I will not fear." The latter was the mantra he gave to me.
— *Carola de Vries Robles [3.39]*

One year Reb Zalman gave a workshop about the holiday of Simchat Torah in Los Angeles. He began by teaching us about the *sefirot*. He then arbitrarily divided the fifty of us into ten different groups, and explained that each group represented one of the ten divine emanations.

Our assignment was to create a song together, or a dance, a prayer, a poem, an incantation—whatever we might collectively invent in our individual groups to reflect the qualities of our *Sefira*. I was assigned to *Malchut*, which is also known as *Shekhinah*. This *Sefira* collects and releases into existence the combined energy of all of the *sefirot* together as they merge and manifest through concrete action on earth.

Two hours later, all of us performed our interpretations of the *sefirot* for the entire group. Reb Zalman purred with pleasure, commenting on the originality and creativity.

He then announced that as a culmination to the workshop we would rehearse for the upcoming holiday of Simchat Torah. We were invited to gather into one large circle and Reb Zalman brought out two Torah scrolls. He explained that we would make seven rounds, taking turns holding the Torah. We would together utter the last word of the last book of the Torah and then immediately intone the first word of the Torah, of the book of Genesis that describes how God created the world.

During that process he encouraged us to image that, as we were making the rounds, we were simultaneously creating new beginnings in our own lives. Reb Zalman stopped in front of me and handed me the Torah. Could he have known or intuited that I was just beginning a new and daring chapter in my own life?
— *Ruth Broyde Sharone [3.40]*

Reb Zalman entered and turned on some soft classical music and began with, "Close your eyes...release your breath...now imagine a path in the forest...follow it to a clearing by a cool flowing stream...look up and enjoy the visit with your *bubbe* (grandmother), or *zayde* (grandfather), or any other ancestor you choose."

People in the room were invited to share afterward in small groups with each other. Many openly wept from the meaning and beauty of their encounters.

When asked to talk about the process, Reb Zalman explained, "the landscape of prayer is also the landscape of imagination. Imagination is ever present with every story we hear, every lift of our arm. First, we have to imagine our arm lifting, which then directs our arm to actually lift in this world. And yet how few of us pay attention to this. When we strengthen our imagination, we focus our intentions, we deepen our prayer."
– *David Arfa [3.41]]*

Reb Zalman encouraged our *tefillot* (prayers) to become a highly personal point of contact between our mind and the One Mind of the cosmos. This experience he called being "*Nochach P'nai HaShem* – placing one's self in the Presence of God."

Drawing on Hassidic teachings on prayer and meditation, Reb Zalman taught us how to view the daily and Shabbat morning service as a journey through the four Kabbalistic worlds: *Assiya*, Action; *Yetzira*, Formation; *Briya*, Creation; and *Atzilut* – the blazing Emanation of pure Divinity.

For some years at Elat Chayyim, my friend and colleague, Rabbi David Wolfe-Blank, of blessed memory, and I worked on illustrating a Four-Worlds map of *Shacharit* (the morning service) as this multidimensional journey. One question that we brought to Reb Zalman was this: "Okay, we see clearly how the *davenen* flows through the Four Worlds, ascending from morning blessings to the *Amida* and gently descending, and here is a map. But what about *Musaf* – the repetition of an *Amida* after the Torah reading? How does *Musaf* fit in the scheme?" So many of our communities have dropped *Musaf* in favor of augmenting aspects of the *Shacharit* experience that cried out for expansion, so *Musaf* was not even on our map.

"What about *Musaf?*" we asked. "How does it fit here? What does *Musaf* do?"

"Ah," he said. "Let me tell you a story. It was 1994 and Eve and I were going out to do a *shabbaton* for the still-small Jewish Renewal community in Boulder. The program was held at Chautauqua Community House. It was going to be my birthday and my beloved Eve bought me a glider ride as a surprise gift.

It was a stunningly beautiful Boulder day when I went up in the glider. A glider is amazingly light. So graceful. Since they don't have engines, the glider is towed high into the air by a powered towing plane that pulls the glider using a long rope. Once the glider is high enough, inside the cockpit the glider pilot releases the towrope, and the glider plane flies free.

The glider pilot took over as the silent, engine-less plane soared over the magnificent Boulder hills and valleys. High above the hills we circled for what seemed like forever, over the rugged terrain of mountain slopes and valleys. Above us an infinite expanse of blue adorned with white clouds. We sailed into eternity. Then we began our luxurious circling descent. All was beautiful. It was like a fluid prayer.

Yet as we descended, suddenly to my surprise, the pilot steered our glider away from the valley toward the outskirts of Boulder, and *gevalt* – right over a vast teeming automobile junkyard! What was happening? Why this? Then I got it! The hot sun baking the metal carcasses was generating a huge thermal updraft. We caught the heated thermal and it carried us way up again! We were back up in the sky, and had another hour of flight, and then a sweetly graceful descent.

"That," said Reb Zalman, "is *Musaf.*"
– *Marcia Prager [3.42]*

Reb Zalman's understanding of *Eloheinu*: "The Reality that Gods us."
— *Moshe Waldoks [3.43]*

I recall Reb Zalman saying, "Don't just surf the waves of the energy in a service. Go deep, study, and learn Hebrew. Compared to serious practitioners of Buddhism, here we're still at the level of kindergarteners!"
— *Eileen Nathanson [3.44]*

On many occasions Reb Zalman would rise from "the rebbe chair," move over one seat, and absorb the "rebbetude" of whoever took his place. And then that one would move over, and someone else would teach.
— *Raachel Jurovics [3.45]*

A painfully agitated community member joined the prayer circle. During announcements, she pleaded aloud, "Reb Zalman, I must see you. During the night, I had terrible nightmares and they are not leaving me."

With great kindness and calmness, Reb Zalman replied, "We do not have to stay with our troubling dreams. Right now, with all of us here, we can all help lift the weight of these dreams. Sound good?"

After the whole room said "Yes!" in agreement, Reb Zalman continued, "Let us all say together these words from the Talmud: 'Good it is and good may it be. May the Compassionate One turn it to good; seven times may it be decreed from heaven that it should be good and may it be good.'"

The dreamer wept.
— *David Arfa [3.46]*

The beautiful B'nai Or *Tallis*, sometimes called the "Joseph's Coat," or Rainbow *Tallit*, was designed by Rabbi Zalman Schachter-Shalomi in the 1950s. Over the years, I have met many Jews who bought a B'nai Or *Tallis* simply because it was beautiful, or because they liked rainbows, without realizing that there is a legend in the making behind this robe of rainbow light. [See front and back cover of this book]

The story begins many years ago, back in the 1950s, when Reb Zalman was still a Lubavitcher *Hassid*. One day, he was meditating on the midrash (commentary): "How did God create the world? He wrapped himself in a robe of light and it began to shine." Suddenly Reb Zalman had a beautiful inspiration, almost a vision, of a prayer shawl woven in vibrant rainbow colors.

Reb Zalman's very first colored *tallis* was made in the 1950s from an Anderson clan tartan. It was very nice, but he still preferred stripes, not only because that is traditional for prayer shawls, but also because he somehow sensed that it should have bands of color, like a spectrum. Reb Zalman later presented the plaid *tallis* to a Scottish convert to Judaism named Anderson. Other experiments included embroidering colors on a regular *tallis*, or appliquéd stripes. With each new design, the rainbow vision became clearer.

Around 1961 or so, the present design was ready for the weavers. But in those days, *tallis* makers were all very orthodox people who were not about to participate in this "crazy idea." Reb Zalman trekked from one Brooklyn manufacturer to another, but was flatly refused by all.

"What is this you want? A Purim *tallis*?" one pious old *Hassid* asked at the Munchatzer *tallis* factory. "Is this some kind of new sect or something?"

Each of the colors, as well as the width and arrangement of the stripes themselves, was based on the seven lower *sefirot* of the Kabbalistic Tree of Life diagram [A stained glass window that illustrates the *sefirot* is beside Reb Zalman in his tallit here: http://wellspringsofwisdom.com/rainbow-rainbow-tallit/]

In 1983, when I interviewed Reb Zalman at the old B'nai Or House on Emlen Street in Philadelphia, Pennsylvania, he explained the *tallis* he'd designed to me as follows.

Gershom: So, you had in mind that the "robe of light" that God wraps himself in to create the world is the spectrum—that it is literally the Primal Light?

Reb Zalman: Right. And the spectrum itself has black lines, too, like you see on a spectroscope. Once I started to see it, I asked myself the question, which ones should have black lines? I saw the black lines as a *k'li,* a "vessel of creation." So which of the *sefirot* need to be contained? Certainly not *Gevurah* (Strength) and *Malchut* (manisfestation), because they themselves are vessels. On the other hand, *Tiferet* (Beauty) and *Yesod* (Foundation) need strong ego-boundaries. Then there was the question of which stripes should be wider, and how they should be spaced….

So it comes out like this—the *atara* (embroidered "collar" strip) on the *tallis* is *Keter,* (Crown) the Source of the White Light, which flows into *Hochma-Bina,* still white and represented by the white cloth as it is draped over the head. Then enters *Hesed* (lovingkindness), which is the wide purple stripe.

Gershom: There are two shades of purple. Why is that?

Reb Zalman: Because it represents *Bereishit,* "In the Beginning," the First Day of Creation. So, the deep purple represents ultraviolet, just coming out of darkness. The lighter lavender (in the center of the deep purple) already has some light mixed in, the first light becoming visible to the human eye. And the whole stripe is very wide, because the nature of *Hesed* is broad and sweeping. Which is why it needs the black lines to contain it.

Now, the next stripe is *tekheilet* (blue) representing *Gevurah.* This stripe represents the Second Day of Creation, when the "waters above" were separated from the "waters below." And since *Gevurah* is by nature a container, because it also represents *halachah*

(Jewish law) and strength, it doesn't need the black stripes bordering it.

Following the Creation story, the next stripe is the Third Day of Creation, *Tiferet*. Vegetation was created then, represented by green.

God also said "It is good" twice on that day, so there are two green stripes, with the white light of *Keter* coming through the middle. *Tiferet*, as the heart chakra, needs a vessel, so there are also the black lines.

Next comes *Netzach*, the Fourth Day, when the sun, moon, and stars were created, so they are represented by yellow. The fifth day was when egg-laying animals were made: all the fish, reptiles, birds, and insects. So I represented the *Sefira* of *Hod* with orange, like egg yolks.

Notice also that *Hod* and *Netzach* are very close together, almost like one stripe, and that they are mirror images of each other. You can't really separate them. In fact, people confuse which is which, and there's a lot of disagreement, some systems interpreting them exactly opposite of other systems.

Gershom: Yes, I see how you have designed them very close together, almost like one stripe, but there is still some white light coming through between them. Like Aaron and Moses. Aaron does the form of the ritual and also channels the blessings. Moses gives laws but also receives revelation. Each has both active and passive elements, like the left and right brain, but more balanced, more integrated. That's why you can't really separate them, right?

Reb Zalman: Right. Now, the red stripe is *Yesod*, which can also represent Ego, so naturally it needs a very strong vessel to contain it. And because the placental mammals were created on the Sixth Day, this one is red, for the blood of life.

[Gershom's note: *Tiferet* and *Yesod* also represent the Higher Self and the lower self, which is why the pattern of the red stripes "below" exactly reflects the green stripes "above," only smaller.]

And last of all, we come to *Malchut*, which is Earth, represented by brown, because all things turn brown and return to the earth when they die. King David is also associated with *Malchut*, not only because he was a king, but also because he received everything [an attribute of *Malchut*] and has nothing of his own—not even his life. There's the midrash that the first Adam gave seventy years of his own life to King David, so that David's very life came from *Adamah*, the earth; thus the brown color.

So, the pattern kept coming through clearer and clearer to Reb Zalman, and the quest for a weaver continued outside the Orthodox community. The very first *tallis* in the B'nai Or pattern was made from reindeer wool by a woman in New Haven, Connecticut. This was lovely, but Reb Zalman still was not satisfied, because the cloth came out more like a blanket than a prayer shawl, and it hung rather stiffly. So the search went on.

Then one day, while visiting Montreal, Reb Zalman looked in the phone book and found the listing of "Karen Bulow— *Vetements Religieux*"—a religious vestment company? Would they be willing to do it? After a brief conversation over the phone, Reb Zalman ran ecstatically into the street and hailed the first taxicab! Yes, they could make it, but he would have to buy five of them, because it wasn't worth setting up the loom for only one. "Of course, yes, I'll gladly take five!" he said with delight.

At last the five original *talleisim* were woven: Reb Zalman got one, Abraham Joshua Heschel got one, Everett Gendler got one, Arthur Green got one. And the fifth *tallis*? I don't know. Perhaps it belongs to all of us, because these five *talleisim* opened the door for Jews everywhere to begin personalizing their prayer shawls and expressing their own visions of Jewish spirituality.

A few months later, Reb Zalman was hired as a "religious environmentalist" at a Ramah summer camp. So here was this Lubavitcher *Hassid*, combing the Manhattan garment district for colorful remnants, especially scraps with stripes and bright colors, so that he could teach Jewish kids how to make their own *talleisim*. With a rented sewing machine and a trunk full of cloth under his bunk, he set up his "tallisarium," the very first grassroots do-it-yourself prayer-shawl-making venture.

Years passed, and those Jews taught other Jews, who taught still others. Reb Zalman never copyrighted his design, so eventually it was picked up and produced by a *tallis* factory in Israel named Talitnia and marketed as the "Joseph's Coat" *tallis*. (Although nowadays, some manufacturers have toned down the original psychedelic neon colors to more muted tones.)

Today, multicolored *talleisim* are commonplace—so much so, that a young man once walked up to the now gray-haired Reb Zalman and asked, "Where did you get your rainbow *tallis*? I also have one. Yours is exactly like mine!"

Reb Zalman smiled lovingly. "Yes, *Baruch HaShem*, I also have a rainbow *tallis*...." He paused, a faraway look in his eyes. "We're both wrapped in the Creator's Robe of Light."

The vision had come full circle.
— *Yonassan Gershom. "Wrapped in a Robe of Light: The Story of the B'nai Or Prayer Shawl," lightly adapted and reprinted with permission from his book* 49 Gates of Kabbalah. [3.47]

One day when Reb Zalman was leading the Torah service, the portion was filled with images and stories of the Holy Temple, the work of the *Cohanim* (priests), and the animal sacrifices that were brought as gifts by the people. He brought us into the world of imagination so that we could spiritually witness the ancient power of the Holy Temple.

One person, in a moment of enthusiasm, spoke up, saying, "Reb Zalman, this is just like my trip to the recycling center this morning! I came with my plastic, paper, glass, and tin offerings, and holy guides were there to direct me so that all my gifts could be transformed and made fresh. Through the holy interconnections of all of our actions—dozens of people streaming in with their offerings, volunteers helping us make sure the plastics made it into the right bin, and so much more—together, we made the place holy and our community a holy community."

In response, Reb Zalman smiled his broad smile.
— *David Arfa [3.48]*

As Reb Zalman embraced the feminine aspect of God, he soon started modeling a new, gender neutral way, calling God "*Yah*" in place of the traditional masculine pronunciation of God's name as *Adonai*—My Lord.
— *Michael Lerner [3.49]*

Reb Zalman loved to turn liturgy into accessible chants and gave us:

It is Perfect.	God, let me do for YOU.
You are Loved.	God, let me feel for YOU.
All is Clear.	God, let me think for YOU.
And I AM Holy.	God, let me be for YOU."

— *Carola de Vies Robles [3.50]*

Reb Zalman entered the retreat at Elat Chayyim with a spring in his step, with a palpable sparkle and energy. He was about seventy years old then, leading us for a week in exploration of the beauty and elegance of prayer. He'd have us meditate out in the field, and upon returning, he'd guide us in creating a group haiku, which became an ongoing linear service. This involved each of us calling out one word to represent an insight from our meditation. There was a depth of the mystical in this exercise.

Reb Zalman continued by demonstrating the many facets he experienced by pausing to savor each word of a prayer. He had us each partner with another person to nuance a prayer by each person, alternating one word in the prayer with emotion in our voices. He instructed us to take in the imagery until the prayer was completely experienced.

Reb Zalman also took a piece of liturgy, prayed it aloud with feeling in Hebrew, translated it in his interpretive English and then equally fluidly into other languages, one after the other. He seemed careful to ensure every person felt seen and heard.

Reb Zalman modeled listening and tasting each moment through every sense and texture, and encouraged us to do so, too. He expressed himself with his arms, his body, his expressions, the shifting tone of his voice…soft and loud, using so much energy in expressions of joy and sadness. He told us it was okay to be expressive.
— *Julie Schechter [3.51]*

Melodies

I started at the Reconstructionist Rabbinical College in the Fall of 1968, a member of its first class. That same fall, a college friend doing graduate work at Brandeis invited me to Boston to experience Havurat Shalom, the "community seminary" Rabbi Arthur Green (later to become my teacher and the second to sign my *smicha*) had formed. On that Shabbat morning, the prayer leader was Reb Zalman and I remember how the words of *El Adon* revealed new meanings when he sang it to the tune of the folksong "Dona, Dona."
— *Daniel Siegel [3.52]*

In 1975 at High Holidays, one of the first gatherings of the Aquarian Minyan in Berkeley, California, Reb Zalman had us read psalms to each other, in partners, line by line, so that each person really got what the line said, and communed with their partner in doing so. He also led us in singing Psalm 150 to the tune of "Michael, Row the Boat Ashore," the unique vernacular of the moment.
— *Ahouva Steinhaus [3.53]*

During the early 1970s, Reb Zalman visited our newly formed Fabrangen Jewish Free-Culture Center in Dupont Circle. He wanted to see what we were doing, to learn from and with us. I recall he led us in singing *Kiddush* to "Home on the Range."

And, in the late 1970s, Reb Zalman and I and others convened a gathering at Pendle Hill, a Quaker retreat center in Wallingford, Pennsylvania. We jammed together as musicians. We did Hassidic music with me on the guitar and Reb Zalman playing the piano, flute, and keyboard.
— *David Shneyer [3.54]*

Reb Zalman taught: "The words of a *tefillah* are an excellent vehicle to remember the *niggun* (wordless melody) — which is actually the main part!"
— *Hal Miller-Jacobs [3.55]*

In 1962 and 1963, I was an older camper at Camp Ramah in Connecticut. Both summers, a "religious environmentalist" visited the camp, a Lubavitcher rabbi by the name of Zalman Schachter. For the most part, I stayed away from him as he took kids to town to buy material to make their own *tallitot* and then to tie the *tzitzit* (specially knotted strings) themselves, or taught them what were the essentials of a *Shacharit* so that they could put on their *tefillin* and *daven* and still make the school bus on time. As a good yeshiva boy, I thought his methods were gimmicks for beginners and not for someone who studied Talmud daily.

But I couldn't avoid him when he shared a different kind of melody for the first blessing of *Birkat Hamazon* (grace after meals) with the entire camp at Shabbat evening dinner, and so I learned an alternative to the table thumper which stayed with me.

It was only recently that I finally asked him whose melody it was and he told me it was his own!
— Daniel Siegel [3.56]

It had been a beautiful Shabbat at the Kallah in Colorado, but as I entered the noisy dining hall Saturday evening my heart sank. Fluorescent lights glared. No one seemed to know that this was *Shalosh Se'udos*, the mystical Third Meal of *Shabbos*, a liminal space in time, full of longing and reflection.

I moved through the dinner line smiling, but my heart was crying out, "Where is the Third Meal of *Shabbos*?" Just then, someone I barely knew tapped me on the shoulder and whispered into my ear, "Reb Zalman wants a few people in the courtyard for the Third Meal of *Shabbos*."

I rushed to the courtyard. There wasn't a soul in sight, except Reb Zalman sitting alone at a picnic table. He nodded at me, indicating that I should approach and sit down. I had never been close to him before.

We sat together in silence as the sunlight faded. Gradually, a small number of people gathered in a tight circle around the table. Someone brought a plate of fruit. Blessings were murmured as we passed the food around.

Then Reb Zalman began to tell a story. Though he spoke slowly and clearly, I had trouble following the plot, and to my dismay heard myself thinking, "I don't like this story!"

Just then, Reb Zalman dropped the story abruptly and began singing, a slow, unhurried melody. I listened intently, but with limited Hebrew all I could catch was the word *Keter*, meaning crown, the name of the highest of the *sefirot*, the emanations that pervade the universe and the self.

Keter was repeated several times. In the next verse I caught the word *Hochma*, meaning wisdom, the next of the *sefirot* on the Kabbalistic Tree of Life. Like *Keter*, the name *Hochma* was repeated. And so on through the ten *sefirot*.

Years earlier I learned the *sefirot* from Reb Zalman's booklet *Gate to the Heart*. Now, as he slowly sang his way through the Tree of Life, I wept and trembled. At last he made his way to *Malchut*, the final *Sefira*, the essence and ground of Shabbat.

Later that evening I saw the person who had tapped me on the shoulder with the summons to *Shalosh Seudos*. I asked, "What was that song?" He wrote something on a slip of paper. But there were no search engines back then, and it was years before I found the song *El Mistater*, an exquisite composition by the 16th century Kabbalist, Avraham Maimon of Tzfat.

Seven years later, speaking about the *sefirot* on the phone with me, Reb Zalman mentioned that same song. I said, "I heard you sing it at *Shalosh Seudos* at the Kallah."

He was quiet for a few moments, and then said, "Yes, *Shalosh Seudos*…"

When I told him that I had set it to a Sephardic melody, he said at once, "Sing it to me!"

And so, years after that extraordinary Third Meal of *Shabbos*, I sang the song back to him. When I finished, Reb Zalman said, "That's a beautiful melody. Make a recording and send me a copy."
— *Naomi Steinberg [3.57]*

We were sitting in a circle at a Four Worlds workshop being given by Reb Zalman in the 1970s. He directed us to chant a *niggun, to* do a particular guided meditation, and then to move our bodies with a given intention. Following his instructions, something shifted and I was on a journey, an inner journey. At one point he said, "Now we have arrived at the gate of the next World, *Briya*— Creation Consciousness." He spoke about the qualities of this World and then began another *niggun,* and we joined in.
— *Nahum Ward-Lev [3.58]*

The person who modeled the *Homo Davenus* for Havurat Shalom was Reb Zalman. Polish-born, raised in Vienna, interned in Vichy France, and trained as an early emissary of Chabad in the United States, Reb Zalman had already broken with ultra-orthodoxy when, on sabbatical from the University of Manitoba, he joined Havurat Shalom, which had just been called into being by Art Green and his fellow rabbis, Albert Axelrad, of blssed memory, and Joseph Lukinsky.

As it happened, I had already met Reb Zalman at a Jewish theology workshop held in the Laurentian Mountains, just north of Montreal. The workshop was closed to the public, but we members of Shomrei Ha'umah, a group of high school students who met in the basement of Rabbi David Hartman's home, were allowed to attend as flies on the wall.

Looking more like a beatnik than a Hassid, peppering his speech with Yiddish, Reb Zalman was a unique presence among that august group of scholars and thinkers, including Emil Fackenheim, Yochanan Muffs, Jakob Petuchowski, and David Novak.

The next time I met Reb Zalman was in early March 1969 when I joined a carload of Brandeis students who had begun attending Sabbath services at Havurat Shalom in Cambridge. It was *Shabbat Zachor*, the Sabbath before Purim, which recalls the enmity and gratuitous cruelty of the Amalekites in Deuteronomy 25, and Reb Zalman was the *ba'al tefillah* (prayer leader).

What I remember from that service is how it ended, with a Mourner's *Kaddish* unlike any I had ever heard. Reb Zalman concluded by singing the *Kaddish* to the melody of "*Zog Nit Keyn Mol*" ("Never Say"), the hymn of the Vilna partisans, written in 1943.

At the same time, he took a melody that was resolutely secular, composed in the Soviet Union, and harnessed its power for spiritual ends, setting it to *Le[i]t Atar Panui Minei* [*Tikkunei Zohar, Tikkun 57*: (Even in suffering "No space [is] devoid of God.")]
— *David G. Roskies, adapted with his permission from "A Jewish World of Infinite Possibility,"* Tablet Magazine: *http://www.tabletmag.com/ jewish-life-and religion/261461 /havurat-shalom-at-50* [3.59]

4

Traveling through Time and Space

Reb Zalman traveled widely, exploring world religions and cultures, while inspiring and guiding many Jewish seekers along the way.

At the 1989 Kallah Reb Zalman told this story of how he arrived in New York in 1941 at age sixteen. He got off the ship and found his way to the subway, but when he came out in Crown Heights he was lost. Then he saw a cop. He hesitated, because "Where I was coming from we avoided cops." But, "this was America, so maybe it would be okay."

He went up to the officer and in his rudimentary English asked, "Please sir, vhere is de 770 Eastern Parkvay?"

And the cop looked at him and said, *"Nu yingele, vilst gehen zum Lubavitcher Reb'n?"* (So sonny, you want to go to the Lubavitcher Rebbe?)

"And that," Reb Zalman added, "is why July Fourth is an important holiday for me."
— *Gideon and Sara Eisenberg [4.1]*

Reb Zalman, how was your trip to Germany?

"It was good."

Did you have anything retriggered for you from during the war?

"Yes, while sitting on a train. I heard the conductor asking for passports and fell back in time. I became fearful I'd be arrested for some error in my papers."

And then what happened?

"I realized where and when I was when a man with dreadlocks walked by. So I told my child-self, 'Look you made it through that narrow place. Let's remember to be grateful.'"
— *Goldie Milgram [4.2]*

One year, for Pesach, I drove the four hundred-plus miles north to explore becoming part of the nascent B'nai Or community in the West Mt. Airy section of Philadelphia. The drive was tedious, as the speed limit was still 55 mph on the highways, and the southern states were notorious for using speed traps to augment their local coffers with out-of-state contributions.

The morning after the holiday, I was getting an early start to return home. Reb Zalman was already up, chanting his morning prayers in his *tallis* and *tefillin*. He paused to greet me warmly, and noticed my suitcase at my side.

"You're leaving. Are you going to try to make it in one day?"

"Yes, if I can. I may have to pull over to rest."

"Do you have *tzedaka* — charity for the trip?"

Reb Zalman dug into his pocket and carefully counted out into my palm a dime, a nickel, and three pennies — eighteen cents. He explained, "It says in the Talmud that messengers of *tzedaka* can come to no harm. Now you are my messenger, and you'll put the money in a *pushke* (a donation box) when you reach home."

Reb Zalman then paused, considering the coins in my hand. When he looked up at me, there was a twinkle in his eye, and he said, "For this amount, you're covered up to 55 mph."
— *Rivka Walton [4.3]*

While traveling on a twelve-hour bus ride with Reb Zalman, I recall him removing the glass cover of an overhead reading lamp in order to playfully introduce me to the notion of *Shevirat HaKeilim*. He explained that this was the Kabbalists' understanding of the breaking through of the original light of creation.

As Reb Zalman showed me the glass bulb, he then asked me to imagine the power of the Source flowing through this fragile vessel. He continued to elaborate on how this sudden surge of energy would release the primordial light of creation, thus shattering its fragile container, similar to the glass bulb he held in his hands. These fragments he added, would themselves contain

sparks of that original light. "The task of humanity," Reb Zalman continued, "is to find and repair these shattered fragments."
— *Carol Rose [4.4]*

The Lama Foundation is a commune in New Mexico that is two-thirds of the way up a mountain, overlooking the distant Rio Grande. On the way there for an overnight, I accidentally hit the edge of the road, blew a tire. It turned out that there was no jack in the trunk. After quite some time an old sedan came rambling up the road. The man in the back seat bid us to get in and come up to the Lama Foundation with them. He said they'd help us fix the car the next day. That man was Reb Zalman.

During our trip up the mountain, Reb Zalman mentioned that he would be heading up the evening's program, which would include playing tapes of Jewish music from throughout the ages.

That evening Reb Zalman also revealed that the night before he had participated in a Native American peyote ceremony held out in the desert. He connected the experience to his Jewish roots when he said that the peyote "gave me the feeling that I was back 3000 years in time as one of the Israelites in the desert."
— *Alan M. Dattner [4.5]*

In 1981 I was living at the Lama Foundation, an interfaith spiritual community in New Mexico. We had just heard that a rabbi was coming to Lama to do a personal hermitage and would probably spend some time in community with us as well.

One day, as we were getting ready to do our afternoon *Salat* (Islamic daily prayers), an older man entered the prayer room. He was wearing a long dark satiny robe, head covering, and had a white beard and shining eyes.

Was this that rabbi?

He asked if he could join us for prayers. We all looked at each other thinking how interesting it was that a rabbi would want to observe our *Salat*, and welcomed him to join us. As we moved into our prayer rows, he stepped forward and walked right up to a place in the front row.

Who was this guy?

Apparently the rabbi was not just planning on observing our prayers, but joining us.

But how could...

Standing just in front of me I was surprised that he seemed to be keeping in perfect time with the varying sets of precise movements—bows, prostrations, kneeling, and standing. And while I was supposed to be looking inward, focused on my own prayers, I couldn't help but notice he was actually reciting the phrases from the Koran, in Arabic, by heart, with everyone!

Who was this guy?

We were soon to find out; he called himself—Reb Zalman.
—*Andrew Gold [4.6]*

I was about to leave Judaism for the second and final time. The first, at age twenty-three, was after turning from a modern orthodox upbringing to an ultra-orthodox life and the second, a decade later, after a failed attempt to return to the modern orthodoxy of my youth. During that decade between, I'd worked as a waiter, gotten into psychology, yoga, martial arts, astrology, then teaching pilates and studying new age philosophy. As I pondered leaving Judaism again, a friend said there was a rabbi I had to meet, and when I heard the name, I realized I had an unread book written by him on my shelves—*Spiritual Intimacy*. I became blown away by parts of it.

In 2004 I went up to Elat Chayyim to experience and meet with Reb Zalman for Shavuos. He was wearing knee-high argyle socks. He had a walking stick and a little Native American pouch for his hearing aids, and something kilt-like on, yet from the neck up he looked like a *Hassidishe* rebbe. I noticed his beautiful hands, very suntanned and with a ring. His eyes were so inviting, and his voice warm and expressive.

I sat in the living room at the old Elat Chayyim and began to tell Reb Zalman my journey. This was the first time in my life I felt that I wasn't alone in my experience and that I'd met somebody else who had been there before.

Reb Zalman was excited to meet me, too. He said he felt a kinship with me and that he needed people who "got it" to teach and become rabbis. As we talked I saw that he had wisdom to share and insight toward a new way; that my questions were his questions and that he had answers. And, when he heard I was an astrologer, he wanted me to do his chart.

As we spoke, every time I would cry, Reb Zalman would say, "A *mikveh* (ritual bath) of tears. David, a *mikveh* of tears."

Reb Zalman conquered me with his spiritual chiropractic. I was looking for a rebbe and I found one. He made it all new again.
— *David Ingber [4.7]*

I first met Reb Zalman in a mosque in Marin County on Bolinas Road. It was the late 1960s and I was spiritual path shopping, and had trekked up from Los Angeles. He was comfortably mixing the ancient mystical paths of the early and modern Hebrews, *Ivriim*, (from the Hebrew root for boundary crossers) with Sufi talk, Christian mysticism, Buddhist and Hindu approaches. Mixing *Yesh me'Ayin, Fana, Baqa,* self-abnegation, and rebirthing!

I became a *shamash*, a helper of Reb Zalman when he would come to Los Angeles, picking him up at the airport and driving him to various meetings or teaching sessions. One time, when he was coming to Santa Monica to do something for *Shabbos,* I mentioned that I did not have a *shul* to go to, and that I was going to stay home and do some Torah reading. He then offered that we get together and do some text study.

When we met, he brought out a piece of text from *B'nei Yissachar*, a traditional Hassidic text. As I read the Hebrew aloud, he interpreted and connected the dots for me with his advanced understanding.

Then he went to another level and started to draw together teachings not intrinsically in the text. From *Sefer Yetzira* (early Kabbalah), we learned that AShaN is an acronym of how our connections with this world are easily made obscure. How? The acronym decodes as *Olam*, world (A), *Shana*, year (SH), *Nefesh*, soul (N). Reb Zalman explained that this means we are being guided by the author to become conscious of our immersion in the spacetimespirit continuum.
— *Ivan Ickovits [4.8]*

It was 1994, and Reb Zalman was very ill; he said it was from a lung problem he'd developed while in a detention camp under the Vichy French. And he was in mourning, as one of his closest friends, Rabbi Shlomo Carlebach, had died the previous month.

We were working at Reb Zalman's apartment in Philadelphia when he came out of the bedroom in the midst of a bronchial cough, waving two sheets of printed paper at me. He said, "You can put that editing project aside for now, I need you to go to New York for me tomorrow to speak for me at two events. The first is the *shloshim* (a traditional thirtieth day after death memorial), and the second — to speak at the installation of Shohama [Wiener] as President of the Academy for Jewish Religion. You can create your own speech for Shohama; I've written the one for Shlomo and will rehearse you in it now."

Weeks earlier, I had been shocked to learn that Reb Zalman had ever had anything to do with the rabbi who had assaulted me as an adolescent, no less that the man was Reb Zalman's best friend?! It seems the Rebbe had sent them out together on *shlichut*, as outreach emissaries. I was relieved to hear that Reb Zalman's organization did not book Reb Shlomo to teach.

"I can certainly do the one with Rabbi Shohama Wiener, though I only met her at Eve's bridal ritual for a few minutes, so you'll need to prep me. Reb Zalman, please choose someone else to cover you for the *shloshim*." There. I didn't want to distress him about his friend who, now gone, couldn't harm anyone else. Let him just find someone else.

Reb Zalman looked straight at me, his color grey, coughed up something awful into a handkerchief and said, "Not you, too."

In response, I suggested names from Reb Zalman's circle who could easily and elegantly give his speech at the *shloshim*.

"No." He said firmly in his you-will-be-doing-this-because-I've-already-decided voice. "Let's go to my computers, and we'll fix this so you can honorably represent me."

Reb Zalman changed the document that began "*Shaliach shel adam k'moto*" that halachically (per Jewish law) made me essentially his temporary clone. About a third of the way through wrote that he, Reb Zalman, encourages the Carlebach community to not only take care that his family would have enough to live on, and not only laud and spread Reb Shlomo's music and teachings, they must also do *tikkunim*, healing repairs, on Reb Shlomo's unfinished business.

I went.
— *Goldie Milgram [4.9]*

Jenny: "Where is God?"

Reb Zalman: "God is in the bonds between all of you."
— *Jenny Goodman [4.10]*

I was first introduced to Reb Zalman in 1969 in front of the Havurat Shalom in, I believe, Somerville, at the time. He was under the hood of his car performing an earthly *tikkun*.
— *Mitchell Chefitz [4.11]*

Reb Zalman's silence on two important issues gradually weakened my relationship with him. A tipping point came toward the end of the 1990s. I attended one of the first gatherings of his rabbinic network after two weeks in Hebron where I witnessed settlers tossing urine, stones, and pipes at Palestinian families shopping near the Tomb of Abraham.

There was a big gap in our perceptions of what was happening in Israel and how Jewish religion was being used in relationship to the conflict.

When Reb Zalman asked me to attend the next ALEPH Kallah in Colorado, I drove up from New Mexico with my son. During the opening session he gave a loving retrospective of his friendship with Rabbi Shlomo Carlebach in front of 800 people.

Unfortunately, I was carrying the stories of women described being abused by Rabbi Carlebach. They had asked me "to do something." Reb Zalman and I were not able to bridge the distance in our understanding of how to respond to issues of sexual violence in the Jewish community.

Years later, feeling the distance, I journeyed to Hawaii to spend time with Reb Zalman. One afternoon, we met privately for a half an hour. He wondered whether or not nonviolence is good for Israel, whether or not it can keep Jews safe. "Well," he chuckled, "you are from the prophetic branch of the family."
— *Lynn Gottlieb [4.12]*

While attending a retreat with Reb Zalman in the Florida Keys, he was standing beside me at sunrise.

"The sun doesn't rise," he advised, overhearing my words. "The earth turns."

Later hearing him speak of astrology, I asked how on one hand he saw the earth within a galaxy of solar systems, and on the other hand the earth as the center of a planetary system.
Reb Zalman shrugged and said, "Different ways of looking at things."
— *Mitchell Chefitz [4:13]*

In 2008, a weekend *shabbaton* with Reb Zalman in Hawaii held a promise of Paradise. The conference hotel was on a plateau of volcanic rock next to the most popular snorkeling spot on the island.

There, Reb Zalman, age eighty-two, announced that he wanted to make his first life-time attempt at snorkeling. The surface leading to the water was so sharp, jagged, and hot that we had to wear shoes to walk there. Reb Zalman looked delightfully outrageous decked out with purple water sandals, neon blue swimming trunks pulled up almost to his chest, translucent red glasses, a brightly patterned *kippa* (skull cap), and his wooden cane. Grinning, Reb Zalman strode along the lava flow, forging ahead onto wobbly rocks, eyes focused on the beautiful scene.

Upon arrival we waded slowly into the shallows to practice breathing through the snorkeling tube. We then ventured a little deeper out onto the reef to view the tropical life. I could see Zalman's eyes widen behind his mask as the yellow, purple, and red multicolored fishes swam under our noses.

Suddenly Reb Zalman slipped. His head was bobbing and arms swirling as I swam to him, grabbed his arm, and guided him back to the ledge. Steadied, he was fine, signaling thumbs up to me, and happily, he returned to snorkeling.

Eventually we returned to shore. Reb Zalman emerged, grinning and dripping. He took off his gear, put on his glasses and *kippa*, and accepted his cane.

"How was it?" David (my husband) asked.

"Wonderful." Zalman glowed. His eyes were huge behind the red glasses. "Such diversity," he said. "And they all get along."
— *Debra Gordon Zaslow [4.14]*

5

The Life Cycle

Reb Zalman's reflections, guidance,
and innovative approaches to life's
transitions and rites of passage.

Engagement, Weddings, Marriage

Our wedding invitation read: "…in the midday summer sun, we shall sing, dance, and rejoice in celebration of this cosmic union."

In order to support and help us create our "cosmic union," Reb Zalman loaded up his Volvo, hitched to the back of his car the trailer he would often travel with in those days, and drove 625 miles from Philadelphia to Knoxville, Tennessee, to officiate. His entourage included his then wife Elana, and their three children — Shalvi, Barya, and Yotam.

Close to midnight on Saturday evening, Reb Zalman came to us saying he had a concern about the timing of the wedding ceremony the next day. He explained that when he checked the Ephemeris — an astronomical calendar which gives the daily positions of the planets, their movements, and their relationships with each other — he had discovered a potential problem.

There is an astrological phenomenon called "Moon Void of Course," when the Moon is not in a significantly angled relationship with any of the planets. This can occur for a period of minutes or a full day, or even more. When this particular astronomical phenomenon takes place, according to contemporary astrology, it is common that appointments get cancelled, i.e., we might go to a store and cannot find what we are looking for, and things that are set in motion do not come to fruition.

Reb Zalman explained to us that since the Moon would be "Void of Course" at the time we were to sign our *ketubah* (Jewish marriage contract) the next day, it would not be an auspicious time for beginning a marriage. Reb Zalman had an idea — instead of waiting for the next day, he wanted us to gather all our witnesses and others in our wedding party at midnight, so that we could perform the ritual act of *kinyan* (acquisition), that is traditionally done before signing a *ketubah* on the day of the wedding.

We quickly gathered about twenty members of our wedding party, including several rabbis. It was obvious Reb Zalman had done some advance scouting, as he led all of us out the back door of the hotel toward the grounds of the Knoxville World's Fair site. He had us climb a set of stairs until we found ourselves standing on a platform at the base of the Sunsphere, the central symbol of the 1982 World's Fair.

Reb Zalman next lined up the men and women to form two separate circles. With bride and groom in the center, Reb Zalman had the women walking in a clockwise circle singing in Hebrew and English from the *Song of Songs* 2:2: "*Ka-tapuakh b'atzei ha-yaar keyn dodi ben ha-banim* — Like an apple tree among the trees of the forest, so is my beloved among the young men." At the same time, the men were walking in a counter-clockwise circle, and continuing to the next verse chanting, "*Ka-shoshanah ben ha-chochim, keyn ra'ayati ben ha-banot* — Like a lily among the thorns, so is my darling among the maidens." This went on for a while, during which time Reb Zalman had us do *kinyan* with our witnesses.

Reb Zalman included our signing of the Lieberman clause — a codicil to the marriage contract ensuring that both parties would agree to a Jewish divorce, if it ever came to that. As the ritual came to a conclusion, Reb Zalman also threw a set of *I Ching* coins to give us a prognosticative omen on our marriage.

The wedding ceremony took place the next day. One highlight was Reb Zalman blowing *shofar* under the *huppah* (wedding canopy) after reading the *ketubah*.

Our relatives from both Canada and Knoxville had never quite seen a wedding ceremony like this!
— *Geela Rayzel Raphael and Simcha Paull Raphael [5.1]*

Halé and I were married in a New Age ceremony in 1976. By the time 2000 rolled around we had three adult children and multiple mortgages. Realizing how deeply meaningful it would be if we were to be married again under the *huppah* with Reb Zalman presiding, I called him.

His deep sweet voice boomed, "Stevela, it would be my pleasure, my privilege, my honor. There's only one problem. Your wife is not Jewish. I'm an Orthodox rabbi and must marry two Jewish people. Would Halé be open to becoming Jewish?"

"Reb Zalman," I replied, "I didn't marry a blonde from Palatial, Connecticut, who grew up with a golden retriever. As you may remember, Halé is Turkish and her family, although completely secular, is from a Muslim culture. Her best friends have always been Jewish. She married me for God's sakes. We have raised our children Jewish. Every Friday night she not only participates in our family *Shabbos* with full heart but she makes the challah from scratch."

There was a pause, and for a moment silence ensued.

Finally he boomed, "Turkish?…Muslim?…Mazel tov…!"

Then with a full voice he said, "Stevela, the Christians are our children. The Muslims are our cousins. I have the deepest respect for the Turkish Sufis. Would you and Halé like me to wear my Sufi robes for the ceremony?"

We knew that Reb Zalman had been ordained as a sheik in the Sufi Chishti Order by Pir Vilayat Inayat Khan, a profound spiritual teacher.

"Of course," I said, with tears in my eyes.

Then I added, "Reb Zalman, in the traditional conversion ceremony it is asked of the convert whether she will renounce all previous spiritual and religious affiliations. I know my wife quite well and I assure you her answer will be 'no'."

"Stevela, this is not a conversion. This is an initiation. Halé is a mature soul. She is a fully developed spiritual person. A vital aspect of her soul is already Jewish, probably from birth. She is simply affirming her Jewishness and consciously taking it on. I want to speak with her about what her new name will be. In addition, you may want to ask whether either of her parents' ancestry comes from Salonika or Izmir, because there were many Jews in those parts of the world who converted to Islam during the time of the false messiah, Shabbetai Tzvi."

I, of course, knew about this history but never thought it had relevance to my personal life.

Later that day I faced my beloved. "Reb Zalman asks," I said, "were either of your parents' families from Izmir or Salonika?" I didn't explain the history of Jews in Salonika that Reb Zalman had just alluded to.

She looked at me for a full moment and then said, "My father's family is from Salonika and my mother's family is from Izmir."

I found a book about the Jews of Turkey that documented exactly what Reb Zalman had said. In fact, before Shabbetai Tzvi's bizarre conversion to Islam, more than 90% of the residents of Salonika were Jewish and another high percentage of the population of Izmir were as well.

On a subsequent call with Reb Zalman, he said wisely, "This doesn't necessarily mean Halé is Jewish but it's wonderful to know. She'll still take the dip (*mikveh*), and so will your children to verify that the family is Jewish."

Fine with us.

And the name for my bride? With Reb Zalman she settled upon *Tzofiyah, Sofia, Sofiya, Sophia*, from Proverbs 31, meaning Wisdom, one who watches, and kabbalistically: "I am willing to be awake," or "I will awaken."

Thus it was that in June of the year 2002 we met with Reb Zalman and a small number of both women and men rabbis in the Indian Springs Hot Springs in Idaho Springs, Colorado. And we all took the dip.

The next day we were remarried on the mountain overlooking the Continental Divide at Artist Point just outside of Boulder, under the *huppah*. Our children held the *huppah* poles. The ceremony, which Reb Zalman added to in a traditional way, was beautiful and meaningful on every level.

Reb Zalman, his face beaming, also gave us full blessings and blessed each of our children. *Selah.*
— *Steven L. Schatz [5.2]*

It was 2005 at Elat Chayyim and Reb Zalman was teaching. The word went out that on the coming Shabbat morning, before services, those requesting a personal blessing should gather in the small room off the main dining area. When we arrived, the space was already filled to bursting.

All eyes turned to the opening door as Reb Zalman entered. He was grandly attired for the observance of Shabbat, in a long black coat and *shtreimel*. He was accompanied by a man he had personally ordained as a *Baal HaBracha*, Master of the Blessing.

Each supplicant arose as Reb Zalman approached them. All watched as one-by-one, he gently gathered their hands into his and listened to their whispered, often tearful concerns. He, in turn, gave each a blessing in Hebrew and his associate followed with a translation into powerful, interpretive English.

Halfway around the circle, Reb Zalman came to stand in front of my wife-to-be. As she stood, so did I. Not yet knowing our desire, I received an imperious wave of his right hand, intended to keep me seated. To his surprise, I remained standing, slipping my arm through my beloved's. We whispered to him, and to this day I

cannot tell you what words were utt
Zalman took less than a nanosecond
to be a marriage blessing for the two
before him.

Reb Zalman's face lit up. Eyes sparkl
straightened and strengthened. Hand
one. The magic of his Hebrew words
were not merely accepted. We were j
loving union as an integral, evolving
— *Deliah Golda Rosel* [5.3]

"So the point is — and
get — that often wh
such privacy th
doesn't work
way, it is a

"An
t

Reb Zalman officiated at our wedding in 2003, and at one point he
taught, "Why is it that we use wine? There was a high priest for
the whole world. He was known as Melchizedek, and he was 'the
priest of God, the Most High.' And he inducted Abraham *Avinu*
(our father) into the mystery of bread and wine...just as wine has
fermented, bread, the same way, has fermented with the yeast.
And on the one hand you would say, 'Oy, why can't it be just plain
grape juice or matzah?' But there is a mystery in the failures we
have in life that are also our glories....

"If you look at an opal, it has fire, and in one light it looks
gorgeous, and in another light it looks like a cracked piece of glass.
That's the mystery of wine. And *yayin* — the Hebrew word for
wine — has the same numerical value as *sod*, secret.

"So in goes the wine, and out comes the secret. May the secret of
what brings you together become manifest to you as you will drink
from this wine."

And,

"The Baal Shem Tov pointed out that the word for man, *ish*, and
the word for woman, *isha*, both share the letters of the word *aish*,
fire. So long as the *yud* is there with you, (gesturing toward Zisha)
and the *hey* is there with you, (gesturing toward Zahava) God is
present. [Talmud Tractate *Sotah* 17a]

this is very hard for most people to really
en they are in their physical union, they want
t they don't even want God to be there. That
very well because every time you are together in this
a prayer so holy, a holy moment.

d for the week at least of the wedding, cover yourself with the
lis at that time to make it really a *davenen* together—where the
two bodies and the two souls *daven* together."
— *Jay (Zisha) and Sabrina (Zahava) Gold [5.4]*

Overhearing a difficult marital moment, Reb Zalman asked, "Do
you sing together? I've come to understand how deeply important
it is for a couple to sing together."
— *Goldie Milgram [5.5]*

Pregnancy, Babies, Children

One Yom Kippur morning we were sitting in the children's service. I was hoping to go to the Torah service when the teacher announced, "Reb Zalman loves kids. He has no problem with the families of young children attending the Torah service and sitting toward the back in case a quick exit is necessary."

Reb Zalman was our guest Rabbi for many years during the high holidays. He led the service all dressed in white. As the Torah was taken from the ark, there was singing and dancing and a feeling of merriment. My daughter, Hyla, was bouncing in my husband Steve's arms with a huge smile on her face. When those gathered became quieter, I pointed ahead whispering, "Hyla, look through there and you will see the rabbi holding the Torah." I pointed again, adding, "There is the Torah."

The room was completely quiet now and you could hear a pin drop. It was the moment just before the chanting of the first blessing. Hyla got very excited and in her biggest outside voice she yelled, "Mommy… LOOK IT'S THE TORAH!!! THERE IS THE TORAH!"

Although we were sitting in the back, she had a loud voice and it carried to the front. Many heads turned around and stared at us sharply. I could feel the shock and my heart began to sink. The room was filled with people and many eyes were on us now. I put my hand over Hyla's mouth but she moved it away and continued to yell with exuberance, "IT'S THE TORAH!"

As we went to the back of the room through an opening in the curtains surrounding the prayer space, unbeknownst to us, Hyla grabbed onto the fabric and we kept walking. Suddenly we heard a huge crashing sound and to our horror, Hyla had pulled down the drapes, metal pipes and all.

Now the entire congregation was looking at us. We heard someone shout, "Wait!"

That someone was Reb Zalman. He ran to where we were standing and motioned for us to come back into the room. We walked up the aisle with our spunky toddler. He reached out for her chubby little hands and held them in his.

Then, he turned to the congregation, rubbed his beard and said, with a twinkle in his eye, "We should all be so excited to see the Torah."
— Karen Golden [5.6]

The first time my wife and I met Reb Zalman we were pregnant with our first child, in the early 1980s. He stopped us as we were walking across the campus of Brandeis University where we were all presenting at a conference. We made introductions, and then he stared at my wife's belly.

"First one," she said.

"Is it a boy or girl?" Reb Zalman asked. He caught himself at the end of the question and before we had a chance to respond he said, "Of course there are so many more than two possibilities." Then he laughed and moved on to other subjects.
— James Stone Goodman [5.7]

Our three-year-old son Jonathan came with us to the ALEPH Kallah in Fort Collins, Colorado, in 1995. We held his *upsherin* there, the Jewish tradition of a first haircut ceremony, among friends and with Reb Zalman's participation.

Jonathan, with his long, red curls, stood on a chair, and held cookies shaped like Hebrew letters that were slathered with sweet honey. Taking turns, long-time and new friends gathered around him, laughing, chanting, and preparing for the ritual.

Just after everyone had snipped a tiny bit of his red curls and moved on to their next activity, Reb Zalman appeared. He bent down to speak with Jonathan at eye level and then asked him two very simple but profound questions. First, he asked for permission

to cut some hair. Jonathan said it was okay, and then he further empowered Jonathan by asking him to point to the place he would like Reb Zalman to cut.
— *Rosalie Harris-Eisen and Efraim Eisen [5.8]*

We were the happy, busy parents of two young children when I discovered that I was pregnant with a third child. My husband was ambivalent about the news and thought about this for a few days. He then announced that he had a "proposal." Trying to make his point in a humorous way, he created a pseudo-document that he asked me to sign basically stating that we would agree to have a third child, but not a fourth one. I eagerly signed on to the plan.

The following days, though, had me thinking about the responsibility of making sure I did not become pregnant again.

We began talking about how to handle this. I decided to walk around the block and discuss the matter with Reb Zalman. I told him about baby number three and the need to prevent baby number four. I shared with him that my husband was thinking about getting a vasectomy.

Reb Zalman: "This would not be a good idea."

"Why not?" I asked.

Reb Zalman: "If you divorce, your husband would marry a younger person who would probably want to have children. He would have to have his vasectomy reversed—not usually pleasant and sometimes unsuccessful. I recommend you get your tubes tied instead."

I repeated this advice to my husband, who immediately answered that he would schedule a vasectomy the very next day.
— *Shoshana Silberman [5.9]*

Reb Zalman had agreed to do a baby naming for our daughter during one of his services.

The service began and continued for some time. When our baby got fussy, I stood up to take her out so she would not disturb anyone.

"Wait," Reb Zalman said, and I stopped. "Sometimes, God has a different plan than we do. Apparently, this baby needs naming right now."
— *Laurie Sanford [5.10]*

B'nei Mitzvah

In 1940, I loved going to synagogue. When I saw the boys were getting ready for their "mitzvah," I went to the local rabbi and said, "I would like to prepare for my 'mitzvah' as well." He looked at me with a very stern, disapproving expression on his face and said, "You should be ashamed of yourself for asking. You are a girl."

One day when Reb Zalman invited the Jews at the Lama Foundation to say something about our relationship to Judaism, the experience above is what I shared. And I added, "even though I continue to find a deep source of comfort in being Jewish, my heart connection with Judaism was deeply tainted."

Within a few days, there was a whispering campaign on campus that I got wind of, people were telling me that Reb Zalman wanted to hold a Bat Mitzvah for me at the Lama Foundation. Really? I had mostly forgotten how to read Hebrew and had raised my children in a more secular than religious home.

In response to the rumors, I went to Reb Zalman and hesitantly asked if it was indeed possible for me to become Bat Mitzvah. He looked at me and said with a deep chuckle, "I thought you'd never ask."

Reb Zalman assigned me a tutor to help me prepare daily for several hours over about three weeks. I began learning the appropriate phrases, became comfortable with saying them, and studied the meanings of the Torah portion.

I was in my late fifties.

On the Friday afternoon before my Bat Mitzvah, Reb Zalman announced that I needed to have a *mikveh*. So late in the afternoon, we went down to the Rio Grande River, where there were some hot springs. We quickly immersed ourselves—women in one spring, men in another. Because of the chill we got out rather quickly and started to dress. Reb Zalman came over to me and said, "Not so fast." He led me by the hand to one of the hot springs where three times I submerged myself under water while he gave the blessings.

On that *Shabbos*, a celebration also transpired. We had ecumenical people of all orders coming from around the area, Albuquerque, Taos, Santa Fe, and beyond, as Reb Zalman was already beginning to become well known. I wore the one flowered dress I'd packed. They made leis for me and adorned my head with flowers. Reb Zalman even had them raise me up in a chair.
— *Neshama (Rose) Lipari [5.11]*

Reb Zalman told a story about how he had "Bar Mitzvahed" a Sufi leader's son. He spoke about how interesting it was exploring similarities in the Jewish and Sufi traditions with the people of the Sufi village — about how this highlighted our Biblical and Koranic tradition about our peoples being brothers and sisters.

Reb Zalman also spoke about the rituals of taking on the commandments, becoming a part of the shared spiritual traditions of these peoples…and the impact of creating a Bar Mitzvah for the child of this Sufi spiritual leader. He went on to give each of us permission to create new traditions, to borrow and "Jewify" what we might treasure in our own Judaism, be it a tradition from another's religion, music, or forms of chant and meditation.
— *Julie Schechter [5.12]*

Birthdays

One year, the party happened in the middle of a snowstorm. People still came. The weather, however, had dampened the proceedings, so the party had a kind of too mellow mood to it.

At ten o'clock, Reb Zalman burst through the door and waved a cassette at us. "Put this right on," he said, with a big smile and a bigger twinkle in his eye. On came the most glorious and grand Viennese waltzes. Reb Zalman took the hand of one of the birthday celebrants and began waltzing her around the living room. He then bowed to his partner and took the hand of the next. Again, round and round he danced her, laughing and having fun, as two old friends would. When the waltz ended, he took the hand of the third and then to get everyone dancing called out, "*Nu*? Am I going to have to do this with every woman here?"

Later, we asked him where he got that cool tape. He told us he had just stepped off a plane from Berkeley, where he was visiting friends from the Aquarian Minyan. He then took a cab from the airport. The driver was playing a tape of Viennese music. Reb Zalman, who grew up in Vienna, loved it immediately. He asked to see its cover, but it was a home made tape. "I'd like to buy it from you," he said. The driver, at first, demurred, but Reb Zalman said, "I'll give you twenty dollars for it."

And that was the tape we were listening to, as we danced on through the night.
— *Ya'acov Gabriel [5.13]*

Divorce

Well, that was it, I was getting divorced. I called Reb Zalman to tell him and to ask his advice

"Hello, Reb Zalman."

"Hello," he said. "How are you?"

"Reb Zalman, I'm getting divorced." I said.

"Oh," he said, "so am I."
— *Laurie Sanford [5.14]*

The *Zohar* says that the "Throne of Glory" weeps at the dissolution of a first marriage. Yet, many of us take that action even after successful years together, so that we can move forward on a new path. After twenty-seven years in a good marriage, a few years of separation, and a secular divorce, I asked my husband for a *"get,"* which is Hebrew for a religious divorce process and documents that are vital should one wish to remarry under Jewish auspices.

Knowing my concerns about the gender bias in that process, he was surprised by my request. He agreed, feeling it was my need, as a potential lineage holder of the Jewish spiritual path. Ironically, I felt it would help him with his very Orthodox family, especially if he remarried.

For the ceremony, I flew from San Francisco to Philadelphia with Reb Zalman, as he was nearby in California at the time. Upon arrival at P'nai Or, surprisingly, Reb Zalman had set up two documents and two sets of witnesses — male and female. Despite my discomfort at not having an integrated approach, he insisted on having one signed by males only, in case I would marry outside of liberal Judaism one day.

The writing, signing, and ceremony took all day, culminating in the reading and burning of letters we each wrote describing the positives we had received from the marriage.
— *Leah Novick [5.15]*

Alas, years later, our marriage, despite the strength of Reb Zalman's blessing, did not continue to flourish.

What happens to the energy of any blessing whose focus has been dissolved on the physical plane? When I called, Reb Zalman himself picked up the phone and we spoke for about ten minutes.

He assured me that I had already done more than what was required legally, religiously, and spiritually. It wasn't so much his words as the energy of his comfort, concern, and understanding about the spiral nature of life and love [that mattered].
— *Deliah Golda Rosel [5.16]*

"Reb Zalman, would you feel comfortable doing a *get* for me and my soon-to-be *wasband*?" He cracked up at the new word, as he had at *hubbatzin* and *feminal* and *infeminate* during our earlier meetings, and then became reflective and silent.

I'd never asked Reb Zalman for professional help before, viewing my work for him in the category of "work-study" for a great professor. He'd been my favorite teacher, at the Reconstructionist Rabbinical College, where I'd graduated with the title "rabbi."

Reb Zalman then said, "Here's how it will go. You'll bring some friends and colleagues and I will secure a scribe for the *get* (Jewish divorce document). I could do the writing, but there's someone in training I'd like to observe, and while we do this I want you to learn how to officiate a *get* with a scribe involved. And I would need you to make sure that there are male colleagues present."

"Why male and not assorted genders?"

Reb Zalman explained the importance of Jewish documents being designed to be taken as valid across the spectrum of Jewish life and how an egalitarian *get* could affect the ability of either of us to marry outside of a liberal Jewish context, and a few other potential complications. I continued to advocate for full gender inclusion in the document and process. And I also told him that my soon-to-be *wasband* would not be present and instead accept his copy by a *shaliach* (emissary) acceptable to him.

Eventually Reb Zalman sighed and said, "I bridge two worlds, the Old and the New, and serve a unique function that makes it so that I cannot do as you suggest. I sometimes have had women write out their own *get*, a Document of Release of their own, that they can do while the formal *get* is being created. Would you want to do that?"

"Psycho-spiritually wouldn't both partners to the marriage benefit from creating their own document of release as an exercise while the scribe creates one unified formal *get*?" I asked. I continued, "Reb Zalman, I understand the position you find yourself in. Thank you for being willing to do this. And, given your circumstances, I think it will be better, given that I'm a feminist rabbi and not a rebbe, to call upon a colleague who will be able to use a fully inclusive, egalitarian document and ritual. There's so much else we can do together, so let's continue in our usual way."

"Thank you for understanding, Goldie, *leibn*, let me know what you design as your ritual. I'm curious, and with your permission, will appropriate whatever I can within the constraints I have set for myself."
— *Goldie Milgram [5.17]*

Aging and Eldering

A gathering of Spiritual Eldering presenters was scheduled. It was to be a time of enrichment, and Reb Zalman would be coming to answer our questions. We discussed possible questions beforehand to use his time efficiently and broadly.

My hesitant question was, "How do you deal with your own mortality?"

Before he answered, Reb Zalman looked at me and said, "Thank you."
— *Justin Freed [5.18]*

One January in the early nineties we met at Murrieta Hot Springs in southern California with various visionaries and leaders of the aging and elder care movements, including Betty Friedan. Reb Zalman had called this meeting because he felt that the elders of his generation and their wisdom had perished in the Holocaust, and he wanted to reimagine how elders should prepare and learn to help themselves and others become wisdom receivers and givers.

We talked, we experimented, trying out ideas and exercises and filling many flip charts! Later I attended the first such formal program, which took place for several years at Canterbury Retreat Center in Florida, in what would become the Spiritual Eldering project.
— *Ahouva Steinhaus [5.19]*

When Reb Zalman began teaching "Aging to Sage-ing," many mature health professionals came to the workshops. At a weeklong program at Bryn Mawr College, the participants extolled the positive qualities of eldering.

However, at the closing ritual when one of our musician-rabbis called for "elders" to come out to the quadrangle, the only two people who emerged were Reb Zalman and myself!

Over the years Reb Zalman continued to urge colleagues, especially those approaching their later years, to be open about their aging process.

At one point he organized a conference call among us to talk specifically about the body. Reb Zalman told us how his religious teachers never spoke of the physical issues, so he wanted to be sure to cover that base.

He also wanted us to deal with death. At one Ohalah gathering he had us all on the floor listening to him speak as if already on his way out!

Later in his life, between ages eighty and ninety, almost every phone conversation involved a description of his waning energy and often challenged physical state. This was not by way of complaint; he explained it was to help us on our own inevitable journeys.
— *Leah Novick [5.20]*

Reb Zalman described himself as a *beynoni* (partially evolved), not a *tzadik* (righteous person), as he shared some of the ways he struggled with willfulness, the "evil *yetzer* (inclination)." At the end of one Kallah, he announced that his time for attending such gatherings was over. He specified that he would be focused on completing his writing projects, handing over many of his leadership functions to others, preparing for his dying — that is, doing his Sage-ing work. And, most important for me, he was doing *teshuva*/repentance/*karma* repair, with his family most of all, and with those he loved, and with his students.

Reb Zalman offered, "If there is *teshuva* I need to do with any of you, let me know and we'll do it."
— *Shaya Isenberg [5.21]*

I arrived as the service was beginning. Only one seat was available, next to Reb Zalman, on a bench at the kitchen table. He looked at

me, then my *tallis*, tested the warp and woof of it between his fingers. "Now, this is a *tallis* to be buried in," he said.
— *Mitchell Chefitz [5.22]*

As a newly ordained rabbi, I sat across from Reb Zalman at a hotel in Colorado, asking his advice about how to guide the community I was going to be serving. He looked at me, radiating the sunshine of his kindly smile. I can still hear him exclaiming, "I like your tears!"

In response to my eventual sharing, Reb Zalman added, "Don't try to lead; guide gently, don't expect them to change, offer them spiritual tools that will support them as they are aging."
— *Diane Elliot [5.23]*

Reb Zalman stayed in touch with his students and prayed for their wellbeing aloud whenever he'd even see their pictures. While working with him, he'd sometimes mention one of his students. He'd often then Google that person just to look at their picture and pray for them.

Sometimes Reb Zalman would pick up a book, for example, *Flow*, or *The Holographic Paradigm*, and look up and say, "I need to speak to this author!" I'd go through his Rolodex of contact information, dial the number, and pass him the phone — sometimes for politicians and spiritual leaders from a variety of religions, too. At times he would call people just to tell them about a project they could collaborate on with him or another, to share a memory, and often he would tell them "I love you" or "I miss you."

And, at a certain point, Reb Zalman began making *teshuva* calls with an array of people. He told me, this "is an important part of eldering, the clearing, and cleaning up of old errors. Try never to leave pain in the soul of another from something you did or said, even if it was a long time ago and you weren't so mature then."
— *Goldie Milgram [5.24]*

"You cannot do spiritual work of becoming an elder without coming to terms with mortality. That sounds abstract; but when I was being wheeled into the operating room on the gurney, I had to come to terms with dying. It's a little bit more direct. What happens is that our consciousness gets a jolt that is necessary when we are in that situation, because we begin to see more than the moment of death into a larger scheme. You cannot do the work of Spiritual Eldering without doing your philosophical homework that says: 'What is my life all about?' I don't mean academic philosophy—but what was it all about? Where do I fit in? Because once I get a little bit more of a glimpse of that, I can say 'yes' to both living and to dying."
— *Janice Rubin. Her transcription from selected pieces, Audio Files 1154, 1155 of her September 2011 interview of Reb Zalman. [5.25]*

Aging, Reb Zalman taught, includes preparing to upload yourself, your story, and your wisdom for future generations and discover what is new in this phase of being.
— *Carola de Vries Robles [5.26]*

During the introductory week of Spiritual Eldering with Reb Zalman, held at Omega Institute, he offered radical, personal honesty about facing aging and mortality. He told us, "Letting go of denial is essential. He also leavened his teachings with humor, e.g., "The mind is a marinade. Do you want to marinate in *kvetch* (complaining) or in joy?"

It wasn't just his wisdom and honesty that mattered; it was his sweetness and kindness, akin to an Eastern European grandparent. His vision was one of a joyful, lively aging.

Reb Zalman told us, "We have particular tasks at each stage of life. As elders we have singular contributions to make. These derive from the redemptive meaning to be found in our mistakes in life— for they are what were necessary to acquire and pass on wisdom.

You don't become a sage simply by growing older. That is the work of Spiritual Eldering."
— *Janice Rubin. Her transcription from selected pieces, Audio Files 1154, 1155 of her September 2011 interview of Reb Zalman. [5.27]* "

"I wrote the book, *From Ageing to Sage-ing*, and in it I discuss how every one of the months of the year is like a seven-year *shmita* cycle (Biblical cycle of rest for the land). The first *shmita* is January, when the first teeth come out and the second teeth come in. The second *shmita* is at puberty, and the third is at twenty-one, and so on.

"We have good models for what people should do until what we call 'September,' which is when we reach our sixties…we don't have good models for what happens in October and November and December. So I wrote that book to help people learn to become an elder in what we call the October Years, and to give back to the planet in the November Years — as teachers, as peacemakers, and so on. But then comes December, which I couldn't write about, because I wasn't there yet. So now I'm working on what I call the December Years."
— *Justin Freed [5.28]*

Death, Dying, Afterlife

"I am very glad that the work of the *Chevra Kaddisha* (burial society) is happening in the communities. The whole business of turning over this work to undertakers, of running away from the gravesite and not filling it in—all of this is trying to keep people away from that final reality. There is a wonderful custom at the end of *shiva* (initial mourning period) where you ask the people on the seventh day to get up from *shiva* and walk out of the house and go around the block, away from the house. In this way you say to the *neshama* (soul), 'Go in peace, go in peace, don't forget your family. Be a good intercessor for us and go in peace.'"
— *Janice Rubin. Her transcription from selected pieces, Audio Files 1154, 1155 of her September 2011 interview of Reb Zalman. [5.28]*

"My sense is, if people have a sense of [the mitzvah of] *Kavod Ha-Met* (respect for the dead body), while they are doing the *tahara* (Jewish approach to preparation of the corpse for burial), they should be really aware that the *neshama* is there in the room....

"Sometimes it may be necessary to say some words to the person, such as the beautiful *pesukim* that you say to the body from *Shir Hashirim* (Song of Songs), and so forth. But to be able to also say, 'Be not afraid of the other place. There are neshamas waiting to show you and to help you around. And yes, your soul will have to undergo some purification, just as we do the purification here with your body. So, some purification is necessary, but be not afraid, because it is there to lead you to the greater light and the greater awareness.'"
— *Janice Rubin. Janice's transcription from selected pieces, Audio Files 1154, 1155 of her September 2011 interview of Reb Zalman. [5.29]*

"It seems that people are now more open to thinking about *Hasharat HaNefesh*, that there is something more after life. The first few hours after the last breath are very important for the doulas, for the people who are working to be able to do these encouraging things for the *neshama*. Even while the body is cooling down and moving into rigor [mortis], it is important to speak to the soul. If the next of kin can touch the body in a good and loving way, that is important too."

— *Janice Rubin. Janice's transcription from selected pieces, Audio Files 1154, 1155 of her September 2011 interview of Reb Zalman. [5.30]*

Reb Zalman: "Am I interested in having *tahara* done to me while I am alive? Well, I am somebody who has been Rolfed, and done Feldenkrais, and all that."

— *Janice Rubin. Janice's transcription from selected pieces, Audio Files 1154, 1155 of her September 2011 interview of Reb Zalman. [5.31]*

"Why don't we do cremation? It begins with Titus who didn't want to be put together by God and resurrected and punished for what he did in the *Beis Hamikdash* (the Temple that stood in Jerusalem).

"My *zayde* was a *shochet* (kosher slaughterer) in Oświęcim [town of Auschwitz]. My uncles were the first ones who were taken in to build the camp, and they died there. When I was a little child, my parents took me to see my *zayde* in Oświęcim. So I have that connection there. It was only by the grace of God that I am around, and all of the different ways that *hashgacha pratit* (personal destiny) made it so that we moved west instead of going back to Poland after Hitler.

"So I had the *hergish* (feeling) that I would like to share with the cousins [ancestors who died in the Holocaust] that end [cremation]. So when people say, 'Then you won't be resurrected,' my answer is, 'If they won't be resurrected then don't do me any favor—don't resurrect me either.' The whole notion of green corpses crawling out of graves makes no sense to me at all. Once you understand the spiritual stuff—that the astral and etheric bodies remove themselves from the flesh—you have the sense that's resurrection enough.

"We have to throw off the body. Otherwise, if you believe in reincarnation, then which body am I going to inhabit when I come back? I am saying it in this way because I don't want to reify it, saying that this is a reality of dead people crawling out of graves [as described in Ezekiel's vision]."

— *Janice Rubin. Janice's transcription from selected pieces, Audio Files 1154, 1155 of her September 2011 interview of Reb Zalman. [5.32]*

"I'll tell you a very strange story. One of my friends, who is an acupuncturist, tells me that when he was working in the gross anatomy lab, he was dealing with a cadaver that had been dead for a while. His colleague was examining the kidneys near the window on the other side of the room. My friend took the acupuncture needle and touched some of the kidney points on the body, when his colleague said, 'What did you do just now? Because there was a tremor in the kidney.'

"So when in Kabbalah and *Hassidus* they teach that after death, there is still a *kisdeh d'chayutah*—a little bit of life-force left, which makes fingernails and hair grow—then that has to be respected. One of the problems with people who want cremation for themselves is that it may be too soon to do it before the third day. That would take a longer *shmira* (period of watching over the body), but if they want to do it this way, my suggestion would be that they take some of the ashes and drop them off at Auschwitz or Birkenau, so they could be with the other brothers and sisters who died. That would raise the whole element of what cremation is about to a higher level. There was a time when I wanted this to be done with my remains. But it would be too much of a burden for family afterwards to have to deal with stuff like that. So I am fine to find interment around here [Colorado]."

— *Janice Rubin. Janice's transcription from selected pieces, Audio Files 1154, 1155 of her September 2011 interview of Reb Zalman. [5.33]*

Reb Zalman was continuously planning for his exit. In March 2014, I learned that Sandy Pond, an artist, had been commissioned to paint a room to be used for the spiritual practice called *shmira*. It was painted in soft blue with gold harps and psalms and Hebrew lettering on the walls to offer a sense of peace, comfort, and acceptance.

It turns out that this was the room that Reb Zalman lay in before burial. The room still stands, for those who will need it next, a moving example of [the mitzvah of] *Kavod Ha-Met* and *hiddur mitzvah* (enhancing a mitzvah).

Reb Zalman had such a sense of curiosity and adventure that he even went as far as having a practice *tahara* while he was alive. He wanted the experience.
— *T'mimah Audrey Ickovits [5.34]*

"Goldie, *leibn*, when you are in the Ukraine I need you to go to the grave of Reb Nachman in Uman to ask a question for me. I want to know the end of a piece that he left unfinished. I will write down the title for you."

"Reb Zalman, is there a special way to prepare to go to the grave of a rebbe?"

"Yes. First, you go to *mikveh* before the driver comes to bring you to the grave. Then, on the way, you pray *tehillim* (psalms) in the order of Reb Nachman's *Tikkun Klali* (prescription for the petitioner's complete renewal). When you arrive, remove your shoes before approaching the grave."

The answer to Reb Zalman's question was indeed provided during a graveside meditation. And, for the next trip, Reb Zalman had given a different assignment.

"Reb Zalman, I again did what you asked and as you taught. Something so troubling happened. It was when two of my students, sisters, took me out for a day and at one point we were at a playground located on two hills covered with snow and ice, as were the roads. When I asked why they had brought me there, they told me that as teens they'd gone to visit an aunt in Kiev, and while they were away the Stalinists slaughtered everyone in their village, including their family. They said the children were shot and buried in one mound, and the adults in another. As I'd begun to teach them about the different types of *Kaddish* on the retreat they were attending, they realized they'd had no form of closure and had brought me there to help them with this.

"I had them do some Gestalt work upon the mass grave and when perhaps all possible words and tears had been said and shed, explained we needed a *minyan* of ten people to say the Mourner's *Kaddish* and would do so back with our Project Kesher group at the old tuberculosis sanatorium that was serving as the retreat center.

"Sending the women out of the icy snow and frigid cold back to the car, I walked the area of the mass graves. In Yiddish, as you had requested me to do at Babi Yar, (which would be too far afield to reach on this trip), I implored any souls that might be hovering in the vicinity to reincarnate in order to help transform the world. When I did, I heard disembodied, annoyed voices of all ages and genders, in Yiddish, telling me that I had no right to disturb them. They also said things like, "Do not concern yourself with us. We neither slumber nor sleep. We are the guardians of this place.'

"I was so frightened by this experience that, Reb Zalman, I started shaking like a dog in a thunderstorm! They also spoke to me later, back in the United States, and saved my life by warning me to drive slower on a slippery day. Reb Zalman, I'm worried. Should I be committed? Have I lost a sufficient hold on sanity?"

Reb Zalman replied, "Not to worry. I suggest that you phone Anne Brener, a spiritually oriented psychotherapist in Los Angeles. She will know how to help you. What's more important at this point, given the advent of Perestroika, is to focus upon finding a rich person to fund your trips to the Ukraine."

A similar assignment was to go to Rivesaltes, the camp where Reb Zalman was interred under the Vichy French during World War II. He said, "There was a river nearby, where every three weeks or so, we were marched to bathe ourselves. On the way there I saw the slaughtered young Spanish freedom fighters. I want you to go immerse in the river and do a ritual to help free their souls that are hovering there, still in trauma."

It took half a day to find the camp and as long to find the river, as its path had changed. Many whom we asked to show us the way tearfully apologized for their parents' role helping to build, supply, and run such camps — filled primarily with Jews, homosexuals, Roma, and political prisoners.

Locals lunching on the riverbank helped me to select from among the abundant reeds and crudely weave them into foot mats in order to wade out into what was at times waist-high watery mud. My destination was toward a sizeable patch of pooled water a good distance away within the riverbed. The river wasn't flowing at all due to a major drought.

Arriving in the center of the still water, suddenly thousands of tiny eyes popped above the surface…frogs floating everywhere! Soon their faces had pointy beards and soulful dark eyes. When a light breeze began, their visages flickered holographically — from all frogs to all Spaniards, repeatedly, back and forth.

Reb Zalman had told me to begin with calling upon *Ribono shel Olam* and that doing this would create a shower of the pure white light of divine love. He had also given me the Spanish words to encourage the remaining souls to ascend, and instructions to sprinkle water in all four directions.

Doing so, I also paraphrased a passage from *Ezekiel* that I imagined might allow the souls the memory of embodiment necessary for their souls to finally ascend: "I will sprinkle pure water on you, and purify you…and turn your heart of stone into a heart of flesh."

We first emailed back pictures and a brief report. The sigh Reb Zalman gave with lidded eyes while hearing the report upon our return to the States was so deep and long.
– *Goldie Milgram* [5.35]

We were going to a Buddhist meditation retreat. She was a close girlfriend, a spiritual adventurer, and I was her companion. However, when we arrived at the retreat center, the Buddhist retreat had been cancelled, and in its place was a retreat on Kabbalah. A rabbi was leading the weekend, on the topic of Kabbalah.

He was like no rabbi I had ever met before. This rabbi was… well… radiant.

He was wearing a long green robe and a large yarmulke that did not quite lie flat on his head, and an incredibly happy smile. He was huge.

This was Reb Zalman, who was leading the weekend, on the topic of Kabbalah.

During an intermission, I went up to him and asked, "How can you be so happy when you were in a concentration camp in your youth and the Holocaust happened? How can you be happy and how does any of this life make sense when things like that can occur?"

"Ahh," he said, with empathy. "There is an entire body of literature about that subject. Would you like to learn?"

"Yes," I said emphatically. "Yes!" In that weekend, I also learned about a Judaism that believed in astrology, and angels, and *karma*, and past lives, and reincarnation, and in an actual literal return of the messiah on the battlefield in Israel.

Before leaving the weekend, I asked Reb Zalman, almost shyly, feeling a little ashamed of my lack of knowledge, "Would you teach me to say the *Kaddish* prayer in memory of my father?"

"Yes," he said.

A week after returning home, a package came from Reb Zalman. In it was a tape cassette in which he had spoken the *Kaddish* very, very slowly so that I could learn the words.
— *Laurie Sanford [5.36]*

On Suicide

"I will tell you a story. I was with a family whose daughter had committed suicide. It was very hard for them. She had suffered for years with eating disorders. At the last day of *shiva*, after all the people had left, I said to the family, 'Do you mind if I become a speaker for the dead?' They didn't understand what I meant. So I explained to them when they asked, 'What's the reason why we are covering the mirrors? People say so that the mourners should not be vain.'

"I said, 'That's not the reason. The reason is: just as when people have near-death or out-of-body experiences, the experiences are invisible but the experiencer can see, [so] in Hebrew you call it *ro-eh v'eino nireh*—seeing and not being visible. And I believe that she is here now, and she wants me to talk to you for her. So I am asking you, for her, to forgive her for the pain she has caused you, and to tell you that she forgives you for not understanding where she was.'

"You can imagine that I didn't leave the house immediately afterward. And, at the end of the *shloshim* we had another conversation about that."
— *Janice Rubin. Transcription from selected pieces, Audio Files 1154, 1155 by Janice of her September 2011 interview of Reb Zalman. [5.37]*

Conversion, *Mikveh*, and Integral *Halachah*

Reb Zalman told me this story from his life that he called "How the River Swallowed My Watch."

"Once upon a time," said Reb Zalman, "I had a watch which showed the phases of the moon. And it got lost in an interesting circumstance when I was teaching in Freiburg im Breisgau in Germany for Temple University.

"A young man studying there impressed me a great deal with his eyes and his bearing and his beard. He had introduced himself as a Jew by the name of Klaus. He invited me to his home. I went to visit him in his home, and met his lady by the name of Uta; she was a German lady [i.e., not Jewish]. So we had this wonderful conversation and a year later I go back there again, we meet again, he tells me she, Uta, would like to convert to be a Jew so that they can marry and have a baby.

'Wonderful,' I say. 'Great! Let me see who are the rabbis here.'

"He tells me that she started with so-and-so, but they are making it really hard. Would I help? I start to make suggestions. In the end she converts— the liberal rabbi and the *hazan* (cantor) who comes to Freiburg did the conversion, and subsequently they had a wedding and everything was *kosher v'yosher* (kosher plus).

"Then there was this meeting on peace that was to happen in Malta. But because I was on the program, along with a couple of other people, the Maltese government didn't get permission from Khadaffi. It's interesting; Khadaffi sort of had control over Malta. They moved the whole show to Amsterdam, and there is where that Peace Meeting was happening. So it was there that I gave a talk on 'Peace and Shadow.'

"While there, I got a telephone call from from Uta and her husband, Klaus. There seemed to be some kind of grave emergency. They wanted me to come to them right away and to see them in Amsterdam. I tell them, 'Wait a minute. I'm going to be in Basel. Freiburg is next to Basel. Come and see me in Basel and tell me what it's all about.'

"It turns out that, by his first marriage, Klaus had a son. And, his son would ask from time to time who are his grandparents. And he would say they died in the Holocaust. It turned out that the son didn't quite swallow this, and he poked around and found out about his grandparents.

"He went into the neighborhood of Hamburg or Altona, where they lived, visited them, found out that they're not Jewish, and in fact that they were SS people. So he comes back and confronts his father. And for the father the jig is up. Somehow now he has to do something about this. His wife didn't know the story. She didn't know that *he* wasn't born Jewish. And so I hear his story in the following way:

"Klaus had gone to University, was very much into New Age and Beat and so on and so forth, and sometimes would hang out with black people and others. Once he comes into a tavern in the town where he was studying and takes a black guy with him. Someone in the back of the tavern starts saying, 'What do you bring this trash here for?' — in German.

"Klaus turns around to him and says, 'How dare you, after the Holocaust, speak in such a way?'

"And the other guy says, 'I suppose you're Jewish, too, yourself!' and starts giving him a hard time. So Klaus finds himself in a situation, if he denies it that he is Jewish, he plays right into the hand of that guy. So he doesn't say a word, and the word spreads around that he is Jewish.

"A few weeks later, a woman who is with Klaus on the teaching faculty of the High School says she needs to talk with him in private. She says 'I'm going to Frankfurt to shop for Pesach.' She herself hadn't let on that she was Jewish. Can she bring him some matzah and stuff like that?

"So now the word was out that he's Jewish. So what's he going to do? He says 'Sure, please bring me matzah for Pesach,' and he was delighted to be able to do a *seder*.

"Next thing, the professor says to him, 'I have to assign a course in Old Testament and, after all, it's so much closer to you, sir, would you be interested in teaching this course?'

"Again he is in that awkward place. Now, in Germany you have to pay taxes according to your religion. So, on the tax report it says your religion tax is to go to Catholics, Protestant, Jewish. So, why should he pay taxes for anyone who isn't Jewish? He marks Jewish, and he's begun to pay taxes, and as far as the Internal Revenue Bureau is concerned, he's now Jewish.

"So one day, Klaus sends a note with a copy of the tax report to the president [of a local congregation], who writes back to him, 'Sir, would you please come and we'll have an *aliya* for you. We're delighted to know that you live in our city, and we understand that you are a teacher of religion, and would you take over our *Talmud Torah* (Hebrew school)?'

"In Germany, when you study anything in religion, you have to take the appropriate language, like Latin or Greek. His university concentration had become Jewish Religion, so he'd taken the Hebrew course, Hebraicum. So he's now teaching in the Talmud Torah and he is now officially accepted as Jewish. So he does a *bracha* over the Torah, fine, and he does all that stuff as a Jew, and he is known as Jewish.

"With Klaus' son coming back and blowing the lid on the whole thing, he doesn't know what to do. And that is why he now comes to me. So I say to him, 'Why don't you level with the congregation. It's an amazing story.'

"He says, 'I can't. I won't. It is not possible.'

"So I invite him to come to Simchas Torah in Philadelphia and to *daven* and to be with us for the retreat that we'll be having. When I ask Klaus when was he circumcised? He says he didn't want, heaven forbid, if he had an accident on the *Autobahn*, them to find him uncircumcised, so he had himself medically circumcised earlier. So in Philadelphia I would [guide] the *tevila* (immersion), and draw the [covenantal] drop of blood to make it a kosher *bris milah* and do another wedding for him with Uta.

"So, there we were, we were doing his *mikveh*, dipping in the Schuylkill River. I had gotten this wonderful watch from Max Sampson—it had the moon phases. As I was going down to do this *mikveh*, I took off the watch because I didn't want to take it into the water with me. And the watch with the moon phases slipped and fell between the cracks, and I never was able to retrieve it, and that's how The River Swallowed My Watch."
— *Ruth Hirsch, as told to her on July 20, 1990 while recording in Reb Zalman's Philadelphia apartment. [5.38]*

Soon after I moved to Denver in 1998, I received a call from Reb Zalman. He wanted to know if I was available and willing to be a witness for conversion at the old *mikveh* on the west side of town. I agreed, and the time was set about two weeks hence on a Sunday afternoon.

A few days before the planned *mikveh*, I called and asked if we would also be doing a *beit din* at the *mikveh*. Reb Zalman said, "No. We are taking care of that for them in Boulder in advance."

It was a sunny Colorado day in February 1999 when I arrived at the Mikveh of West Denver. Outside, I found Reb Zalman and many others. It turned out our "guests" included Rabbi Michael Goldberger of Dusseldorf, Germany, and seven German citizens— four women and three men.

As we walked into the *mikveh*, Reb Zalman explained that while many of them have Jewish fathers, this immersion is still important. And he advised that all of the women would immerse at once on one side with him supervising from outside the door and a woman witness inside helping. And then, all of the men would immerse at once under his supervision on the other side of the facility.

So in the room with the men, Reb Zalman explains we need to do *hatafat dam brit*, drawing a covenantal drop of blood. He turns to me and says, "Do you know how to do this?"

"So far, not this." I reply.

Reb Zalman had the three men strip and jump up on the long counter in the dressing room. He then showed me three demonstrations of how to do *hatafat dam brit*.

Shortly thereafter, Zalman invited all three men into the men's *mikveh*, and then went in with them. Two of the men appeared young, perhaps in their thirties, and one was an older man. Reb Zalman spoke to them in German, giving them teachings and *kavanot* (spiritual intention) for their immersions. I understood little. The word *Birkenau* stood out when he spoke with the older man.

After the men got out and dressed, the older man showed me his old German ID. Turns out he was in Birkenau as a child with his Jewish father! Here was this man, a child of an interfaith marriage before WWII, and a concentration camp survivor…. and all these years later…. he is officially converting to Judaism! Reb Zalman explained that this was a great *tikkun* — bringing all these Jewish souls back into the fold of Jewish life and community.

The women held a spirited ritual on their side. And then altogether we had a joyful brief celebration…and then went on with our lives, not one of us the same.
— *Steve Booth-Nadav [5.39]*

When in 2012 I asked Reb Zalman to share his practices for immersing in the *mikveh* he replied:

1. When he is personally doing *mikveh*, he stands in the water of the *mikveh* and bows to the four cardinal directions in this order: East, South, West and ends with "North from where evil develops" [Jeremiah 1:14] and that this sequence also parallels the Four Worlds.

2. Each time he bows he takes upon himself one of the four modes of the death penalty in this order: stoning, burning, decapitation and strangulation. And then he added that sometimes he begins with burning.

3. When I told him that my practice before immersing was to recite the verse, "I put my soul in your hand and you have redeemed me, YHVH, God of Truth" [Psalms 31:6], he said this is oriented toward the same goal as the practice he described. He explained that this is because the essence of the practice of immersing in the *mikveh* is giving your life (*mesirat nefesh*) through which you can be reborn. The *mikveh* waters serve as amniotic fluid.

4. Regarding birth he said that when a child is born its skin is covered with vernix, which reflects the aspect of *mashiach*, the anointed one—for every child exits the womb anointed.

5. And he said that he follows the practice of the Baal Shem Tov, to immerse with open eyes. He added that a person should use common sense to decide if it is safe to do so in any specific *mikveh*.

6. Reb Zalman further said that even though our communities do not uphold the practice of impurity following marital relations (*niddah*), it is still good to go immerse in the *mikveh* after engaging in such. And if a person cannot immerse in a *mikveh*, one can at least pour nine *kavin*, units of water, over themselves, as is the known practice.

7. When he officiates at the conversion of a *ger tzedek,* it is Reb Zalman's practice to immerse together with the *ger.* And he himself says the blessing on the immersion of converts—*al tevilat gerim*—with them as their guide.

8. And similarly, when a female partner immerses for purity following *niddah,* he immerses with her on the second immersion after she does the first alone.

9. And he said that one should pray for the needs of other people in the *mikveh,* for the *mikveh* is *Bina,* the supernal Mother, the place where all judgment is sweetened.

10. Reb Zalman also taught that the time to pray for another person or people is when you are holding your breath under the water.
— *Ebn Leader [5.40]*

Many years ago, a local rabbinic colleague and friend asked me to serve as one of the three rabbis for a conversion of one of her congregants. This person was an Asian man who had married a Jewish woman. Through her, he developed an interest and then a great love of Judaism. He grew to love to celebrate Shabbat and the Jewish holidays in their home. He became active in the synagogue. He learned Hebrew and he attended Shabbat services regularly with his wife. He loved the sound of the Torah being chanted aloud and began learning the Torah trope (musical symbols) and how to chant from the Torah.

This person was fully ready to convert, but there was one huge obstacle in his way. Try as he might, he could not come to terms with the circumcision ritual.

This couple had a son together. They were joyfully raising him as a Jew. Tragically, the woman became seriously ill. She had developed a virulent form of cancer. On her deathbed, her husband promised her that he would train their son for his Bar

Mitzvah and he, himself, would be called to the Torah as a Jew to honor their deep connection to Judaism.

This man went into therapy explicitly to overcome his terror of adult circumcision. Unfortunately, after two frustrating years, he was no closer to overcoming this obstacle. With his son's Bar Mitzvah approaching, he desperately was seeking a way to convert. This was the story his rabbi told me when she invited me into his conversion process and asked, "What should we do?"

So I said, what I always said, when knowing not which way to turn, "Let's call Reb Zalman."

Reb Zalman listened very carefully to the story of this desperate man. He asked some very incisive questions about his situation and level of commitment. Then there was a long silence at the other end of the phone. Reb Zalman was considering what could be done to honor the Jewish tradition he loved so much with compassion for this struggling soul.

Finally, Reb Zalman declared, "God wants us to be creative to help this *neshama* embrace *Yiddishkeit*. I want to suggest that you conduct the *Beit Din* and then take him to the *mikveh*. Before he immerses, open up the Torah text to *Devarim* (Deuteronomy) Chapter 10, verse 16 and have him read aloud: '*U'maltem eyt orlat l'vavchem, v'or-pi-chem lo takshu ode*—circumcise your hearts and do not resist Me any more.'"

This was the verse that the apostle Paul used as a midrash (a commentary) to abolish circumcision as a necessity for conversion.

Reb Zalman, who required circumcision for infants and for conversion under normal circumstances throughout his life, to the best of my knowledge, then said, "I know what you are thinking. This verse has been a source of pain for our people. These words need healing…this lovely man needs healing. Let's bring them together and bring healing to our tradition."
— *Dan Goldblatt [5.41]*

6

Deep Ecumenism

Reb Zalman modeled and encouraged his students
to experience the people, philosophy, and practices
of the world's religions, the importance of
interfaith dialogue, and within Judaism
—respectful pluralism.

Questioner: "Why are there so many religions?"

Reb Zalman: "Because God needs an ecology [of paths]…"
— *Aryeh Hirschfield, of blessed memory; from Beth Hirschfield [6.1]*

In the fall of 1992, while sitting in Alicia and Itzhik Magal's cozy, colorful sukkah in Los Angeles, Reb Zalman and Eve arrived for a short visit. I hardly knew Reb Zalman, but after some initial conversation, I took courage and blurted out a request.

"There's a new interfaith project I'm working on," I ventured. "Perhaps I could write to you about it."

"Tell me about it now," he replied, with an engaging smile. "I'm here now."

I told him, "I'm working with a black minister named Delores Gray, and we want to take a group of Christians, Muslims, and Jews on an interfaith peace pilgrimage, beginning in Egypt, continuing through the Sinai, and then ending in Jerusalem. As we symbolically retrace the steps of Exodus, we will share our own faith stories along the way, engage in intimate interfaith dialogue, celebrate Easter together in Jerusalem, and then, as a culminating event, conduct an interfaith Passover seder for people of all faiths."

Reb Zalman looked at me, smiling bemusedly, "You're *meshuga*— crazy! You know that, don't you?"

"I know," I replied sheepishly, acknowledging my incurable idealism with a shoulder shrug. "What can I do?"

Reb Zalman leaned over the table, bringing his head close to mine, and whispered like a co-conspirator, "Don't worry, Ruth, I'm *meshuga* too, and when enough *meshugaim* get together, then we'll all start to feel sane!" Reb Zalman took up a pen and drew on the paper tablecloth the layout of the tables he recommended for the culminating seder. He was hooked! He couldn't make the first one in 1993, so he and Eve joined us in 1994.

As a prelude to the seder, they led a two-day Passover workshop in Jerusalem for our interfaith group and local residents. Among the local participants were the Arab mayor of Jericho, Rajai Abdo, and his wife. For many of the participants it was the first occasion they were meeting a Palestinian at close range.

The culminating seder was scheduled for the following evening. Half an hour before the event began, a crew from Israel television showed up and asked to interview both Reb Zalman and the Palestinian mayor. Their questions became more and more pointed, as they probed into the mayor's political position regarding Israel. The mayor started to squirm and suddenly Reb Zalman rose up majestically in his long white robe, like an ancient prophet. In an angry tone of voice — which I had never heard before from Reb Zalman — he scolded the interviewer.

"The mayor and his wife are guests of honor in our home and they should be treated with respect, not interrogated about their political views."

Known to be compassionate in his dealings with people of all backgrounds, and slow to anger, Reb Zalman's outburst took many by surprise.

The reporter from Israel TV apologized and the rest of the interview was conducted with utmost respect and no further provocative political questions were posed. (Afterwards, Reb Zalman sought out the Israeli reporter to apologize to him for having embarrassed him in public. The journalist accepted his apology and thanked him sincerely.)

More and more *shabbaton* guests began to arrive, including other Israelis and Palestinians, Black Hebrews from Dimona, and a wide array of visitors from such far-flung places as Ethiopia, Sri Lanka, and India.

No one knew exactly what to expect since it was not a traditional Passover seder.

An updated seder plate, designed by the workshop participants, dominated the main table. In addition to the well-known Passover symbols of hard boiled eggs, parsley, salt water, bitter herbs, and matzah, the plate also included an olive branch for hope, a broken chain symbolizing the breaking of all bondage, and almond milk to replace the lamb shank "so no blood would be shed" — at the suggestion of the Palestinian mayor.

A reading followed the festival *Kiddush* prayer from both the Kor'an and the Lord's Prayer in Aramaic. At Reb Zalman's request, more than fifty memorial candles were lit, symbolizing the many troubled places in the world, and in honor of all peoples struggling to be free from tyranny. As Reb Zalman looked out at the interfaith, multicultural, multiracial gathering of some one hundred people, he declared it to be a "seder of the future, not a seder of the past." [Highlights of the innovative Interfaith Seder were later aired by Israel TV and CNN's World News.]
— *Ruth Broyde Sharone [6.2]*

"[Muslims] say, '*Lá iláha illallah*, there is no God but God.' We say, '*Ein keloheinu, ein kadoneinu*, there is none like our God, there is none like our Lord.'"
— *Jay (Zisha) and Sabrina (Zahava) Gold [6.3]*

The summer after my Bar Mitzvah, my parents sent me to the Eagle's Nest Boys' Ranch in the Texas hill country for a month, not knowing that the director and staff of the ranch were fervent evangelical Christians. And during the final week of camp, we learned we'd be spending our last weekend together at a revival meeting. I was deeply traumatized by that experience, and, as a Jew, felt shame at having had to participate, as well as guilt that I was not a Christian.

Decades later, while giving a weekly course on the world's religions to a group of high school juniors, I began to panic a few days before teaching the class on Christianity. Having gotten to know Reb Zalman better while we were both active with Havurat Shalom in Boston, I called him to ask for his help. After I explained about that long-ago revival meeting, we made a plan for the contents and flow of the class. Reb Zalman was the first person I had ever told about the revival experience.

On the following Sunday morning, I followed the plan. I readied a different classroom than usual. I pulled the window shades down, turned off the overhead light, placed a large pillow in the middle of the room, turned on a recording of Gregorian chants, and lit candles and incense.

Upstairs in the usual classroom, I greeted my students, took attendance, and then led them quietly to the darkened room on the lower floor, and sat on a large pillow. The students silently took seats in a surrounding semicircle on the floor.

After about five minutes of Gregorian chant from the New Testament, still following Reb Zalman's directions step-by-step, I slowly read aloud selections from Jesus, his Jewish teacher's Sermon on the Mount:

And large crowds followed Jesus from Galilee and the Decapolis Jerusalem and Judea and beyond the Jordan River. And when he saw the crowds, he went up onto a hill, and when he had sat down, his disciples gathered around him, and he began to teach them. And this is what he said:
  Blessed are those who are not bound to their desires, for theirs is the realm of God.
  Blessed are the gentle, for they shall have the earth as an inheritance.
  Blessed are those who mourn, for they shall be comforted.
  Blessed are those who hunger and thirst for justice, for they shall have their fill.
  Blessed are the merciful, for they shall have mercy shown to them.
  Blessed are the pure in heart, for they already see God.
  Blessed are the peacemakers, for they shall be recognized as children of God.
  Blessed are those who are persecuted in the cause of righteousness, for theirs is the realm of God…." [Matthew 5:1-14]

After a period of silent reflection and on into the day, long-needed awareness and healing began to take hold.
— *Burt Jacobson [6.4]*

During a few private minutes at a retreat in Ashland, Oregon, in 2010, Reb Zalman asked me, "Zelig, *leibn*, what's on your heart today?"

I told him that in the fall of 2010, a Lakota holy man had given me a *canupa*, the sacred pipe of the Lakota people. Receiving a *canupa* is an initiation into relationship with and commitment to a sacred code of conduct. So I asked Reb Zalman, "Is it okay for a Jewish leader to participate in such ceremonies and commit to such a path?"

Reb Zalman recalled attending a multi-faith gathering of spiritual leaders where one morning he snuck up onto the hotel roof to *daven Shacharit*. Somewhere in his *davenen* he noticed a native man also on the roof praying. After they finished, the native man came over and asked to see his instruments.

Reb Zalman recounted to me how this man picked up his *tefillin*. "Rawhide," he noted aloud. Then, feeling Reb Zalman's *tzitzit*, he commented, "Noble knots." Next he picked up the *shofar* and blew a few notes, and then nodded and gestured toward the eagle bone whistle he had blown on the roof earlier. The native man expressed appreciation for the meaning and power of these Jewish sacred objects, and how Jews have maintained connection to their indigenous ways, even in modernity.

"So, Zelig, *leibn*, you see, we are closely related to our indigenous brothers and sisters, and still have some of our indigenous ways intact. Your job is to help us recover what we lost."

Then, in January of 2014 during a session of *yichidus* with Reb Zalman, I silently passed him my *tefillin* from one hand and the canupa from another hand. With eyes closed, Reb Zalman drew my *tefillin* to his heart, and then said to me, "*Tov*, these are good," and then asked me to put them on.

After wrapping myself, he peered at the *Shadai* (Hebrew letters *Shin, Dalet, Yud*) wrapped onto my hand and affirmed, "A good teaching."

Again with eyes closed, he drew the canupa to his heart, holding it there much longer. When he opened his eyes, I saw that Reb Zalman twinkle in his eyes, and he said, "This is very good."

He then reached to the side table and picked up an eagle feather wrapped with red yarn and gifted it to me. Reb Zalman then concluded by blessing me to grow in my ability to help us remember our indigenous relationship to mother earth.
— *Zelig Golden [6.5]*

When Reb Zalman visited my university to teach, during a question and answer session, an Orthodox student asked him with a censorious tone, "Why do you hang out with Christians and Muslims? Why do you *daven* with them?"

Reb Zalman's response, gently spoken was, "I can't get all my vitamins from the same place." This he called Deep Ecumenism, that we are not here because we expect, at the end of time, that God will return to say to Jews or Christians, Muslims or Buddhists, etc., "You were right all the time!"

Reb Zalman would say that whatever the Torah's idea of "chosenness" might mean, it's not that "Daddy loves me best."
— *Shaya Isenberg [6.6]*

May 2011. Ashland, Oregon. I was one of the rabbis and community leaders invited to participate, along with Reb Zalman, in an interfaith Daime ceremony with the local Church of the Holy Light of the Queen. This church is the first of its kind to have been given a religious exemption from the Controlled Substances Act enabling its sacramental use of ayahuasca (legalized in 2009 under the Religious Freedom Restoration Act).

Ayahuasca originates in the Brazilian rain forest and induces colorful psychedelic visions and a feeling of oneness with the universe, with nature, and with all beings. The community consumes it ritually. Their shared visions can result in revelation of individual and communal truths, as well as personal growth and evolution. Our gathering was the first time that rabbis were participating in a highly organized, completely legal, and controlled ayahuasca ceremony.

Upon entering the sanctuary, I realized that our synagogue had been transformed by the Daime community. The customary open seating had been rearranged into quadrants, with each section segregated by gender alternating male/female/male/female. Everyone from the Daime church was dressed in identical uniforms of white and blue, and they were respectfully seated, quietly, in their places.

We Jewish participants came in our white Shabbat clothing, with many of us wearing our *tallitot* as well. We were a mixed group of all adult ages and seemed to cut across all socioeconomic groups. As the members of the Jewish community entered, we each were individually led to specific seats by members of the Daime community and handed a hymnal, with an insert containing the *Ma'ariv* evening service.

In the center of the circle was a long table covered with a white cloth, upon which was sitting a very large wooden cross, along with a vase of vibrant flowers, and a jug of herbal brew. Beside the table, Reb Zalman, calm and centered, sat to the left of the leader of our local Santo Daime Church.

After we took our seats and were welcomed, Reb Zalman stood and respectfully thanked the ritual leader. He introduced himself to the Daime community, and then addressed the Jewish community affectionately — aware of how jarring and uncomfortable the sight of a large cross in the center of the sanctuary was for many of us.

"*Yiddin* (Dear Jews), we all see the cross through eyes scarred with PTSD, post-traumatic stress. Let go of that fear. Be present right here." He went on to reassure us that it's perfectly acceptable to pray in the presence of a cross, and encouraged us to open our hearts and minds, let go of our past feelings of discrimination or persecution associated with our traumatic history, and to renew our approach to the cross.

Reb Zalman pointed out that its sacred geometry is similar to that of the Star of David. The *Magen David* has one triangle pointing upwards toward the heavens, and the other triangle pointing downwards toward the earth. When we combine the two, we unite heaven and earth. Similarly, he encouraged us to think of the cross as uniting heaven and earth with its vertical pole, and to see the horizontal pole as representing the uniting of all sentient beings on earth.

Now we were ready to begin the ceremony.
— *Sue Mauer Morningstar [6.7]*

In the summer of 1979, Yehudit and I made our first trip to Israel as a family, with our thirteen-month-old son, Yeshayah Simcha. It was a hopeful time in Palestinian-Israeli relations, a year after Anwar Sadat's visit to Jerusalem and a couple of years before the war in Lebanon.

A highlight was the ten-day Festival of Peace, held at Moshav Meor Modi'im, which included a field trip to Hebron with Reb Zalman to pray in the Ibrahim Mosque, which is built over the gravesites of Abraham and Sarah, Isaac and Rebecca, and Jacob and Leah, at the Cave of Machpelah, and to visit a sheikh Reb Zalman had previously befriended.

We had arrived during Ramadan, and the streets were nearly deserted due to the fast and the siesta time. At first, we were unable to gain access to the interior of the mosque, where the sepulchers are located, so we davened *Mincha* (afternoon prayer) in the midday sun by the wall of the tomb. Afterward we were given a tour, made possible by Reb Zalman's intervention.

The next stop on our pilgrimage was the small house of worship where the Sufi sheikh Reb Zalman knew held services. He was reputedly 130 years old! As we walked through the narrow, cobbled streets, Arab children ran alongside us, grinning and chanting, "*Shalom! Shalom! Shalom! Shalom!*"

Reb Zalman carried Yeshayah on his shoulders until we reached what we took to be a small mosque, a thick-walled stone house, plastered and whitewashed inside. We took off our footwear at the entrance and walked in. An atmosphere of quiet contemplation enfolded us. We stood awkwardly, tourists and seekers, waiting for orientation.

A member of our group from Modi'im knew some Arabic and translated the greetings and explanations of the Muslim cleric in charge. Reb Zalman made formal greetings in exchange, and we sat and awaited the arrival of the sheikh.

Some fifteen minutes later, there was a stir at the door. Three or four young men appeared, escorting a frail, stooped, nearly blind but still vigorous old man clothed in a white gown, who entered the doorway, stumbling over our shoes. We were embarrassed; we hadn't realized our footgear would block the entrance. Fortunately, he did not fall. We all stood in awe and respect while Reb Zalman embraced him, held his hands, and joyfully greeted him with words of blessing and thanks.

There followed some hospitable offerings of liquid refreshment, and the main event commenced. Men and women grouped themselves separately, according to the custom of the place, and the old sheik led us in *zikr*, the rhythmic chanting of the names of God and phrases from the Koran in Arabic, accompanied by drum and tambourine. When it was time to go, we bowed our way out, with many thanks.

While waiting for transportation, we convened in small groups. The one Israeli member of our party confided that after our arrival at the little mosque, while preliminary introductions were being made, he had heard the name of one of our hosts and realized that it was the same family name as many of those who had attacked the Jewish quarter of Hebron in 1929. That riot led to the slaughter of sixty-seven residents and the confiscation of their property.

Simultaneously, our companion related, he had noticed a large stain on the rug. He had been unable to take his eyes off it and had morbidly wondered whether it was from the blood of the slain. He was still upset as he described this experience.

In response, at Reb Zalman's suggestion, we formed a large prayer circle in an open space and even drew into it two of the three Israeli soldiers on guard duty there. We chanted and sang. We then walked in a loose procession up the hill on the edge of town to a bus depot as night was falling. Soldiers in jeeps drove alongside of us, concerned for our safety. Although we sensed no danger, they escorted us the rest of the way, and two or three of our company rode in and on their vehicles.
– Reuven Goldfarb. Lightly edited and reprinted with permission from from J. The Jewish News of Northern California [6.8]

Reb Zalman explained the history of Rachel's Tomb to us on a 1986 bus ride from Jerusalem to the outskirts of Bethlehem, where the tomb was located. Rachel was the favored wife of our patriarch Jacob and had great difficulty conceiving children. After many years of barrenness, she gave birth to Joseph, and then Benjamin. Tragically, she died giving birth to Benjamin and, unlike the other foremothers and fathers who were buried in the ancestral Cave of Machpelah, Rachel was buried by the side of the road, near Bethlehem.

And Rachel died, and was buried on the way to Ephrat, which is Bethlehem. And Jacob set a pillar upon her grave: that is the pillar of Rachel's grave unto this day. [Genesis 35: 19-20]

"Sometimes, the *tzuris* (trouble) we go through gives us the gift of helping others with similar problems," explained Reb Zalman. "*Rachel Imenu* (our Mother Rachel), who had trouble becoming pregnant, and who died giving birth, merited to become a spiritual intercessor for others in need of healing. In the words of the prophet Jeremiah 31:15, 'Rachel is weeping for her children.' That's why we're going to visit her tomb, now covered by a huge rock and enclosed in a building sacred to Jews, Muslims, and Christians. Of course, we pray to God, but we can get extra power for our prayers for ourselves and for others by asking our ancestors to help."

We entered the building that had been built around Rachel's tomb, and saw there the tombstone, an enormous oblong rock, with red thread wound around it. Surrounding the rock were Orthodox women, heads covered, praying from little books of *Tehillim*, their voices soft and plaintive.

With his holy determined and innovative spirit, Reb Zalman pulled a large skein of red thread from his satchel and convinced the Orthodox women to remove their thread and let us have a turn. And they did. Unheard of! The rock and the tomb were under Orthodox Israeli control!

Reb Zalman placed us around the rock, all the while humming a *niggun*, and told us to focus on opening our hearts and souls to plead for healing for someone near and dear to us. The soulful atmosphere of Mother Rachel's burial place helped us do so, as we joined him in the melody and walked slowly, all of us helping wind the thread around the stone seven times.

When we concluded the winding, Reb Zalman softly intoned a Hebrew prayer. Then we resumed our *niggun* as we unwound the red thread from the stone, back into the shape of a skein of yarn. Step by step, step by step.

Before we left, Reb Zalman cut off a piece for each of us to bring home.
— *Shohama Wiener [6.9]*

Reb Zalman told us: "Used to be, when I would go to Israel, I would go up to a place outside of Nablus, called Balata. Balata was one of those 'refugee camps.' In Balata there lived Sidi Murshid Hassan, of blessed memory — *salaam alaihu* (peace be unto him). Many of you were there that Yom Kippur afternoon [September 15, 1975/5736, Aquarian Minyan, Berkeley] when we did *zikr* with Murshid Hassan. Just as we were praying the *Avoda* where the High Priest enters the sanctuary, he came and led a *zikr* with us, and we, at that time, got as close as one can get to the inner sacred space.

"Alas, he passed on. Hardly any great and universalist Sufis around among Palestinians — only the hard-rock fundamentalists are around, and it's very hard to have dialogue with them. You see, I wish that we would again have our counterparts among Palestinians so that we would be able to do like we did at the time in Hevron, years ago.

"We went to Hevron and there found the grave of Shibli, one of the Sufi saints. And there was an old blind Sheikh there (he sat there telling his beads), and when I came and sat in front of him, he turned to me — he had felt that I was there and asked me whether I knew Nur (Steve Durkee) and Mariam (another spiritual friend).

"I said, '*Aiwa.*' Yes.

'What do you want?'

"I said, 'I want to say *zikr* with you.'

"And he said, 'Then come, on Thursday at four o'clock.'

"We came back, a whole group of us, on Thursday at four o'clock, to that little *shtiebele* (small prayer space), the *Zawiyah*. And there the Sheikh sat on the side. And the Qadi of the mosque had come. He had this red fez with a white turban wrap around it, and he wanted to find out whether it's kosher for them to say *zikr* with us. "We are trying to get to talk to each other, but there isn't a translator there. The young Arabs didn't want to admit that they knew Hebrew, so I couldn't give it over to them in Hebrew to translate into Arabic. So they brought the public health official, a doctor, to translate.

"He came in, and he hadn't said his afternoon prayers. So he began, '*Allahu akbar, Allahu akbar* (God is great),' and, standing at his side, I said the prayers along with him. He finished his prayers, and then comes the hearing. And at the hearing, they say, 'Who sent you?'

"I respond, 'The One, be He Blessed, Who sent our father Ibrahim out of Ur of the Chaldees.'

"He said, 'What do you want?'

"I said, 'I'm here to say *zikr* with you.'

"'Why don't you go with your own people?'

"I said, 'I davened this morning with my own people.'"

"So why do you want to say *zikr* with us?'

"I said, 'Because when I'm outside of the Holy Land, I find my *Ihwan*, my brethren—Sufi brethren—to say *zikr* with them there, and to be in the Holy Land, and not to have a chance to say *zikr*, with you, is sad. I'd like to be able to say *zikr* with you.'

"'Are you a Muslim?'

"I say, *'La. Ana Mu'min.'* I'm a believer. I'm not a Muslim, I'm a believer.

"And he asks, 'What do you believe in?'

"And I say, *'Ash-hadu.'* I bear witness. *'La illaha ill Allah al-ahad.'* There is no God but God, and that God is One.

"Okay. Not too bad.

"'So, do you observe the *Shariyat* [the Muslim guide to righteous conduct, equivalent to the *Halakhah*]?'

"The *Shulchan Aruch*, you know? Do you know *Shulchan Aruch*?

"The term *Shulchan Aruch* (the prepared table) is also found in the Koran, where there is a *Sura* that's called *Ma'ida*, which [also] means the prepared table, and in that Sura is written what Muslims may and may not eat. Do you hear that? There's a *Sura* called *Shulchan Aruch* in the Koran!

"So they ask me, 'Do you observe the *Shariyat*?' I say, *'Aiwa.'* Yes, I do.

"'What level of *Shariyat* do you observe?'

"I say, 'I observe the *Shariyat* of the *banei Ishaq* (sons of Isaac) and the *banei Yaqub (sons of Jacob).'*

"So he says to me, 'Then why not follow the *Shariyat* of Islam?'

"I say, 'Because it is not fitting, it isn't *Adab*, it's not fitting for a son to go in paths different than his father. So I come from the *banei Ishaq* and *banei Yaqub* and not from the *banei Ismail*, and so I have to follow the *Shariyat* of my parents.'

"'What about *Tariqat* (Sufi path of spiritual learning)?'

"So we were talking about the higher levels of the Sufi. I said, 'With that, I'm with you at one.'

"Then somebody gives a kick on the side and says, 'Ask him! Ask him! What about *Rasuliyat* (prophethood)?' What has he got to say about Muhammed? Ah, they got me, ah!

"So I say, '*Ash-hadu.*' I bear witness. '*La illaha il Allah, wa Muhammed-ar Rasul'Illah.*' There is no God but Allah. Muhammed is His messenger.

"So they say to me, 'Then you're a Muslim!'

"And I say, '*La. Ana Yahud.*' No, I'm a Jew.

"'Then how could you say, how could you say such a thing?'

"So I said, 'Allow me to go back with you in your history. There was Ismail, the son of Ibrahim Khalil Allah, Abraham the friend of God. Ismail still had the *Tawhid*—the knowledge of the Oneness of God—but his children fell into the dark ages, into the *jahiliya*, into the unknowing. And so, they had lost their way to the Oneness of God. So, *Ya Rahman, Ya Rahim*, the Merciful, the Compassionate, sent out a messenger to the children of Ismail to bring them back to the *Tawhid*—to the Oneness. I believe that he was a true messenger.'

"The Imam said, 'I don't want to talk anymore. I want to say *zikr* with this man!'

"And they brought in the drums, and we start to say *zikr*.

"Another time, in Hevron, and I want to talk about that because it hurts so much. There was a group of people that went on a pilgrimage with us. And we came to the tomb, and I said to the people, 'Wait a little bit.' And I went in to the sheikh of the tomb. He has a little office there. And I said to him, 'May I speak to you for a moment?' He speaks a very good English.

"'Yes. What can I do for you?'

"I said, 'I've come to ask your permission to do our pilgrimage here.'

"He said, with a bitter heart, he said, 'You need my permission?' pointing to the guys with the Uzis outside.

"And I said, 'You, and your family, and your ancestors, have been the keepers of this sacred tomb for all these years, and it isn't fitting that I should ignore that.'

"He got up from behind his desk and gave me a hug, and a kiss on both sides of the cheek, and then took me and the group around Machpelah, an ancestral Israelite burial cave.

"What a difference there is in the approach! How important it is not to forget that."
— Transcribed by Reuven Goldfarb with the assistance of Rodef Shalom Eliyahu McLean and Rabbi Pam Frydman and clarifying editorial input from Reb Zalman. Revised excerpt from an audiotape of the Farbrengen, an event featuring Rabbi Zalman Schachter-Shalomi and Rabbi Shlomo Carlebach, co-sponsored by The Aquarian Minyan and the Berkeley Hillel Foundation, March 19, 1994. [6.10]

It was a Friday afternoon in November 2012. Reb Zalman opened the door to where I stood holding a two hundred-plus year old Czech Memorial Scroll Trust Torah #1118, from Prague. "It's good to see you again," he said with a smile that moved from his mouth across his face and gently passed through his eyes. He offered to hold my "cargo" while I removed my shoes. He then invited me into the kitchen, a sanctuary filled with the fragrances of Shabbat dinner.

Reb Zalman had a different gait about him, moving more slowly than a year prior, yet eagerly shuffling to the table. There he bent over and with one arm, swiftly slid all that was upon it to the side.

"Now," he said, "Let's see what you have brought here today for me to see."

Together we undressed the Torah. He let her rest on the kitchen table a moment. Then, in a flash, parchment rippling, he unrolled it across the entire table. He leaned in, exploring the text across exposed columns, sharing his observations. His whole being shifted with a special "aliveness," wonder and excitement, eyes wide with enthusiasm.

"Extraordinarily beautiful script! Ah, yes, if you would write things at the time of the Great Rabbi Loew, that's the kind of script…yes, heavy on the horizontals and narrow on the verticals…. And the stitching, ah, yes." He also described more about the *sofer's* (scribe's) calligraphy — beautiful and straight, without a lot of extra curly script.

Eve invited their carpenter, who was working outside, to come in and see. When he entered the room, both Reb Zalman and Eve did a "couple's dance" of eager sharing about this Torah's special characteristics with him. Reb Zalman became even more animated, turning the scroll and looking ever more closely at the letters.

In Spanish, Eve then said, "I thought one who appreciated good handwork would enjoy seeing the Torah." Reb Zalman followed, "And these wooden handles are also turned on a lathe." The man's face was awash in joy.

When the carpenter departed, we dressed the Torah and joked about the mantle being "Dalai Lama red." Reb Zalman then carefully placed the Torah back on the kitchen table and invited questions.

As this scroll would meet another older Czech scroll at the interfaith Abrahamic Initiative in Denver in a few days, he asked me to read this passage there: "*Lech l'cha* — Go away from your land…to the land that I will show you….And you will be a

blessing to the nations. I will bless you and make you great. You shall become a blessing."
– *Stacy Grove [6.11]*

I had convinced an important business entrepreneur in Rio to donate money for bringing Reb Zalman to teach in Brazil. The orthodox community became furious and brought pressure on our synagogue not to do so. For the first time, all the orthodox rabbis, who had their differences, decided to engage in a united effort and wrote a pamphlet denouncing the plan, entitled, "Judaism is like a mother — there is only one! Fighting Hellenism on this Hanukah 1987." Reb Zalman was not aware of this context when he arrived with his not-yet-official wife, Eve.

There would be three major events: The *shabbaton* in the outskirts of Rio; an open talk to take place in the huge synagogue sanctuary; and a performance at Circo Voador, a circus kind of arena for rock concerts, etc., and open to the whole population, Jews and non-Jews.

Tikkun Olam (healing the world) was the *shabbaton* theme, and this program drew mostly young people, some tent camping. Reb Zalman was at his best, speaking Portuguese that he intuitively constructed out of Latin roots with his unique smile. He was delighted by the challenge of communicating without knowing the language.

Add to the mood moments such as when a woman asked him for a blessing to neutralize some poltergeist occurrences in her house after her mother had passed away. Reb Zalman, turning to the open sky, began to talk to the woman's soul asking her to let go of any unfinished business down here on earth — which was immediately "replied" to by a gust of wind in the midst of the clear and sunny day.

There were rumors that we would get the unpleasant attendance of a more radical group of Jews that were coming to disrupt the event. The event was packed with people and it all came as a shock to the synagogue's board, since there were more people signed up for that talk than for our Yom Kippur *Neila* service.

In the afternoon before the talk, knowing of Reb Zalman's mystical interest in *pri ha-arets* (the native and unique fruits of the land), we prepared several indigenous fruits from Brazil for him. Delighted, he began saying the *Shehecheyanu* prayer for each of the fruits he was tasting for the first time, and savoring.

When we got to the synagogue it was packed — a Yom Kippur during a Decemberish Rio summer. He got onto the stage, and there was silence. Reb Zalman started to talk about *tikkun olam* and after five minutes into his talk said, "Okay, I will take three last questions...."

What?!!!!

I sped to his side and he whispered in my ear, "...the fruits...."

"What about the fruits?"

"They didn't do well to my stomach...it will have to be just these few last questions."

The final questions were easily responded to by Reb Zalman, who quickly left the place. Frustration and disappointment were on faces all around. As hundreds of people were vacating the place a car stopped beside me and lowered the window. It was Reb Zalman who said to me, "I am sorry, don't be disappointed. It doesn't happen that way... it just doesn't happen that way. Change will come in the right time, not out of one single event."

There was still the open performance in the Circus. The rabbi and the board of the synagogue called me for a meeting and told me they had enough with the newspapers and the media. They warned me it was too intense and that they didn't want more exposure. I promised.

Meanwhile, Reb Zalman showed interest in visiting and experiencing the local Afro-Brazilian traditions and the spirituality indigenous to Brazil—a manifestation of his spiritual ecumenism.

Busy organizing the evening event, I asked a distinguished sociologist in Brazil to accompany Reb Zalman and Eve and serve as interpreter for their meeting. He would also participate in an incredible demonstration of faith on the last day of the year when thousands of people go to the beaches to send offerings to Yemanja, the Queen of the Sea. Reb Zalman and Eve would fly home that same night.

That meeting was with Mãe Beata, the priestess of over a million people in an area of the periphery of Rio called Baixada Fluminense. She was a much-respected Mãe de Santo (priestess) involved in a local NGO promoting religious freedom. At that time, Mãe Beata was under severe attack by evangelical groups that preyed on her followers.

It happened that a very heavy rain fell on the area they were heading to. At the very moment that Reb Zalman made his way into the little temple, the storm became stronger and it started to thunder. Mãe Beata immediately begun to chant, claiming that Reb Zalman was aligned with Oxum—the entity of water, rain, and thunder.

As soon as Reb Zalman entered the place he took off his large *kippa,* showing respect for the sanctuary. They began to communicate in a non-conventional language, a kind of spiritual sign language and Mãe Beata asked Reb Zalman to bless her. Because of the religious war she was in, she had arranged for a photographer to be there and document this "official" visit.

The next morning our senior rabbi charged forward shouting "What is this? Didn't I tell you it was enough?!" while holding up a newspaper called *O Dia,* a very popular and somewhat sensationalistic tabloid. Half of the entire front page held a huge picture of Reb Zalman with his priestly hands over Mãe Beata's head ministering a blessing. The heading was "*Axé Rabi!*" (Power Rabbi!) It was a difficult position for the *shul*.

On the last day with Reb Zalman in Rio at their apartment, glancing into the kitchen, I spotted a small wooden boat (a little larger than a sushi one) filled with goodies on the counter. It was a typical offering in the Afro-Brazilian traditions that is given to Yemanja (female Yoruba water deity). The boats are taken to the sea and are left to float randomly toward the horizon. In a sort of naïve way, I turned to the cook and said, "So, you're getting ready for tonight?" And she replied with a conspiring smile, "No…this is for the rabbi and his wife!"

I couldn't believe it. She was preparing an offering for Reb Zalman to take to Yemanja and he was going right to the sea to offer it! I became both worried and angry. How could he do that? Was I exposing my community to some sort of distortion or heresy, i.e., *avoda zara*? What if a member of the *shul* would see this?

I stormed into the room where they were packing to ask him not to do so. Eve sort of tried to make Reb Zalman reconsider it, reasoning that it could put me in trouble and it could jeopardize my job. Reb Zalman nodded as a sign that he agreed.

At dusk, as we left for the event, as the door in the elevator was closing, the cook came running with the little boat in her hands. "Rabbi! You almost forgot this!" She screamed and handed the boat with the goodies to Reb Zalman who immediately took it. The door closed and we looked at each other in silence.

As soon as we got the beach Reb Zalman left the little boat on the sand as we watched the circles of dancing and chanting. All of a sudden, I realized he was gone.

He was at the edge of the water, feet already engulfed by the sea and going deeper. I began to approach them but suddenly stopped…I understood that I should not cross that line, that he had carefully not brought me lest I be further compromised.

And so Reb Zalman and Eve left Brazil. On three more occasions we were able to organize *shabbaton* gatherings in Brazil, and so this land was deeply touched by Reb Zalman's soul. *Axé Rebbe!*
— *Nilton Bonder [6.12]*

The weekend chronicled below occurred in Bloomington, Indiana, in 1979. One of the diverse groups with a huge presence here then was the Rudrananda Ashram—a spiritual tantric yoga community headed up by Swami Chenanananda. Its founder, Swami Rudrananda was killed in an accident ten years prior. He was Jewish.

One day we received a call from the ashram. They wanted to celebrate their founder's tenth *yahrtzeit* (anniversary of death) in a way that honored his Jewish roots, coupled with his transcendent contribution as founder of their community. Knowing Reb Zalman was our Rebbe they asked that we contact him and request that he come to teach for the memorial event, which would be the week of Shavuot.

Thursday:
We picked Reb Zalman up at the Indianapolis airport in our very well used red and white Volkswagen van. This van had a lot of history that was visible from the stories the many bumper stickers expressed. When Reb Zalman saw it, he examined the stickers, offered one of his great belly laughs and said, "What a wonderful wagon."

On our way to our home Reb Zalman shared stories of the Baal Shem Tov's legendary mystical journeys in his own wagon. As we passed Martinsville, Indiana, and explained to Reb Zalman this was the home of the grand dragon of the Ku Klux Klan, Reb Zalman sighed deeply and imparted deep Torah and teachings about hate in the world, and how we had to attempt to neutralize it by creating a *tikkun* and not live in a space of fear. He spoke of connecting to our inner heart space of love and being able to spread this love to all humanity. He went further and explained why at the peace blessing at the end of reciting the *Kaddish*, we now include Jews and *"kol yoshvei teyvel* (all that resides on the planet)."

When we arrived at our home, Reb Zalman went straight to sit on the swing under the shade of a large oak tree. As he was swinging, he offered a teaching on the "four worlds" of our existence that are physical, emotional, intellectual, and spiritual. He explained the "ups and downs" of our holy voyage through life through that perspective.

Reb Zalman also explained that prior to our next incarnation the only way the soul can receive power on its journey is from our recitation of *Kaddish,* and that each time we do so, a spark of energy travels to the soul. He said a person does not have to be Jewish to receive this empowerment for their soul, for through our praise and gratitude to the Holy One of Blessing the message is received.

He explained that we need to be present to ourselves, to our universe, and to God as we constantly go up and down the worlds, just as the swing is moving through time and space.

Later in the day we went to the ashram for the ceremony. Reb Zalman was adorned in a colorful bright Kelly green robe and matching huge green Hassidic-style fur *shtreimel.* As we approached, many heads turned with curious attention.

The ashram was a beautifully decorated sacred space. Multicolored oriental rugs were piled high. The tools and vessels used for prayer were conspicuous. We were escorted into a room that was the davening space. There, Reb Zalman and the current Swami exchanged blessings and greetings.

Since we were Reb Zalman's escorts, we were invited to attend the Memorial Ceremony. There were about sixty people present. Some wore fine robes and some flannel shirts and jeans. Reb Zalman summoned all to form a circle according to their birthday in order to create an astrological flow of space and energy. He said that as the Swami's radiance is traveling through time and space, we will be assisting in opening "the gates" for his travel. He explained the importance of observing the anniversary of a person's soul's departure, their *yahrtzeit,* and how the prayer's sparks energize the soul of the person we are honoring.

After teaching, Reb Zalman went into prayer. He instructed us to raise our hands high when we get to the part in the service where we chant "holy, holy, holy." When we arrived at this place in the service about ninety percent of the people raised their hands high and from a deep place in their *kishkas* chanted, "*Kadosh, Kadosh, Kadosh.*" Reb Zalman smiled. He finished the service and blessed the Swami, the participants, and the ashram. He thanked all with entrusting him with this holy ceremony.

After leaving the service Reb Zalman explained that he had anticipated that most of the participants would be Jewish. He said that Jews are having trouble finding spirituality in the conventional synagogue service, and his hope was that the Jewish renewal movement would provide the spiritual avenue for them to return. He then instructed us that whenever we go to a community outside of our own, if we seek out an ashram, there we will find Jews yearning to open their hearts. He told us to find them and teach that the spiritual path of Judaism is available and accessible to them.

Friday:
On Friday Reb Zalman held court for the many people who wanted to visit with him. Most of his private visits were held in our backyard while he was on his holy swing. As he swung he was teaching and learning new *niggunim* from his many visitors. The dogwood tree, the blooming spring garden, the large oaks, and the birds joined him as he sang the *niggunim* and taught Torah. At this time in our lives, Jackie and I were involved with booking folk music. Reb Zalman knew this and asked if I could arrange studio time for him to record a project that was on his mind for many years. Eclectricity, one of the groups Jackie managed, were folk musicians, and they also sang and recorded Klezmer, European,

Indian, and Gypsy music. They were honored to record with Reb Zalman in the studio. Reb Zalman recorded "Your Glory Shines," which is still available online. The studio owner and sound technician said he never had an experience like recording Reb Zalman and felt his studio was blessed.

Friday night Reb Zalman agreed to go to the local Hillel house for *Kabbalat Shabbat*. We walked with him the four blocks. He again donned his green robe and his huge fur *shtreimel*. The Hillel was filled to capacity with students awaiting Reb Zalman's arrival. It was a wondrous night of prayer, dance, and song. The students did not want the service and dinner afterward to end. They wanted more. So Reb Zalman invited them to our backyard for a *Tikkun Leyl Shavuot* (nighttime study session for the holy day).

On the way home, from the Hillel house we had to pass by Bear's Place, the local student bar and hang out in Bloomington. Reb Zalman knew Eclectricity was performing in the back room and he said, "Let's stop in for a set." We walked through the bar on the way to the room where the band was playing, and all eyes turned as they saw the man with his green robe and *shtreimel*. Reb Zalman said, with all eyes on him, that he felt like an alien from a Star Trek episode.

When we went to the back room and the person at the door requested we pay the cover charge, Reb Zalman looked deeply into his eyes and said, "It's *Shabbos*, we don't carry money." Of course, we were admitted without another word uttered. When Eclectricity saw Reb Zalman, they played some Klezmer songs and asked him to join them for a song they had recorded together earlier. People of all religions were dancing, and although they did not realize it, they were experiencing Shabbat, maybe the first Shabbat ever in a bar.

We left the club and went home. There, Reb Zalman said, "Let's go to the hot tub." As we immersed ourselves, he taught more Torah, and we sang some *niggunim*, until finally he sent us all off to bed.

Shabbat:

We walked about a mile to the local *shul* that served the entire Jewish population in Bloomington. Most of the people were professors from the Jewish Studies Department at Indiana University. They were highly educated and used to a traditional service.

When Reb Zalman came in unexpectedly and uninvited, again dressed in the bright green robe and *shtreimel*, he was greeted warmly. He saw that the chairs were set up in rows. Along the side of the room were tables. He took charge and said, "Let's rearrange." He then proceeded to have each person sit at a table and moved the tables into a circle. He explained that he was creating a *beit midrash*, and this way we each had a place to put our books out in front of us.

He justified this arrangement by teaching that with our heads buried in a book it would be difficult to reach a higher space of *devekut* (cleaving to God). He said that without the distraction of the book we would be able to pray from our hearts.

When the Torah was removed from the ark, he led the procession. He was asked to chant the week's *Haftorah*, (reading from *Nevi'im* – the Prophets). Prior to his chanting of the blessings he asked who needed some extra energy for the coming week and who needed a healing. He took the Torah and invited congregants to hold and hug it. He said, "When finished, pass the Torah to the next person."

Glancing around the room I witnessed tears of joy from the daveners hugging the Torah. It was the first time that most were able to do this, rather than only touching it while it was paraded in honor around the room. He gave a spiritual teaching on the weekly Torah reading and asked us to let the teachings go deep into our consciousness. He then chanted the Torah reading in Hebrew and in his own spontaneous English translation.

Following the morning service, we walked home, had Shabbat lunch, and rested. Saturday night was the celebration of Shavuot.

After *Havdalah*, the ritual ending the holy day, Reb Zalman had us sing and dance to the song, "Everybody Loves Saturday Night." We then had a short service throughout which he scattered fascinating explanations.

From there we went back to the house for our all-night *Tikkun Leyl Shavuot*. Our living room was filled with people anxious to learn and teach. One person after another offered teachings and *niggunim* all night. Some people brought their pajamas.

The outskirts of the room were lined with little children curled up sleeping with covers their parents had brought.

Sunday:
As we approached daybreak we gathered in our back yard to witness the sun coming up. We stood in a circle, and as the sun was rising we sang "Morning Has Broken," with the sun beating on our faces, and God's glory did shine. We then had a creative service which Reb Zalman began by singing the *Modeh Ani* (morning prayer of gratitude) to the tune of "Oh, What a Beautiful Mornin'." As the Torah was opened, Reb Zalman declared a healing service.

Our youngest daughter, seven-year-old Jenni, had been in a serious car accident several months prior and was having trouble walking as a result of her injuries. She had to be pulled in a wagon. Reb Zalman called her to the Torah and Jackie and I pulled her in the wagon to the Torah. I recited the traditional prayers on her behalf. After Reb Zalman gave his powerful *mishebeirach* directed deeply toward her, Jenni stepped out of the wagon and walked away. She ran to the holy backyard swing. Tears of joy poured from our eyes.

While the Torah was open, Reb Zalman asked if anyone wanted to take a Hebrew name, add a name, or change their name. This allowed all who felt they needed to connect more deeply with a matriarch or patriarch to do so, or to add a name that they felt was part of their *neshama*. After the service we schmoozed; some played music, and some sat quietly.

Prior to revving up our wagon to leave for the airport, Reb Zalman said, "I have one more thing that I must do in private." We went into our home and from the window we saw him on the swing traveling up and down. His lips were moving.
— *Jackie & Leon Olenick [6.13]*

I brought my former assistant to meet Reb Zalman. An African-American Evangelical preacher in her own right, she loved working with a rabbi, learning Judaism, and helping out at rabbinic conferences.

Reb Zalman engaged her in conversation and afterward said to me, "This woman is a *tzadeket*, a holy woman."
— *Yocheved Mintz [6.14]*

Questioner: "Reb Zalman, do you consider the sacred texts and teachings of other traditions to be Torah?"

Reb Zalman: "The answer is — YES."

Reb Zalman also taught that many Jews are afraid that such "external" teachings are a possible virus that will infect Jews. He said, "I don't believe in circling the wagons. We can all learn from each other."
— *Richard Kaplan [6.15]*

Reb Zalman taught that everything that exists is "God godding as that." Therefore, the whole universe is "God godding as…." And when we are commanded to love God, "We are commanded to love everyone and everything including ourselves and our 'others.'"
— *Shaya Isenberg [6:16]*

Pluralism

During an independent study session with Dr. Abraham Joshua Heschel, I was introduced to Reb Zalman. He came dressed in traditional Hassidic garb with a *shtreimel*.
— *Michael Lerner [6.17]*

Reb Zalman sometimes approached me to talk about Sephardic Jewry — our different cultures, origins, history, and customs. On one occasion, after some seconds in silence, he said, "You Sephardim are one of the real tribes. You are spiritual by nature. That's why, for natural balance in the universe, you have the greatest among the greatest of rationalists to keep you down to earth, the one and only Rambam (Maimonides)."

Reb Zalman continued, "We *Ashkenazim* have to reinvent ourselves over and over again to explain our place on earth and our role in Judaism, sometimes destroying everything to create something new. That's our weird nature. You are natural; you don't need to reinvent yourselves — because you are organic, and the original seed of Judaism is organic. We Ashkenazim don't know what we are."

I wrote what he said on a napkin, one Sunday afternoon after a lecture he gave to a women's group. He put his signature to what he had said to me.
— *Carlos Zarur [6.18]*

We parked a few blocks from the Chabad *shul* in Boulder, Colorado, and walked the rest of the way. It was chilly and Reb Zalman wore a jacket over his black caftan. As we entered the *shul*, Reb Zalman pulled off his coat and said, "Who wants to learn?" This must have been expected as the men and women, already assembled in their respective sides of the *shul*, swiftly crossed the gender barrier so central to Orthodoxy and came to sit together at a long table to learn the week's *parsha*. One young man stood by the window facing the street to act as lookout for the *shul*'s regular rabbi.

Half an hour later the lookout shouted, "The rabbi is coming." People scrambled to their lawful places. The rabbi entered with his two sons. After a few moments of preparation, the *davenen* began.

The Chabad kids were running all over the *shul,* and after a few minutes I detected a pattern. The kids would run to Reb Zalman and beg him for candy. He would point to some text in the *siddur* and send them off to read it. They would run away, read, and run back again where Reb Zalman rewarded them with Hershey's Kisses he carried in the pockets of his caftan. The longer the service ran, the more they ran to Reb Zalman. The more they ran, the more they read. The more they read, the more Kisses they consumed. The more Kisses they consumed, the more they ran.

Reb Zalman noticed I had substituted watching the kids for praying. He pulled a Hassidic text off a shelf behind him, and handed it to me. "Read this," he said, pointing to some passage.

"Kisses?" I thought. I read. No Kisses. I walked up beside him and made some comment about the text to show that I had read and understood it. No Kisses. He pointed to another passage. I read it. No Kisses.

Even after being called up to the Torah and reciting the blessings, still no Kisses, just decades of wisdom, support, and guidance. But Hershey's Kisses? Not even one.
— *Rami Shapiro [6.19]*

7

The Power of Blessing

Reb Zalman modeled and taught
how everyone can truly and deeply
pray, and give and receive blessings.

"Reb Zalman said, "Richard, I noticed that you were not wearing a *tallis* when you gave your *d'var Torah*. You should wear a *tallis*. Here, try mine." He wrapped me in his large rainbow *tallis* for the *aliya* up at the Torah, when I would then bless and witness the Torah reading.

After the *aliya*, Reb Zalman suggested that I get my own *tallis*. "Pick a fabric and when you are ready come over to my apartment and we will tie the *tzitzit*...."

After tying the *tzitzit* with him, I offered to bless him. He accepted and immediately stood in a receptive pose."
— *Richard Heiberger [7.1]*

When dining out in Los Angeles with Reb Zalman and Eve, a briefcase-carrying suit-wearing man wielding a paperback book accosted us with a sales pitch of stunning complexity and only minimal coherence. He had written and published a book proving that Abraham's little-known wife Keturah was the progenitor of most of the civilized world and Denmark (something about the tribe of Dan).

Now, Reb Zalman was a scholar, so when the bookseller asked rhetorically, "And, how many people know who Abraham's other wife was?" Reb Zalman answered his question immediately. And yet never once in his entire monologue did the impassioned author deign to find out with whom he was actually speaking.

At the end of the pitch, the salesman explained to us that he was going to offer us a very special opportunity. For twenty dollars, he'd not only sell us his book, but also sign it, personally.

"All right," said Reb Zalman. "I'll make you a bargain. I'll buy your book, but I want something extra."

"Of course," replied the self-proclaimed proclaimer. "I'll be happy to dedicate it to you or any person of your choosing."

Reb Zalman replied, "Thank you, but I want something else. Something even more special. I want your blessing."

The fact is, I don't remember what the blessing was, just how Reb Zalman transformed the encounter into a deeply moving spiritual experience.
— *Bernie DeKoven, of blessed memory [7.2]*

I was always seeing Reb Zalman from a distance except when he led *shabbatonim* at Havurah Shir Hadash in Ashland, Oregon. There I would bring the children to him for a blessing because I was their teacher. He would give them a group blessing. They would also sit at his feet when he told stories.
— *Batya Podos [7.3]*

In 1987, when Reb Zalman was gathering people for his first Wisdom School, I went to an introductory evening in New York City. I had brought a friend who had a question for him, so we joined the line of people waiting to speak with him after the talk. Then my friend had to step out for a few minutes, so I held his place in line.

My friend hadn't yet returned when his opportunity to speak with Reb Zalman came. As I had overheard someone farther up the line ask Reb Zalman for a blessing, and I found myself in the position of having my friend's turn, I asked for a blessing, too.

Reb Zalman took my hands, looked into my eyes, and gave his powerful blessing (which may have been two to three minutes of clock time). He revealed what was possible.
— *Ellen Weaver [7.4]*

At my first encounter with Reb Zalman, when he learned that I was a therapist and had just written an article about working with forgiveness in psychotherapy, he said, "You are doing important work."

He had ideas for me to consider. Not only did I listen intently to what he was saying, he listened intently to what I was saying. The dialogue was not just teacher to student; rather, there was a mutuality that I had not often experienced with other teachers.

"I want you to send me your article," Reb Zalman said at the end of our conversation, "and then we can talk again."

"I read your article," Reb Zalman began our second conversation. "I know you have already sent it in, but there are just a few points that I want to go over with you."

Mostly I remember the end of the conversation. "Ed, I want to bless you with the strength to continue to do your work with troubled souls."

Reb Zalman had reflected back how stuck some of my clients were in their own pain, and how difficult it is to release oneself from that pain and move toward forgiveness. And also how stuck I felt that I could not move my clients more toward forgiveness. And how troubled my clients were, and as a result, how troubled I was.

When Reb Zalman spoke to me at ordination, I reminded him of our conversations and the blessing he had given me. I told him that I was still working with troubled souls. He smiled and put his arm around me and just nodded.
— *Edwin Harris [7.5]*

I went to Reb Zalman for advice on a complicated queer model of parenting that would be done together with a lesbian couple. We had a long talk about it and he blessed my children as follows: "Along with the many souls now here with us that are fresh from the horrors of the last century, may your souls be rays of light, brought here to raise up the Light even higher. Children need to be born now to raise the sparks of the souls."
— *Amichai Lau-Lavie [7.6]*

My first experience of Reb Zalman was as a participant in a class on the *Song of Songs* at Elat Chayyim. He was recovering from major bladder surgery. Even so, he sat in front of our group for many hours each day, wearing a warm smile, stimulating us with questions, and emphatically stating his "desire to continue to live and thrive—with God's blessing."
— *Nancy Handwerger [7.7]*

My (now) husband and I were taking a week-long training titled AccuPressure for Couples at Omega in Rhinebeck, New York, and I was surprised to see Reb Zalman crossing the campus coming toward me. So far as we knew, he wasn't on the schedule. It turned out that he had been asked to come sit in on and evaluate a session of a course someone else was giving.

I had been divorced from my first husband for five years. And there at Omega, by my side was a new love, Barry Bub, a physician and psychotherapist. I introduced him to Reb Zalman. Delighted by their mutual interests, Reb Zalman engaged him in conversation on spirituality and the practice of medicine.

After some time, Reb Zalman asked for both of our hands, put them together on top of each other, and said, "You are like two diamonds that will polish each other. It won't be easy; it will be wonderful." He then chanted one of the *Sheva Brachot* (the seven wedding blessings), looked at his watch, bid us to have a great retreat, and left to fulfill his assignment.
— *Goldie Milgram [7.8]*

As Reb Zalman passed me at a rabbinic gathering, he looked at me and said, "God bless you!" And, in his last year or so, Reb Zalman would sign off on his posts by writing something like, "Blessings in the ways that you need them."
— *Debrah Shenefelt [7.9]*

During a Jewish Renewal symposium in Philadelphia that featured Reb Zalman, he sat in a chair on stage before several hundred people and offered us a blessing. He then led us into a brief

meditation, suggesting that we open ourselves to something significant to come into our lives.
— *Nancy Handwerger [7.10]*

The last time I saw Reb Zalman was the last time he would ever come to Ashland, Oregon. He was very ill and on oxygen. We gathered around him to chant *Kaddish d'Rabbanan*, the prayer for blessing all teachers. As our voices swelled with the blessing, he looked directly at me and with a gesture told me not to focus on him, but on all of those gathered around.
— *Batya Podos [7.11]*

During my last visit with Reb Zalman in Boulder, he inquired about those he knew in the Netherlands, and then invited me to share the harvest of my life. At the end of our meeting Reb Zalman asked me to pray for him and bless him. He bowed, and I blessed him and prayed aloud for a "sweetening" of this last phase of his journey in this world.
— *Carola de Vries Robles [7.12]*

Long past the time he could walk from his home to *shul* on *Shabbos*, I was riding with Reb Zalman to a Lubavitcher *shtiebl* in Boulder, Colorado. The shrill pinging of a Tibetan bell that was hanging from Reb Zalman's rearview mirror continually interrupted our time together. Every pothole elicited the ringing of the bell, and while I did my best to ignore it, the tinny clanging finally got the better of me.

"What's with the bell?" I asked.

"It is my blessing bell. Every time it rings I say *Baruch HaShem*, thanks God. This way if, God forbid, I should get into a fatal accident, the bell would ring and the last words I would utter would be *Baruch HaShem*."
— *Rami Shapiro [7.13]*

8

Smicha: Ordination

Reb Zalman realized a new paradigm of holistic forms of Judaism would also require new approaches to Jewish clergy training. He began by privately training and ordaining some of his students and teaching for a variety of seminaries. Reb Zalman then encouraged the founding of the ALEPH Ordination Program, while also consulting and supporting ordinees and colleagues in the creation of their own new forms of training and ordination.

I remember meeting you (Reb Zalman) for the first time, in a little apartment in the Loop. You were lying on a couch and looked up at me and said, "I need a *sofer*. Will you be my scribe?" The next day we walked around a tree seven times, took our vows to each other, and created a Reb Zalman who lived in the past and present at the same time.
— *Howard Schwartz [8.1]*

By the time of the 2009 Ohalah conference, the first Hashpa'ah (spiritual direction) group of trainees was ready to be ordained. The faculty realized that although all of us had been trained, not all of us had a *Mashpia smicha* certificate. When I brought this to Reb Zalman, he was eager to provide a solution. He would personally sign a certificate for each student and each member of the faculty. And so he did and also bestowed on us this blessing: "From where I stand, go forward."
— *Shohama Wiener [8.2]*

One day among those Reb Zalman and I spent together on my first trip to Winnipeg in 1972, he asked me whether I would consider *smicha* from three rabbis, one each being Orthodox, Conservative and Reform. I told him that I wasn't sure I wanted to be a rabbi at all, but if I did this would be a way I could embrace. By accepting the possibility that I could accept *smicha* from him (the Orthodox component!) and, as he used to say, "by giving him permission to start a new lineage, I became his *Hassid* and he became my rebbe." Thus, he called my *smicha* a "Certificate of Collegiality."
— *Daniel Siegel [8.3]*

Beit Shekhinah, a community I established after being ordained by Reb Zalman, introduced feminine and gender-neutral God language, blessed interfaith and same-sex couples, and celebrated with the addition of Sephardic music and a focus upon love of nature. While the group was a success, after a few years Reb Zalman advised I wouldn't be a real rabbi until I led a conventional synagogue. He told me, "In Northern California you can swing from the chandeliers and everyone will say Amen."
— *Leah Novick [8.4]*

Reb Zalman influenced me most through his writing. During my ordination speech I looked into Reb Zalman's eyes and he cried when I relayed a story he'd shared in the book, *My Life in Jewish Renewal*. The story was about when he was a little boy asking his father about prayer and connection to God:

> "Papa, what are you doing?" I asked. "I'm talking to God," he replied. Coming closer I noticed that beneath Papa's *tallit* (prayer shawl), his face was streaked with tears. So I innocently asked, "Does it hurt to talk to God?" Papa smiled wanly and said, "No, it's just been a long time since I had such a nice talk with God. And it feels really good."

— Leslie Schotz [8.5]

I am a sixth generation Ashkenazi Jew, using she pronouns, from Turtle Island, of German, Lithuanian, and Polish descent. I'm not sure what Zalman sees in me when, in 1977, I walk in late to a B'nai Or Sabbath Gathering at Fellowship Farm in Pennsylvania. The Sabbath candles implanted in a sand-filled aluminum pan illuminate the barn. A donkey brays and a cow moos. Out of the corner of my eye, I see Reb Zalman throw a chunk of challah in my direction and I swipe it out of the air. He motions me to eat it. People gasp.

Soon after, I am told that when a Hassidic rebbe breaks off the "kiss" of the challah, and tosses it your way, it's actually an invitation to become a formal student. That night, I choose to enter a process that would lead to rabbinic ordination.

— Lynn Gottlieb [8.6]

Reb Zalman tried to discourage me from becoming a rabbi for he thought I should be making music and exploring Kabbalah. I persisted and went to the Reconstructionist Rabbinical College. Finally, he embraced me and my calling. And then, Reb Zalman gave me impossibly big assignments, which I embraced — especially when he said, "Go and awaken the longing in our people."

— Shefa Gold [8.7]

As one of Reb Zalman's earliest *musmachim* (ordinees), rabbinical training was unconventional, beginning in 1977 and lasting eight years until *smicha* in 1985. The "field work" was centered around driving Reb Zalman to teaching engagements in rural and urban communities throughout Oregon while recording many hours of conversation and listening to the tapes over and over until learning Reb Zalman's teachings and thoughts just about verbatim.
— *Aryeh Hirschfield, of blessed memory; from Beth Hirschfield [8.8]*

Reb Zalman often told the story of the man who came to the rebbe and told him, "My father came to me in a dream and said that I was to be the rebbe for three hundred *Hassidim*." The rebbe responded, "When three hundred *Hassidim* come to me and say that your father told them in a dream that you are their rebbe, then I'll take you seriously."

Reb Zalman would conclude, "There is no such thing as a rebbe without *Hassidim*, nor a *Hassid* without a rebbe."
— *Daniel Siegel [8.9]*

In 1985 I began driving Reb Zalman during his frequent teaching trips to California. At the beginning our conversation was about curriculum, as my daughter and friends were studying with him.

The conversation progressed to the issue of ordaining women. At that time Reb Zalman had ordained only one. Consistent with the strategy used for judicial appointments, I began to bring him the names of women in the Berkeley area who had already studied in yeshiva, women I felt he should consider for *smicha*.

Our discussion evolved as I studied with Reb Zalman and other teachers, sometimes centering on his idea of giving the women a different title than male rabbis. I disagreed, making the case that we needed the community to receive us as equals.

By 1986, three more women had been ordained by Reb Zalman. Also that year, I assisted Reb Zalman with Rosh Hashanah services at the Mount Madonna retreat center in the Santa Cruz Mountains.

At that gathering, Reb Zalman announced his intention to ordain me after I had completed additional studies. That pledge was sealed with the gift of a silver ring inscribed, *"Gam zu l'tova,"* meaning, "This, too, is for the good."

A year later, in the summer of 1987, I was heading to Joshua Tree National Park for the Harmonic Convergence. I don't know how Reb Zalman found me in Los Angeles at a friend's home. Calling at six in the morning, he said, without introduction, "Where do you want to get your *smicha*?"

I replied, "Maybe Mount Madonna," as he had done so much work there.

Reb Zalman responded "No. Your *smicha* has to be very public. How about the San Francisco Jewish Community Center?"

And so it was. There, in 1987, Reb Zalman used the occasion, attended by hundreds, to really make clear his commitment to ordaining women.
— *Leah Novick [8.10]*

Reb Zalman would often visit Berkeley. I had many opportunities to go on long walks with him, to talk Torah, and to receive his guidance. On one of our walks Reb Zalman expressed his desire to begin ordaining. He said he was looking for *talmidim* (students) with solid backgrounds that came from the yeshiva world, who had already cracked the "*sefer* barrier" of Hebrew for sacred text learning. When he asked me if I was interested, I declined. I told him I just wanted to continue studying and being part of the Aquarian Minyan and, of course, continue to have him as my rebbe and *mashpia*.

Several years later, when I was doing prison outreach work, I needed an ordination certificate to serve. I called Reb Zalman and asked him if he could give me a simple clergy certificate and he mailed it to me with a gold seal embossed with "P'nai Or."
— *Sarah Leah Grafstein [8.11]*

Reb Zalman always encouraged us, and drew upon and nurtured our gifts. He spontaneously asked me to tell stories of the women in the Torah at my ordination.
— *Lynn Gottlieb [8.12]*

After some years of connection, Reb Zalman asked me whether I was headed toward becoming a rabbi or a cantor. Much later, I approached him with trepidation, and instead asked for his *smicha* for a professional path that no one had ever taken before. It was an "Esther moment," as they say, speaking of the story of Purim in which the young queen approaches her king with a request that could get her banished or worse.

Reb Zalman asked me to return the next day, whereupon he formally presented me with a freshly inscribed certificate with his personal stamp upon it. The *smicha*, ordination that he gave me was as *Ba'alat Shirei Hama'alot B'hesed Elyon*—Mistress of the Songs of Ecstatic Ascension.
— *Sharon Alexander [8.13]*

After Rabbi David Wolfe-Blank asked me co-lead a High Holiday service in Mendocino, I realized I was ready to study to serve as a rabbi. I called Reb Zalman and said, "I am ready." He was very pleased and responded, "*ma'aseh b'reisheet* (the act of creation) happens whenever it happens." He organized a study partner for me with a similar background, Ketura Eshel. Reb Zalman wanted us to thoroughly study *Otzar Dinim and Minhagim* and *P'nimiut haTorah*" (a five-volume set of commentaries on the Torah).

Ketura and I worked through these *sefarim* (books) and many more, especially in Kabbalah, meditation, and many modalities of healing and serving. Serving the Aquarian Minyan became my designated fieldwork.

I met up with Reb Zalman on many occasions, not only in Berkeley and Philly, but also in Toronto when we were both visiting our families. He would always say, "Open up this *sefer*, read, and explain." Reb Zalman wanted us to be 100% prepared, to be totally trained to do anything a rabbi might need to do anywhere, including conversions and divorces. We mastered all this. He put out a binder with every template we would ever need, which was mostly traditional and in Hebrew, as well as a more creative version in English.

Reb Zalman used to say to me that if his *talmidim* used the traditional formats, our documents would be taken seriously in the *frum* world. He said he wanted to keep *Klal Yisrael* (all of the Jewish people) together.

Years of study and service were passing by, and yet, Reb Zalman was not giving women students his *smicha*. I eventually dropped out of the program.

Ketura Eshel then wrote him a letter about the many males to whom he had conferred his *smicha*. She asked him if the men really knew more than the women. Shortly thereafter I was interviewed for a book "The Feminine Face of God." The author asked me how it felt that in the end I had not received *smicha*. I told her just fine, as I was already doing the type of rabbinic work that I wanted to do and had a great spiritual community that I loved and could contribute to. Then I paused, laughed, and said, "Well, if Reb Zalman ever called me up and finally offered me *smicha*, I suppose I would accept it."

A few days later Reb Zalman called me and said, "I received a dream, and in my dream I was told that now is your time and I want to give both you and Ketura *smicha*." In the past I had seen his ordination documents in Hebrew and English, printed via first generation printers. Because they were hard to preserve, I asked Reb Zalman for mine to be handwritten instead. He agreed.

Ketura Eshel received *smicha* on International Women's Day at a large event in Santa Fe in 1987. I was instructed to come to Philadelphia for a week that year in August, together with a fellow student, Yitz Husbands-Hankin, so that we could prepare and be tested together. The intensity of that week surpasses anything I have ever experienced.

I was given a room near Reb Zalman's house, in the home of a female rabbi I admired, who was against Reb Zalman giving private *smicha*. She said I would be better off getting a recognized *smicha* by going to a regular seminary.

Yitz and I went everywhere with Reb Zalman that week — to the pool and movies with his kids, even to food shopping. Everywhere we learned something from what he said. At the end of the week, on thirteenth of *Tammuz* 1987, we held a small ceremony in his home with just a few people present. We davened together, rolled the Torah until we came to a spot that felt right, read and gave our personal commentaries.

When it came time for my personal blessing of ordination under Reb Zalman's *tallis*, he first said, "I want you to know that it has taken me a long time to arrive at this place, to be able to look my rebbe straight in the eyes and say to him that the time for women to be rabbis has arrived."
— *Sarah Leah Grafstein [8.14]*

I traveled to the retreat center to meet Reb Zalman for the first time, for *yechidus*. He drew me out about my Orthodox roots and extensive training in Jewish studies and Jewish education as he contemplated my request for ordination, saying, "You are coming to me to *kasher* your *chazir feesel* — to make your 'pig feet' kosher, i.e., to ordain a woman, an action which is traditionally unkosher."

I told him that on my spiritual path I cannot uncover my hair and that I need to wear long skirts. He told me he couldn't take off his yarmulke or his *tzitzis*, the fringed daily prayer garment worn under his clothes, either. And, at the end of the session, he told me that it would be an honor to ordain me.
— *Bonita Nathan Sussman [8.15]*

I first met Reb Zalman at his Philadelphia home on Emlen Street, which also served as the old B'nai Or Fellowship headquarters. It was the beginning of Hanukah 1987, and he invited me to light the first candle of the big menorah in the front window.

That began a series of visits and learning and classes and retreats with Reb Zalman over many years. He invited me into a rabbinic track of studies on more than one occasion, but I declined, unable to envision myself in that role in a community. We agreed on an alternate plan, given my earlier training: cantorial ordination, with additional competencies also included in the *smicha* document, as was his way.

Years later, my ordination was witnessed by a gathering of Reb Zalman's previous *musmachim*. At the end of the ceremony, I leaned back into Reb Zalman's arms as he conferred the *smicha* as *Chazan*, Cantor. Minutes later, I said to him, "This felt like falling into a benevolent abyss."

Reb Zalman laughed deeply in response, with his characteristic twinkle of the eye.
— *Robert (Micha'el) Esformes [8.16]*

After arriving to work in Boulder in the fall of 2008, with the encouragement of my peers, I emailed Reb Zalman and asked if I could study with him. Seeing him shortly thereafter, he invited me to come over to his home.

Reb Zalman interviewed me in his basement study, asking about my background, what I had studied, and what I had yet to learn in the rabbinic program. He then invited me to come study with him once or twice a week. I had only one question. "Reb Zalman, I know your time is precious. Can I pay you something?"

Reb Zalman closed his eyes, thought for a moment, smiled, looked at me, an underemployed rabbinical student, and said, "From you, I don't need money."

"So what can I offer you?" I asked.

"Winter is coming." Reb Zalman replied. "When it snows you'll come over and shovel the driveway."

And so it was – singing *niggunim* while shoveling, with a warm drink and time together with Reb Zalman and Eve inside afterwards.
– *Ilan Glazer [8.17]*

Only one time did I have a one-on-one talk with Reb Zalman. In Boulder in 2011, at a Shabbat fundraiser, he called me over to talk with him and asked, "What is your story?" I explained that I had served on the ALEPH board for many years, helped with a local Renewal *havurah,* and led and hosted services in San Diego. I told him that many people wanted me to get into the ALEPH Ordination Program, but that I had a hard time with languages, being mildly dyslexic. I asked, "What should I do?"

Reb Zalman looked at and into me, and said that we have plenty of rabbis, and that he wanted me to go home and work for my local, larger Jewish community. If I could teach a little about Jewish Renewal, that would be good also.
– *David Rafsky [8.18]*

In the 1980s several of us in Washington, D.C., created Maalot – A Seminary for Cantors and Judaists. Reb Zalman encouraged me to receive *smicha,* even though I did not want it and refused him three times. He understood, and respected the fact that I had received a "*smicha* from the people."

In 2001, in the wake of the attack on the World Trade Center towers in New York City, I found myself being called upon to represent the Washington (D.C.) Jewish community at interfaith programs, panels, and healing services. It was then that I called to ask if Reb Zalman was still willing to give me *smicha.*

I received Reb Zalman's *smicha* at the Ohalah Conference in Boulder, Colorado, with Reb Zalman and faculty from the ALEPH Ordination Program. I gave a brief Torah teaching and then, as guided, leaned back into their hands while all present chanted his invocation formula for *smicha*. In celebration, I'd brought a bottle of schnapps with me, so we closed the ritual with a *l'chaim* toast — to life!

— *David Shneyer [8.19]*

Reb Zalman was teaching a small group of Renewal rabbis a particularly dense and opaque text about the *sefirot*. He would call on one of us to read, to translate, and to explain a few sentences.

We gamely tried to do what he asked, but it was like slogging through molasses. There were lots of stops and uncomfortable silences, and then Reb Zalman would patiently correct us and ask us to continue.

Finally came the time, after about twenty minutes of stammering embarrassment, that we mutinied. "Reb Zalman, it's too hard," said one anguished participant. "I can't follow this. Please, can you read it to us, and explain it?" The rest of us nodded in agreement.

In the past, we had pressured him and eventually he would cave. This time, however, he would not be moved. We continued to whine and to nudge him, like overtired seven year-olds begging for chocolate. He finally got annoyed.

"This is not okay," he said frowning. "You don't want to struggle. You want me to explain everything. You don't want Kabbalah. You want crack Kabbalah."

We stopped whining.

— *Jack (Ya'acov) Gabriel [8.20]*

I heard Reb Zalman identify a crucial difference between the Ba'al Shem Tov and the *mitnagdim* (his opponents). Everyone, the Baal Shem Tov averred, is obligated to do *teshuva* constantly. The *talmidei chachamim* (traditional Talmud scholars) among those opponents were outraged at the thought that their scholarship was not sufficient to justify their pre-eminence in Jewish community

and that they too, needed to do *teshuva*, as if they were ordinary, lowly *amei ha-aretz* (rabbinically uneducated boors).
— *Shaya Isenberg [8.21]*

Reb Zalman supported his students' development and visibility as teachers. At Elat Chayyim, observing my leading of the *Kabbalat Shabbat* service, he told me how he saw the *Shekhinah*, the Divine Mother, working through me. Years later, he directed me to write a paper on what he termed "The *Shekhinah* Theology of the Future," and he had me present it at the 2008 Ohalah Conference.
— *Leah Novick [8.22]*

Before an audition for a cantorial position, I had an appointment with Reb Zalman. He served a hearty and yummy lunch, his signature dish, wonderful vegetarian cholent.

After lunch he decided that I couldn't go to the audition so longhaired and a bit unkempt. So he directed me to the bathroom, where he lovingly and competently cut my hair.
— *Robert (Micha'el) Esformes [8.23]*

9

Toward a Jewish Future

Reb Zalman understood the evolution
of Judaism to require solid grounding
in both tradition and science, as well
as love and awe from and toward
All that Is and Will Be.

Reb Zalman taught that the Earth is a living organism. Just as each of us has lungs, kidneys, and a liver, so too, our Earth has Buddhism, Christianity, Islam, Judaism, and more. Just as we need individual body parts to do their specific jobs well to be healthy, so too, Reb Zalman taught, that the Earth requires that each tradition bring in the blessings that only it is able to bring for Earth's health. As Reb Zalman liked to say, "We can only get it together, together."
— *T'mimah Audrey Ickovits [9.1]*

Reb Zalman taught that the world's different traditions are part of an overall "organicity." Each of our religious traditions is an organ in the larger human organism. Moreover, he explained that each is needed for the evolution of human consciousness, necessary for us to save ourselves, to save the planet and all the family of species.
— *Shaya Isenberg [9.2]*

Once Reb Zalman told me, with great sorrow, "The Jewish people are starved for mythology. Myth is the collective dream of a people, and who wants to lose their collective dream?"
— *Howard Schwartz [9.3]*

In the early 1990s Reb Zalman convened a group of about twenty rabbis who had been connected to him over the years. He called us members of the RabCab, rabbinical cabinet. At one such gathering in Boulder, we were having a discussion about where we would place the Jewish women sages, such as the *Imahot* (the Biblical four/foremothers), on the Kabbalistic Tree of Life model. My guidance was to place *Rivkah*, based on her courageous actions, into the *Sefira* of *Gevurah*, the attribute of strength and judgment. Reb Zalman did not agree.

At the third meal of *Shabbat*, *Seudah Shlishit*, Reb Zalman and I debated my choice, back and forth. Finally, he deferred to me, acknowledging that my insights were powerful, and that I, too, was entitled to innovate like the sages of the past.
— *Leah Novick [9.4]*

"I think that there is another [way of] understanding what the life in *Olam Ha-t'chiya* (resurrected world) means. Most important is that our planet becomes resurrected, as it were, that our Mother, the Earth, becomes divinized and conscious. To think of ourselves as individuals is a mistake anyway, because we are at best cells in the larger being. These cells have been renewed from an amoeba to an ever-higher form, and each time spirit also grew.

"In the first situation we say that Samuel the prophet was in the Netherworld. According to Kabbalah, he should have been in the highest heavens. What was he doing in the Netherworld? Because humanity and the spirit mass had not yet advanced to that level. But as it (spirit mass) grew more and more, we are now looking at reincarnation in a different way than we did before. So it isn't necessarily as important that my individual soul becomes resurrected, as it is that in each lifetime we pour our experience into the treasure vault of life on the planet. It is really the planet becoming more and more conscious.
— *Janice Rubin. Transcribed by Janice from selected pieces from Audio Files 1154, 1155 of her September 2011 interview of Reb Zalman [9.5]*

Although I had recently moved to California, Reb Zalman urged me to come to Philadelphia in 1981 to spearhead B'nai Or—a "religious fellowship" he had envisioned since the sixties. We found it challenging to do this from scratch with an amorphous collection of people, ideas, and the several cats in his home where the office was initially housed.

His office was a maze of early computers and wires and extension cords. We laid a foundation for an organization that was, and is, as multidimensional as he was. This evolved from B'nai Or, Children of Light, to P'nai Or, Faces of Light, to ALEPH: Alliance for Jewish Renewal—a multifaceted container for his many-faceted vision.
— *Ahouva Steinhaus [9.6]*

The 1988 Ruach Conference for Jewish Spirituality in Leeds, UK, drew those who were seeking something different for the times. We were drawn to a smiling, bearded, hippy-looking, kind, open,

Yinglish-speaking, Orthodox-looking rabbi with an infectious smile and wit—Reb Zalman. He taught that Judaism today requires a "paradigm shift," and, that "truth transcends denominational boundaries."

Reb Zalman told us, "Put up a flip chart sheet on the wall and invite anyone who wants to participate in exploring Judaism in a new way to sign up for a gathering in London." And that list was the birth of the Britain's first intentional Jewish Renewal spiritual community, which exists to this day—The Ruach Chavurah.
— *Janet Berenson [9.7]*

One way that Reb Zalman used to speak of renewing Judaism was as a means for each of us to enact our unique innerness about the evolving Judaism in which we all have a part, to enact our particular role in the process by which Divine Providence reinvigorates Judaism. He explained that if we fail to trust our *kishkes* transparently before the Holy One, how will we and those with whom we share this precious planet ever learn to live together in love, or meaning, or ecstasy? And, he asked, without learning to trust our *kishkes*, how will we find the *koach* (inner strength) to do our part to nourish the Godfield that sustains all Being?
— *Raachel Jurovics [9.8]*

It was the spring of 1977, and Reb Zalman's first *shabbaton* in Eugene, Oregon, was at my house. Twenty or thirty people, mostly young Jewish hippie types, gathered for this weekend retreat and celebration of the Sabbath. Above the mantle hung a four-foot beautiful tapestry of patchwork greens, a voluptuous fabric portrait of rolling hills and mountaintops, titled "Mother Earth." "That's so beautiful." Reb Zalman commented. "It really captures the feeling of Gaia, our Mother."

The Shabbat celebration began with lighting candles, making *Kiddush* and *HaMotzi*—traditional blessings with wine and bread, and honoring Gaia. The weekly Torah portion was *Tazria/Metzora*, heralding a time of healing and transformation. Reb Zalman shared a full evening and day of prayers, songs, and stories with our spiritually hungry group.

Early Sunday morning, crowded into my red VW bug, five of us careened up the winding highway with Reb Zalman sitting in the passenger seat, giving over Torah teachings. We were en route to Cougar Hot Springs for a *mikveh* of healing and renewal that he would lead in a pristine seven-layered series of pools high in the Cascade Mountains.

We hiked, we bathed, we sang, we prayed. In the early morning silence, deep in the forest, the rebbe had us call out the *Shema*, our voices echoing through the trees.

There, Reb Zalman slowly reached to his hand, removed a silver ring, and placed it on my finger. "*Gam Zeh Ya'avor,*" it read in Hebrew — this too shall pass. In the ancient grove of fir and cedar trees, it was a mystery to contemplate.
— *Shonna Husbands-Hankin [9.9]*

I remember telling Reb Zalman in the mid-1980s of my difficulty in saying the words of prayers, especially, the idea of saying *you* to the language for God in most *siddurim*.

By this time Reb Zalman's teaching had already incorporated a strong appreciation of the Gaian Hypothesis — that earth is in some ways conscious and self-regulating. He asked me whether I could say *you* to the universe. He had a way of giving people permission to experiment, and to this day, having been given his blessing, I still bless by praying, "*Baruch ata olam,*" meaning "Bless you, world" or "O blessed world."
— *Herb Levine [9.10]*

I first met Reb Zalman, with his family, in a hot tub in Marin County, California, in 1977. A good friend who was sure I needed to connect with Reb Zalman, even though I was primarily immersed in feminist political organizing nationally, arranged the visit.

After chatting as we soaked, Reb Zalman turned to me and asked, "What are you going to do to help Jewish renewal develop?" I barely knew what it was, but even so I responded, "When I move to California, I will work on creating a Jewish renewal retreat center."
— *Leah Novick [9.11]*

During a meal at the RabCab in a large B&B in the Colorado Mountains, I was surprised when he spoke fervently about the Gaian hypothesis. He described earth as a homeostatic, possibly sentient, living organism, and called it, "Our Mother."

For over a decade I'd been having dreams where a male voice would tell me in English that "Earth is not the mother, it is a placenta, and the people will need to get off the planet." For the first time I spoke the dream aloud in a public space, at the meal, to Reb Zalman, in front of my colleagues.

"Could be," Reb Zalman replied. "But that is beyond my event horizon. Sustaining Gaia is important now."
— *Goldie Milgram [9.12]*

It was on Shavuot at the Isabella Freedman Retreat Center, when I turned to Reb Zalman and muttered something about interest in Naropa University, where he was teaching. Softly, in his Old World accent, he replied, "Nowadays, you can take all of the courses online."

Over the course of the next couple of days, contemplation of the future and of humankind's current technological advancement permeated Reb Zalman's activities and musings. Even as he and Eve spoke of ancient mysteries, like the mythical account of the revelation received by our people before Sinai, Reb Zalman spoke concerning the meaning of Jewish tradition in the age of computers and globalization.

Speaking of Torah to an assembly of young Jewish farmhands, he alluded to our people's outdated hardware and of the Jewish people's need to once again "update the manual" that God delivered to Moses.

The evening before Reb Zalman and Eve's departure from Isabella Freedman, together with them a small group of us watched *Star Trek: The Next Generation.*
— *Jeremy Zorn [9.13]*

Reb Zalman shared with us that Judaism is a "living, flowing religion" and that "each generation gifts Judaism [with] new spirit, new soul, new words, new prayer, new vision...."
— *Julie Schechter [9.14]*

Reb Zalman spoke often of the mutual yearning between The Holy One and the human being and provided images to illustrate our efforts to connect. He likened the process to that of a radio's transmitter and receiver, as they move to "align with one another in order to create a clear channel through which a signal can flow." He also described the depiction of God and the earthling on the ceiling of the Sistine Chapel, as their hands reach longingly toward each other. He quoted the Talmudic tale, which says that as much "as the calf wants to nurse, the cow wants to give milk."

Reb Zalman told us that the flow of our own *kavanah* creates the alignment that enables us to unite with God. He taught that living life in accordance with the Divine Will is the goal, and *kavanah*, is our tool for getting there and bringing "the is" into alignment with "the ought." This "mind-steering" effort, he said, is an "authentic form of Jewish meditation," as we "*l'khaven et ha-matara* — aim at the target."

Not only does "*l'khaven*" have the same root as "*kavanah*," he told us, but he also made a case for the etymological connection of *KavaNah* to the word "*SheKhiNah*" as well as to the words "*KeN* — yes," and *mishKaN* or dwelling place for God. He taught us that through our *kavanah* or spiritual focus we each establish ourselves as a *mishkan*, thereby saying *ken* (yes) to the *Shekhinah*. Reb Zalman

said, "'*Avneh mishkan b'lev* — I will build for You a sanctuary in my heart,' and if that *mishkan* is established, then there is *kavanah*."
— *Anne Brener and Ivan Ickovits [9.15]*

"Spirit isn't different than matter. We are talking about levels of vibration and attunement. There is vibratory stuff that has to do with flesh and the body. There is lower level vibratory stuff that has to do with chemistry and with physics and with biology. Still lower, we are talking about atomic and subatomic. Then there are places of subtlety and of consciousness that are higher and higher to the point that a very few specially privileged people wake up for a nanosecond in cosmic consciousness.

"Think of us having this conversation with some people who are cosmologists, saying, 'You people are always talking about etiology — where does it come from?' and yet you are not asking the question of teleology — where does it go to? What is attracting it?" Somewhere you have to say that Divinity is attracting all of creation to become more and more Divine. People don't realize that. So I keep saying that we human being are 'theotropic' beings, just like a sunflower is heliotropic and turns with the sun.

"We are being turned to God in some way or another. I believe that every religion is like a vital organ of the planet. So it is not which one is better, which one is triumphal — we are all integral. We are needed."
— *Rami Shapiro [9.16]*

One day Reb Zalman said, "I feel that my students have passed me in a lot of ways. I take great joy in that."
— *Leah Novick [9.17]*

In early spring of 2000 Rabbi Mordechai Twersky, known as the Hornsteipler Rebbe, organized a Friday morning service in Boulder, Colorado, at the Masonic Lodge. I was in Boulder that week to study with Reb Zalman, so he invited me to tag along as his *davenen* companion. In the early part of the service one of Rabbi Twersky's *Hassidim* (disciples) was leading prayers while Reb

Zalman and Rabbi Twersky stood together off to the side. They both stared out the window, pointing and chatting quietly as the whirring drone of a hedge trimmer was heard outside.

When Reb Zalman returned to his seat next to me he whispered, "*Nu*, Duved, so do you want to know what we talked about?"

"Of course!" I answered.

Reb Zalman said, "Rabbi Twersky pointed at the gardener outside who was trimming the hedges and said 'Look, Zalman, when you trim too much, the hedges don't look so good.'

"So, I pointed to the untrimmed hedges and said, 'True, Mordechai, but when you never trim the hedges the plant gets all choked up in the overgrowth and can't breathe.'"

Reb Zalman nodded and smiled at me knowingly, adding, "You know what I'm saying, Duved?"

I muttered, "Wow!" and looked over at Rav Twersky who was watching Reb Zalman whisper to me.

The Rav looked at us, shrugged his shoulders, and grinned.
— *David Zaslow [9.18]*

One Friday in November 2013, I had asked to be with Reb Zalman and Eve for the day just to hang out. So we did, and one of the most satisfying moments for me was when Reb Zalman affirmed that he felt a sense of satisfaction with his work and with his legacy. He said that it did not matter to him whether people know he is the source of the innovation they may be experiencing in many Jewish settings. What he said was important to him was that the innovation had been seeded and now had a life of its own.
— *Ahouva Steinhaus [9.19]*

Having called us to detour from our cross country teaching itinerary to meet with him, per usual, Reb Zalman had plans, and assignments within them, lined up to discuss in detail. And, he had a story and a message: "As you know the Rebbe (*der Friedeger Rebbe*) brought Shlomo and me into his office to change our *shlichut* from focusing on serving in communities to going to campuses. 'Go see what the youth need, what our people need, and determine how to best give it to them,' he told us."

Reb Zalman continued, "I have never stopped fulfilling the intent of the *shlichut* the Rebbe sent me on. From my perspective Chabad has gone off course. Looking back on my life I am very satisfied and proud of what I have done. The seeds of a good future have been planted."
— *Goldie Milgram [9.20]*

During a conference session, Reb Zalman spoke about the future. "It's not so much leadership I'm worried about," he said, "as we are leader-full. I am worried about the *chevra*; how you will treat each other after I'm gone."
— *James Stone Goodman [9.21]*

Reb Zalman told us, "We must be renewing Renewal itself."

And,

"Trust and let The Future pull you."
— *Carola de Vries Robles [9.22]*

The Tale of the Honey
By Howard Schwartz

Now Reb Hayim Elya of Buczacz rarely traveled. He had spent a
year exploring the Holy Land, and that had more than satisfied his
desire to wander. Still, one city pulled at him no matter where he
went — Zholkiev, where Reb Zalman made his home. And one
year, when he felt a great need to speak to his Rebbe face to face,
Reb Hayim set out to travel to Zholkiev.

His meeting with Reb Zalman was wonderful — they recalled all
the years they had known each other, and how close they had
become. And before Hayim Elya departed, Reb Zalman asked his
wife to bring him a gift. So Rebbetsin Eve went to a cabinet and
took down a bottle of honey. She gave it to Reb Zalman and he
offered it to Hayim Elya.

Now Hayim Elya knew that Reb Zalman had few material
resources, and he knew that honey was a rarity and very valuable.
And he felt terribly guilty to accept such a precious gift. So he
refused. This seemed to greatly surprise Reb Zalman, and he
insisted. Hayim Elya made many apologies, but continued to turn
it down. He left soon after that and set out on his journey home.

It was not until the third day of his journey home that Hayim Elya
realized what he had done — he had turned down a gift of
sweetness from his Rebbe! How could he do such a thing? Surely it
came with Reb Zalman's blessings for sweetness in his life. Hayim
Elya wondered if he had lost his mind. He even considered turning
back, but he had already traveled too far, and the moment of Reb
Zalman's blessing had passed.

By the time he reached home, he was numb. Here he had turned
down a great blessing, and surely the door to evil was open — who
knows what might slip in. But everything at home seemed calm.
His wife was happy to see him and brought him a steaming cup of
tea, to warm him on that cold winter day. When Hayim Elya took
a sip, a taste of glorious sweetness filled him with calm and joy.

He asked his wife what she had used to sweeten the tea, and she got up and brought him a bottle, strangely familiar, and she said, "I found this in the cabinet. I don't know where it came from."

And Hayim said, "I do—it was a gift from Reb Zalman."

Contributor Authors

Bios: Pages 216-255

Vignettes and Stories
Indexed by Author: Pages 256-267

Reb Zalman at Lama Foundation, 1988
Photo credit: David Pascale

Sharon Alexander. I had already become involved with Jewish Renewal some time before actually meeting Reb Zalman. Attending the Joys of Jewishing retreat in the Sierras of California, I was impressed by the white Shabbat clothing and rainbow *tallitot* and the choices in *davenen*, Tai Chi, and meditation in the woods. But what most impressed me was the respect I saw the children exhibit toward one another. I decided I had come home. All the rest—meeting and become a follower of Reb Zalman, starting the Gesher Ohr Chavurah in Boulder, attending Kallahs, meeting my Renewalnik Swiss husband and relocating to Basel, and eventually developing Shir Ecstasy Jospel Choirs and receiving a *smicha* from Reb Zalman—all the rest is commentary. *ShirEcstacy.com*

David Arfa. I first met Reb Zalman during the early 1990s. I was a young environmental educator, fresh from a year of yeshiva in Jerusalem, and came to Philly to be a summer assistant with Shomrei Adamah. There I discovered the vibrancy of Reb Zalman and the entire Jewish Renewal community, and worked for two summers as the Education Director with the Shalom Center's Eco-Shalom Corps located at Elat Chayyim. I continued to learn and began to teach about Judaism's environmental heritage, reclaiming the role of *Maggid*, storyteller. Exploring wonder, hope, grief, and activism through a Jewish lens led me into Clinical Pastoral Education. I'm currently the chaplain at a local behavioral health hospital and lead monthly contemplative Shabbat-inspired hikes. *maggiddavid.net*

Rachel Barenblat. I have blogged since 2003 as The Velveteen Rabbi. In 2008 *Time* magazine named my blog as one of the top twenty-five. I am the author of several poetry collections including, *70 faces: Torah poems* (Phoenicia), *Toward Sinai: Omer poems* (VR Press), and *Texts to the Holy* (Ben Yehuda Press). Encountering Reb Zalman and his work set me on the path to the rabbinate, my second ordination as *Mashpi'ah Ruchanit*, and ongoing work toward continually renewing Judaism. In service of that goal I am a Founding Builder at Bayit: Your Jewish Home and serve Congregation Beth Israel, a Reform and Renewal *shul* in

North Adams, Massachusetts.
velveteenrabbi.blogs.com/blog/yourbayit.org

Janet Berenson. After a conventional Conservative Jewish education at Philadelphia's Gratz College, I chose to reject Judaism in favor of philosophy when studying at Penn. Subsequently, I moved to England and discovered Zen Buddhism, which inspired me to look back into Judaism for wisdom. Meeting Reb Zalman convinced me of the validity of integrating all the wisdom traditions and reviving Jewish practice with a deeper understanding and meaning. I became a professional Jewish educator for the Leo Baeck College and the Movement for Reform Judaism in London, as well as a teacher of Jewish meditation. I wrote *Kabbalah Decoder* (2002) and more recently published some of my short stories and poetry. My Jewish spiritual journey continues through study, prayer, and social action with Finchley Reform Synagogue and The Ruach Chavurah.

Leila Gal Berner. When I first met Reb Zalman, I was studying at the Reconstructionist Rabbinical College in Philadelphia. Deeply intrigued by him, I soon found myself visiting often, learning texts and life wisdom from him. We often took walks in the tree-filled neighborhood, and sometimes he would sing a *niggun* and I would learn from his gentle voice. Reb Zalman became my rebbe. After I was ordained, I served several congregations, taught in several colleges and universities, and now teach and serve as the Dean of Students of the ALEPH Ordination Program. Currently, I dedicate myself to the Four Worlds principles I learned from Reb Zalman and have my feet firmly planted on God's magnificent earth. *aleph.org/ordinations*

Nilton Bonder. I came to know Reb Zalman during my last year of rabbinical school (JTS 1986). During my first Kallah we developed a close connection, mostly by virtue of his adventurous/creative side. On the last of his four trips to Brazil, he gave me a second *smicha* as rabbi, with powers to ordain covering all of Latin America. In that document he changed my family name from "Bonder" to "*Bone-a-dor*" — Builder of a generation). He was very influential in my rabbinical life and an inspiration for my writing career. I have published twenty-two books in Brazil, which have been translated into nineteen languages, with over 1.5 million sold. Two successful plays have been adapted from my books, and a film and TV series are being released in 2018. *niltonbonder.com*

Steven Booth-Nadav. Reb Zalman recommended that I attend RRC, which he said at the time was "the only seminary with a soul." He was a teacher and mentor for me during my years there. I moved to Colorado in 1998, in part to be near him. He always made himself available to mentor me in practical rabbinics, and I enjoyed studying with him and local rabbis. I was deeply honored to host him at Kavod Senior Life in 2012. When the basement of his home flooded in the great Boulder flood (2013), it was a privilege to participate in clearing out the basement and to help him reorganize his books and things afterwards. He called me *Stevele*, which I will always cherish. *wisdomhousedenver.org*

Barbara (Bobbi) Breitman. I was named as a spiritual guide, *Mashpi'ah Ruchanit*, by Reb Zalman. A member of the planning committee for the first four ALEPH *Kallot*, I am also a cofounder of Lev Shomea, the first training program in Jewish Spiritual Direction, a program of Elat Chayyim. I presently train and supervise spiritual directors at the Reconstructionist Rabbinical College and HUC-JIR. I seeded the spiritual direction program at the Rabbinical School at Hebrew College. I am also an Assistant Professor of Pastoral Care at RRC and a psychotherapist.

Anne Brener. As a rabbi, spiritual director, psychotherapist, meditation teacher, and author, I specialize in grief, healing, and spirituality, and assist institutions in creating communities grounded in compassion. I am a Professor of Ritual and Human Development at The Academy for Jewish Religion, California, where I train rabbinical, cantorial, and chaplaincy students. My writing appears in many anthologies on Jewish spirituality and healing and in the *Los Angeles Jewish Journal*. A founder of one of California's first shelters for victims of domestic violence, I also cofounded a Jewish spiritual direction training program and have worked as a hospice chaplain. I presently serve on the ALEPH board. My book *Mitzvah & Mourning: Walking the Mourners' Path through Grief to Healing* is now in an expanded third edition. *ajrca.edu*

Mitchell Chefitz. I had studied the early works of Jewish mysticism, from *Sefer Yetzirah* through *Zohar*, and was just ready to learn Hassidic literature when Reb Zalman appeared in Miami and became a regular visitor and teacher in my home. *mitchellchefitz.com*

Michael Chusid. I am a *shofar* master blaster, *Ba'al Tekiah*, author of *Hearing Shofar: The Still Small Voice of the Ram's Horn*, and I teach *shofar* classes and workshops throughout North America, including by phone and Internet. I am a member of a *havurah* that goes into the desert each year to relive the Passover exodus and reconnect with nature and reinvent tribal, earth-based Hebrew culture. My lineage goes back to Rabbi Nachman of Breslov. Having grown up with Reform, Conservative, and secular Judaism, my discovery of Jewish Renewal was stimulated by Rabbis Jonathan Omer-Man, Stan Levy, Moshe Halfon, Deborah Orenstein, and David A. Cooper, as well as Reb Zalman. *hearingshofar.blogspot.com; passowervillage.blogspot.com*

Alan M. Dattner. When Reb Zalman rescued me beside a flat tire on the road one day, I had long before left the formal Judaism of my childhood behind and had found spirituality through yoga, through Sufi Sam, Swami Satchidananda, and a host of other spiritual leaders I'd met at their events, including Rabbi Shlomo Carlebach. This meeting with Reb Zalman allowed me to merge my spiritual yearnings with a Judaism that included spirit, mind, heart, and personal experience, and also to honor other paths to the Divine. Meeting and marrying Rabbi Shohama Wiener has brought me deep into Renewal Judaism. As a physician, I made sure to include in my book, *Radiant Skin from the Inside Out*, a chapter connecting the condition of one's skin with the condition of the Earth's skin, melding my thoughts with Reb Zalman's concern for the health of Gaia, our living planetary home. *holisticdermatology.com*

Bernie DeKoven, of blessed memory, and Reb Zalman, of blessed memory, were friends. Bernie was an American game designer, author, lecturer, and fun theorist. He was publicly acclaimed for his book *The Well-Played Game*, for his contributions to the New Games Foundation, and for his pioneering work in computer game design. Bernie created an Interplay Curriculum for the School District of Philadelphia and with his family established The Games Preserve, a retreat center for the study of games and play located in Eastern Pennsylvania. He was a lifetime member of The Association of the Study of Play. *deepFun.com*

Carola de Vries Robles. Serving as a professional leader in the personal growth and transpersonal psychology movements, I was Jewish, and also a lost soul searching for spiritual nourishment as a Sufi and Buddhist meditation practitioner. Reb Zalman became my soul-mirror and ally, revealing Judaism as a transformative and heart-centered path, helping me to integrate this learning, and empowering me as a Jewish woman. I became a lay leader in Jewish Renewal in the Netherlands, and teacher of Jewish spirituality and Kabbalistic meditation. Reb Zalman ordained me as a *Mashpi'ah Ruchanit*, and I was given the title of *Eshet Hazon* by wise women sisters at a Kallah. I also trained in Spiritual Eldering and Embodying Spirit. My documentary, "To Remember to Return," honors Reb Zalman and those who helped me turn trauma into challenge and wonder. *caroladevriesrobles.nl*

Efraim Eisen. I met Reb Zalman during the 1991 Kallah in Bryn Mawr, Pennsylvania, having been influenced by Rabbi Aryeh Hirschfield during my sojourn in Ashland, Oregon. I met Rosalie at that Kallah. We married and then began creating Basherte — workshops for single people seeking their soulmates. During our marriage we produced over two hundred workshops exposing people to the Four World encounters that highlighted our workshops. Basherte became the method of our connection, and I composed "Every Being Has a Light," which was the soundtrack that informed our workshop. I received rabbinic ordination through ALEPH, and Reb Zalman continues to influence my life.

Gideon and Sara Eisenberg met at a B'nai Or Retreat and were married by Reb Zalman two years later. We met "in the middle" — Pottstown, between our homes in Manhattan and Baltimore; and "in the middle" — Jewish Renewal, between our upbringings in Modern Orthodox and Reform Judaism. Gideon is a psychotherapist and has pursued his love of *niggunim* from many Hassidic traditions. Sara has rooted her work as an herbalist, healer, and teacher in Kabbalah. *alifeofpractice.com*

Diane Elliot. Before becoming a rabbi, I pursued multiple career tracks — actress, modern dancer, choreographer, world traveler, writer for Facts on File, file clerk, shoe salesperson, meditation teacher, somatic movement therapist, and teacher of Body-Mind Centering®. Ordained by the trans-denominational Academy for Jewish Religion, California, I served for three years as spiritual leader of the Aquarian Minyan, created and directed ALEPH's Embodying Spirit embodied Judaism training, and have recently published, *This Is the Day*, poems inspired by the practice of counting the *Omer. whollypresent.org*

Robert (Micha'el) Esformes. Before meeting Reb Zalman I was simply a wandering Jew. After meeting Reb Zalman, I have become a simple, wondering Jew.
store.cdbaby.com/cd/robertmichaelesformes

Yehudis Fishman. When I met Reb Zalman, I had recently been married in Worcester, Massachusetts. It was on Sukkot when I looked over the *mechitza* (divider between sections for men and women) and saw Reb Zalman for the first time, someone with a rainbow *tallit*. And, he, too, looked over the *mechitza* to see a woman waving a *lulav* and *etrog* — not too common in the sixties. We became friends from then on, until his passing. One of the reasons I relocated to Boulder was to be around him. His effect on my life was profound. While I still remain mainstream observant, I have absorbed much of his open-minded inclusion of many paths and philosophies, both within Judaism and elsewhere.

Justin Freed. I encountered Reb Zalman through one of his creations, The Spiritual Eldering Institute. He appeared in my life at a time of crisis: I had recently had surgery to remove a cancerous kidney and was facing mortality for the first time, at the age of sixty. I had not yet faced the issues evoked by aging, which was generally a taboo subject in society at the time. He provided my first opportunity to face these issues in a liberating way. I enrolled in his training program and became a Certified Spiritual Eldering presenter. His impact on my life was profound. Presently I am a multimedia artist with healing video installations at two Boston hospitals. My mission is to link my art with healing. I exhibit at Galatea Fine Art, Boston. *justinfreed-visualmedia.com*

Jack (Ya'acov) Gabriel. Reb Zalman was my rebbe, my surrogate "non-critical father." When I met him in 1986, at a holiday retreat, I was forty, a recording artist and producer, and a radio personality. Born in a refugee camp in Italy, I was also a child of the Holocaust. My heart was battered. My path to healing was becoming the founding Spiritual Leader of the Woodstock Jewish Congregation. But I yearned for a mentor. Reb Zalman trained me for three and a half years and ordained me in 1990. I have gone on to write, sing, and produce five albums of my own American/Hebrew songs. I've led many different denominational congregations in Colorado, New York, California, and South Africa, teaching Jewish Renewal and mystical awareness.

Yonassan Gershom. When I met Reb Zalman in 1980, he was still the B'nai Or Rebbe, and that's how I will always remember him. That first encounter was truly magical. He was able to see beyond my (then undiagnosed) autism into my soul, and I became his devoted *Hassid*. From him I learned how to apply my visual-processing mind to storytelling, picturing the events and bringing the tales alive. In 1983 he empowered me as a *Maggid*, and, in 1986, I received rabbinic ordination publicly, in St. Paul, Minnesota. He once called me "a master of prayer in the way of Reb Nachman of

Breslov," which proved to be prophetic. Today my wife Caryl and I are Breslov *Hassidim*, living and praying in the woods of rural Minnesota. *rooster613.blogspot.com*

Ilan Glazer. Before meeting Reb Zalman, I was struggling to find a spiritual home. After meeting Reb Zalman, I knew that he was my teacher, and that Jewish Renewal was the rabbinical training and spiritual home I was looking for. I studied with ALEPH and became a rabbi and *Mashpia*. I was privileged to serve as rabbi of Temple Beth El of North Bergen, New Jersey, and Beth Sholom Synagogue of Memphis. I'm now a freelance rabbi, speaker, trainer, transformation coach, and host of the *Torah of Life* podcast, which blends Jewish wisdom with personal growth, healing, music, and spirituality. *torahoflife.com*

Andrew Gold. I was raised in a non-observant family where Pesach seders were about it. In my early twenties I began to feel the call of Spirit. I practiced Buddhist meditation and learned Native American spirituality with local Pueblo elders. While living at the Lama Foundation, an interfaith spiritual community, I met Reb Zalman. He introduced me to a Jewish spirituality and ecumenism that I deeply resonated with. He opened a doorway Home. After receiving *smicha* as *Maggid* and Rabbinic Pastor, I led a contemplative congregation in Santa Fe for many years and founded the interfaith Rose Mountain Retreat Center. Currently I'm organizing fundraisers to support the Hand in Hand Schools in Israel. These life-paths were birthed while "watching the Rebbe tie his shoelaces."

Jay (Zisha) and Sabrina (Zahava) Gold. After a "Reb Zalman week" at Elat Chayyim in 1998, Zisha, who had had a Conservative Jewish upbringing, and Zahava, who would become a Jew by choice in 2000, decided to be Renewal Jews. We joined Congregation Shaarei Shamayim, Madison's Reconstructionist/ Renewal community. We studied Reb Zalman's books and tapes intensively (as we continue to do), and attended many ALEPH events. Zahava created for Reb Zalman a multicolored bead and wire *kippa* based on his B'nai Or *tallit*, and we got to know him well enough that on November 2, 2003, he officiated at our wedding. We're retired now, and his *neshama* remains an enduring presence for us.

Shefa Gold. I have been an explorer of consciousness for most all of my life. Meeting Reb Zalman gave me permission to fully inhabit that role. My degrees are in Philosophy and my heart is in music. At some point on my journey I fell in love with God and knew that I needed to express that love through service. In fact, my whole life is an expression of that love. I have written five books: *The Magic of Hebrew Chant* is my latest one published, and my yet-to-be-published manuscript is called *Are We There Yet? Inspirations for Travel*. I teach others whatever I am working on for myself. *rabbishefagold.com*

Dan Goldblatt. I met Reb Zalman at a *shabbaton* of the Aquarian Minyan. Before that meeting, I was living in Berkeley and working as a filmmaker. He invited me to go for a walk with him and suggested that I consider becoming a rabbi. I laughed. In the years that followed, I worked avocationally for seven different congregations in the Bay Area as Interim Spiritual Leader. One congregation asked me to become their rabbi. I agreed on the condition that I enter the ALEPH Ordination Program and receive ordination from Reb Zalman. I have been the Rabbi of Beth Chaim Congregation in Danville, California, for the past twenty-five years. I am readying a book for publication, *Miracles Happen: Stories That Break Open the Heart*.

Karen Golden. Before meeting Reb Zalman, I had spent seven years in Israel exploring my life's mission and deepening my knowledge of Judaism. I met him not long after I had discovered my callings as a storyteller, educator, and mother, and had moved to Los Angeles. Since then I have worked to inspire thousands of curiosity seekers, both young and young at heart, through my work internationally as a storyteller, musician, recording artist, and writer. I am the founding director of a homeschool learning center, Creative Learning Place. My Jewish roots run deep in all that I do. Each day I try to live by Mother's motto: "It's not what you get, but what you give that measures the worth of the life you live." *karengolden.com; creativelearningplace.com*

Zelig Golden. My vision is for an earth-based Judaism formed by integrating thought, leadership, ritual facilitation, and village-based mentorship to support local Jewish life, regional land-based festivals, nature-based youth programs and rites of passage, and international trainings for emerging leaders. I was ordained as a *Maggid* by Reb Zalman, and as a rabbi and spiritual director through ALEPH, with the support of a Wexner Fellowship, and I earned a Masters degree in Jewish Studies from the Graduate Theological Union. *wildernesstorah.org*

Aggie Goldenholz. I served as co-leader of a conservative congregation in Milwaukee, where I led Shabbat and healing services. I was also a cofounder/leader of the first two women's Rosh Chodesh groups and the co-conspirator of the Milwaukee Women's Seder. I was drawn to Reb Zalman because of his progressive, egalitarian, and compassionate approach. My healing work as a chaplain in an inner-city hospital was enhanced when I was trained and ordained Rabbinic Pastor by him. I continue to mentor residents and teach staff about the spiritual needs of Jewish patients. I offer *bikkur cholim* (care for those who are ill) and mentor volunteers in several hospitals, and also teach children and adults about *bikkur cholim*. I am a co-author of *Tastes of Jewish Tradition* and our community women's seder.

Reuven Goldfarb. I have published poetry, stories, essays, profiles, and Torah commentaries in scores of periodicals and anthologies and won several awards. I edited AGADA, the illustrated Jewish literary magazine (1981-1988), taught Freshman English at Oakland's Merritt College (1989-1997) and two courses as a freelancer in Tzfat: Poetry Immersion and Short Story Intensive (2009-2012). I served the Aquarian Minyan as officer and service leader for twenty-five years and received *smicha* from Reb Zalman as *Moreinu, Maggid*, and Rabbinic Deputy in 1993. Presently I serve as copy editor for manuscripts and books (including *What Do We Know? The Carlebach Anthology*) and coordinate monthly meetings for the Upper Galilee branch of Voices Israel. My wife Yehudit and I host classes, workshops, and a weekly Talmud *shiur* in our home. *reuvengoldfarb.com; reuvengoldfarb – youtube; soundcloud.com/reuven-goldfarb*

Yehudit Goldfarb. When I met Reb Zalman at Brandeis Camp Institute in 1961, I was a second-generation San Francisco Jew from a secular Zionist household. Reb Zalman opened for me a connection with the Living God and taught me Jewish maps of consciousness that helped guide my soul's journey. In June 1974, after his month-long *Tanya* workshop, I cofounded the Aquarian Minyan. Reb Zalman's teachings on Hassidism influenced my doctoral dissertation, a Jungian interpretation of Saul Bellow's novels. At his first Mystery School Retreat in November 1987, I began channeling the Hebrew letter movements (*Otiyot Hayyot* — Living Letters for Healing and Renewal). I was later honored as an *Eshet Hazon,* and Reb Zalman gave me *smicha* as *Morataynu*. I now codirect Maor HaLev Center for Movement, Healing, and Language Arts in Tzfat. *yehuditgoldfarb.blogspot.com; otiyot.com*

Jenny Goodman. I grew up in an atheist, Marxist Jewish home. Encountering Reb Zalman and Jewish spiritual renewal allowed me to experience a form of Judaism that felt real, alive, and non-oppressive, and has led to thirty years of joyful participation in, and often leadership of, a Jewish Renewal community. It has enabled me to find the divine in song and dance and silence, as I never could in words alone.

James Stone Goodman. I was trained as a Reform Rabbi at the Hebrew Union College. I loved my training and studied classical Kabbalah with manuscript excerpts at the college library. When I met Reb Zalman, he encouraged my creative efforts in music and writing. He let me know that I was onto something with the music I was creating and the pieces I was writing. I performed with several musical groups, all of which specialized in original materials based on traditional themes, integrating story and music in a performance art form. Reb Zalman was enthusiastic whenever he heard me and several times contacted me about a written piece he had read. I returned to school and earned an MFA in creative writing from the University of Missouri-St. Louis. I presently serve two synagogues in the St. Louis area. *stonegoodman.com*

Lynn Gottlieb. I am a Jewish feminist, activist, writer, visual artist, ceremonialist, community organizer, and master storyteller. I cofounded Congregation Nahalat Shalom in Albuquerque, New Mexico (1981), The Muslim Jewish Peacewalk (2002), and Shomeret Shalom Peacemaking Order, a Jewish path of nonviolence. A Fellow with the Fellowship of Reconciliation, cofounder of Interfaith Peace Builder delegations to Palestine, I am also a cofounder of The Community of Living Traditions at Stony Point Center, New York. Currently I serve as director of Youth and Family Programming at Chochmat Halev and as president of the board of the Interfaith Movement for Human Integrity in California. My most recent book, *World Beyond Borders Passover Haggadah*, was reviewed as the best Haggadah of 2017.

Sarah Leah Grafstein. I am the founder and spiritual leader of Ruach Hamidbar: Spirit of the Desert in Scottsdale, Arizona, established in 1989. Committed to inspiring, educating, and supporting people to joyfully experience and celebrate their Jewishness, I blend my background in the arts and traditional Judaism with Jewish renewal spirituality, *Hassidut*, and Kabbalah. I also co-lead "Drum Shalom," a Jewish drumming circle. My mentors have also included Rabbi Shlomo Carlebach, and I received rabbinic ordination from Reb Zalman in 1987. An accomplished documentarian, and producer of a growing multi-volume DVD library on the topic of Jewish Renewal, I am currently completing a full-length feature documentary on Jewish Renewal. *ruach.org*

Stacy Grove. I wouldn't be an Interfaith Minister serving a Unitarian Universalist congregation without Reb Zalman's encouragement to listen and follow my heart in the work of Deep Ecumenism and Sage-ing. My training with Rabbi Gershon Winkler in Jewish Shamanic healing, Rabbi Joseph Gelberman in Interfaith ministry, and Rabbi Nadya Gross in her Wisdom School greatly support my work in pastoral care. When Reb Zalman offered specific details for a return visit to a Czech community with Reb Raachel Jurovics in 2008, this resulted in applying for and receiving a scroll from the Czech Memorial Trust in 2009. This scroll is used in Yavneh Jewish Renewal Community Raleigh, NC, founded soon after that journey. I also carry the scroll to many interfaith settings for teaching and storytelling. *HeartSpaceSpiritualResources.org*

Jill Hammer. When I met Reb Zalman, I was attending a retreat at Elat Chayyim in Accord, New York. I had just finished my doctorate in Social Psychology and was beginning rabbinical school. I'm now a rabbi teaching rabbinical and cantorial students at the Academy for Jewish Religion, a Rav Kohenet and cofounder of the Kohenet Hebrew Priestess Institute, and the author of several books, including *The Hebrew Priestess: Ancient and New Visions of Jewish Women's Spiritual Leadership, The Book of Earth and Other Mysteries, Sisters at Sinai: New Tales of Biblical Women,* and *The Jewish Book of Days: A Companion for All Seasons.* I've continued my association with Jewish Renewal and teach frequently at Congregation Romemu and the Isabella Freedman Jewish Retreat Center. *kohenet.org; rabbijillhammer.com*

Nancy Handwerger. I offer meditation classes focused on the inner life of the Hebrew letters. I am a psychotherapist whose work integrated hands-on healing, with certification as a meditation teacher by Chochmat HaLev. Through inspiration in a workshop with Reb Zalman, I chose to become ordained a *Kohenet,* focusing on women's roles in the Torah. I wrote dialogues of Biblical characters, which have been offered as *divrei Torah* during *Shabbat* services and in Torah study groups. In subsequent years, inspiration from Reb Zalman led me to publish a book, *The Hebrew Letters Speak,* which describes meditation practices with the letters. In the book are prints of my paintings of the Hebrew letters. *hebrewlettersspeak.com*

Edwin Harris. Prior to meeting Reb Zalman, I was a practicing therapist during the week and a practicing Jew on Shabbat and

Jewish holidays. Reb Zalman taught me to bring all of me wherever I went, and he opened for me ways to bring my Jewish self to psychotherapy and my psychotherapy self to Judaism. This integration first became evident in my work as a rabbi at Central Reform Congregation in St. Louis. Reb Zalman continues to be with me in my private practice, in my teaching Pastoral Counseling in the ALEPH Ordination Program and at Hebrew Union College in Los Angeles, and as the founding rabbi of the Playa Vista Jewish Community. *pvjc.org*

Rosalie Harris-Eisen. I was living in Eugene, Oregon, when I met Reb Zalman, through early Renewalniks. Little did I know that early meeting would lead me to the 1991 Kallah, meeting my then soulmate, and then toward the development of Basherte, Jewish personal growth work for those seeking their soulmates and their souls. Reb Zalman recognized our unique work with a special *smicha* as Relationship Counselors and Masters of Blessings. I am also blessed to have been brought into the *Eshet Hazon* Circle. Reb Zalman and many of his students continue to influence my life daily, in all Four Worlds.

Richard Heiberger. I am presently co-chair of P'nai Or Philadelphia. I created a euphonic translation of *Kaddish*, occasionally lead Torah study, and give *divrei Torah*. About two years ago Art Green said we need a mythology of origins with a value system. I said, "I can do that." Two and-a-half years and seven ALEPH Rabbinical courses later I am still working on it. My day job is Professor Emeritus of Statistics at Temple University. I wrote the graduate text *Statistical Analysis and Data Display* (with Burt Holland), Springer 2015 (second edition). *astro.temple.edu/~rmh/*

Rita Hindin (Ryzl Hoda). I grew up in a family that was a little more traditionally observant and a little less financially well-to-do than those in the average 1960s Teaneck, New Jersey, home. I first encountered Reb Zalman when I was a teenager. Toward the end of 2017, I was once again actively grappling with what authentic-for-me Judaism would look like, so I opened a not-yet-read Reb

Zalman book that had been dormant on my shelf for about thirty-five years. Once again Reb Zalman's words and ideas are having a profound impact on me and my work at the intersection of food systems and public health, with a heavy emphasis on ethical concerns.

Ruth Hirsch. I remember meeting Reb Zalman; he was then (sometimes) wearing a *shtreimel* and black coat. This was around 1979. It was a Sunday event hosted by the Brooklyn College Hillel, coordinated by Rabbi Meir Fund. The panel included Reb Zalman, Rabbi Twerski, and Rabbi Dovid Din, *olav hasholom*. A carful of us drove there from New Paltz. I was surprised at the bareness of the room, not even a pitcher of water for the speakers. And so I adventured off in the empty building, found a kitchen, and shyly delivered a pitcher of water and glasses to the speakers. Reb Zalman later asked my name and told me that in the original it meant "She who quenches thirst." That was what it meant to him. We remained dear friends forever, loving nature, loving to *daven*.

Aryeh Hirschfield, of blessed memory. Ordained as a rabbi by Reb Zalman in 1985, Reb Aryeh went on to help establish Northwest Jewish Renewal communities from San Francisco to Vancouver and was the founding spiritual leader in Oregon of Havurah Shir Hadash (Ashland) and P'nai Or (Portland). A mesmerizing singer, songwriter, guitarist, and storyteller, he offered concerts and workshops on Jewish spirituality throughout North America and Europe, particularly in the service of healing and reconciliation in Germany and toward Israel-Palestine peace. He was also honored for leadership in local social justice and interfaith efforts. Albums: "Wings of Peace," "As the Deer Yearns," "Let the Healing Begin," "*Batee l'Ganee*," "The Last Night of Chanukah," "*Sulam Hahayrut*: The Ladder of Freedom: A Passover Hagadah," and the DVD, "Reb Aryeh: A Tribute in Images & Music." *rebaryeh.com*

Shonna Husbands-Hankin. After meeting Reb Zalman in 1977, my Jewish spiritual life flourished. I became a Judaic artist, writer, spiritual director, leader, and tour guide, creating numerous Judaic art pieces, writings, rituals, classes, retreats, Jewish and interfaith gatherings. I have led spiritual trips to Israel, Cuba, and Native American settings. With my life partner, Reb Yitz, we cofounded Moshav Shivtei Shalom, and I served as a congregational rebbetzin for years. My recent publication in the October 2016 *American Jewish History Journal*, "Soul Brothers: A Memoir," is about the relationship between Reb Zalman and Reb Shlomo. I was recognized as an *Eshet Hazon*, Woman of Vision, in 1990, and certified by Morei Derekh as a Jewish Spiritual Director in 2006. *wingsofshechinah.com*

Yitz Husbands-Hankin. I am an early rabbinic *musmach* of Reb Zalman, and Rabbi Emeritus of Temple Beth Israel — Center for Jewish Life in Eugene, Oregon. As a composer, singer, cellist, guitarist, and performing artist, music is at the heart of my spiritual life. I served as Musical Director of KITOV, producing two recordings, "Gathering the Sparks" and "KITOV LIVE." In addition to many concerts and guest teaching appearances, I have also recorded "Dancing Through Eden," a compilation of my compositions, as well as those of other contemporary Jewish composers, and I published "Treasure Each Day" as a solo recording and songbook. A past chair of the Committee for Ethical Kashrut of Ohalah, I presently serve on the Ethics and Conference committees and have a strong interest in social activism and interfaith dialogue which inform my rabbinic leadership. *tbieugene.org; store.cdbaby.com/Artist/YitzhakHusbandsHankin1*

Ivan Ickovits. I am a trained physicist, and I worked as a systems engineer in aerospace on many scientific and Defense programs, including Chandra, Space Station, and StarWars projects. In a parallel universe, I have been a student of Reb Zalman since ca. 1975. I received *smicha* ca. 2005. In those years, I had been mentoring and teaching classes in *Sefer Yetzira, Zohar, Bahir, Bnei Yissasschar*, and many other Hassidic teachings, including those of the Ba'al Shem Tov, *Tanya*, Reb Nachman, Magid Devarav L'Yaakov, etc. I have been a teacher to many individuals and small groups, leading meditations, retreats, and sharing my enthusiasm for the integration of physics and the early Kabbalah in the South of France, Languedoc, Provence, Narbonne, and Andulusia, while continuing to live in Southern California.

T'mimah Audrey Ickovits. When I met Reb Zalman I was living a corporate life, hypnotized by a high level career as an electronics engineer. Soon, summer vacations meant attending Reb Zalman's annual retreat at Elat Chayyim. I eventually left the corporate world to become a rabbi. I teach Kabbalah and prayer to clergy in training and other adults, and I actively work on kind, green, traditional, cost-effective, end-of-life options. I founded and lead Holistic Jew, where, through a Jewish spiritual lens, we pray, study, and enjoy mitzvah meals, serving "Garden to Table" produce and ethically sourced meat. I also teach and practice Continuum Movement to expand and refine awareness through moving meditation. *holisticjew.org*

David Ingber. Meeting Reb Zalman changed everything for me. He made Judaism new again and set me on the path to be a teacher and spread the word. Raised Modern Orthodox in New York, I studied and trained at Yeshiva University, Beit Midrash L'Torah, Yeshivat Chaim Berlin, Yeshivat Chovovei Torah Rabbinical School, NYU, and in 2004 received rabbinic ordination from Reb Zalman. Prior to founding Romemu, a large New York City Jewish renewal congregation, I served as a Rabbi-in-Residence at Elat Chayyim. Teaching a renewed Jewish mysticism that integrates meditative mindfulness and physical awareness, I also serve on the ALEPH Board and Synagogue 3000 Next Dor's Working Group of Sacred Emergent Communities, and was named among America's most influential Jewish leaders by *Newsweek* and *The Forward 50*. *romemu.org*

Shaya Isenberg. After childhood connections, I first (re)connected with Reb Zalman through the Association of Jewish Studies. At a Kallah, Reb Zalman called for more Jewish Renewal rabbis, and ten years later I received *smicha* from him and the ALEPH Ordination Program. Bahira Sugarman's and my involvement with Jewish Renewal became central to our teachings of relationships as a spiritual path. I am Rabbi Emeritus of Gainesville P'nai Or, and serve on the faculty of the ALEPH Ordination and Spiritual Direction Programs. In his paradigm shifting work with conscious aging, Reb Zalman asked the two of us to develop and implement the Spiritual Eldering curriculum and Leadership Training Program, and then to develop the ALEPH Sage-ing® Mentorship Program, now The Sage-ing® Legacy Mentorship Program. *yerusha.org/sageing*

Burt Jacobson. Ordained by JTS (1966), I first met Reb Zalman in 1963. Reb Zalman and I joined Art Green and others to start Havurat Shalom (Boston, 1968). That first year Reb Zalman and I often led Shabbat morning services together. A few years later I dropped out of the Jewish world, which had become oppressive to me, and became involved in San Francisco's hippie counterculture. Upon reconnecting with Reb Zalman in 1973, I found him immensely supportive of the path I had taken, and he blessed my journey. I helped him lead Aquarian Minyan High Holy Days services in 1976 and co-led thereafter with other members. In 1984 I founded the Kehilla Community Synagogue, a Jewish Renewal community. My newest book, *This Precious Moment: The Wisdom of the Ba'al Shem Tov*, reconstructs the life and spiritual philosophy of this spiritual master.

Raachel Jurovics. I learned that there was a Jewish Renewal Seminary while reading *Stalking Elijah*, a spiritual sequel to *The Jew in the Lotus* — wherein I recognized Reb Zalman as a teacher with whom I longed to study. A proponent of deep ecumenism before ever hearing the term, I recognized in Reb Zalman an orientation to openhearted religious leadership, and, after receiving ALEPH ordination, my rabbinate has expressed this essential spiritual value in every aspect of practice and teaching. I currently serve as spiritual leader of Yavneh: A Jewish Renewal Community (Raleigh, NC) and as President of OHALAH: The Association of Rabbis, Cantors, and Rabbinic Pastors for Jewish Renewal. I also conduct a multifaith spiritual direction practice predominantly for clergy. *ohalah.org; yavneh-raleigh.org*

Rodger Kamenetz. The first time I saw Reb Zalman I loved him and felt his love for me. He brought me into the Four Worlds on our way back from Dharamsala, and I am still his student. I've written of our sacred encounters in *The Jew in the Lotus* and *Stalking Elijah*. When I began working with dreams, he told me that's what some *maggidim* also do. Later he blessed me as a *Maggid* with a beautiful certificate. After he died, I learned that he'd also named me as a *Ba'al ha-Berakhah* (Master of Blessing). *kamenetz.com*

Richard Kaplan. Reb Zalman gave me the wonderful challenge of putting powerful traditional verses from liturgy, *Hassidus*, and Kabbalah into music, and to this day I delight in doing so. I have been performing professionally as a singer, songwriter, and pianist for over forty years, and I am a cantor, teacher, and ethno-musicologist. My concert repertoire of Jewish World Music includes songs from Ashkenazic (European), Mizrachi (Middle Eastern), and Sephardic (Spanish/Andalusian) traditions, as well as original pieces. Among my many published CDs are "The Hidden One: Mystical Songs," "Life of the Worlds: Journeys in Jewish Sacred Music," and "Tuning the Soul: Worlds of Jewish Sacred Music."

Cherie Koller-Fox. I met Reb Zalman in Cambridge when I first arrived in town. Finding him and the other people around Havurat Shalom was the beginning of my adult life as a Jew when I found myself and my calling. For me, that calling was Jewish education. Reb Zalman came to several of the CAJE conferences that I helped organize, and he found great joy and a measure of *nachas* (pride) in them. I am now the President of NewCAJE. I received *smicha* from the Academy for Jewish Religion and am Rabbi Emerita of Congregation Eitz Chayim in Cambridge. *newcaje.org*

Latifa Berry Kropf. I met Reb Zalman in 1975 when I traveled to Philadelphia to see my Sufi teacher Pir Vilayat Inayat Khan with whom he was sharing the stage. I had not been actively involved in Judaism for many years, but Reb Zalman lit up my Jewish *neshama*, and I started attending retreats and studying with him. These studies led me to help form a Jewish Renewal Chavurah in

Charlottesville, which I have co-led for the past twenty-eight years. I also created a form of embodied practice, Jewish sacred dance, and have had the honor of sharing these dances in many communities and conferences. I received the *smicha* of *Gabbai* and *Torah l'Torah* from Reb Zalman, as well as the title of *Eshet Hazon* from my ALEPH sisters. *jewishsacreddance.com*

Amichai Lau-Lavie. I am the founding spiritual leader of Lab/Shul NYC, the creator of Storahtelling, Inc., and a rabbi, educator, writer, and performance artist. My rabbinical ordination is from the Jewish Theological Seminary of America in 2016. I am a member of the Global Justice Fellowship of the American Jewish World Service, a founding member of the Jewish Emergent Network, a consultant to the Reboot Network, a member of the URJ Faculty Team and the Advisory Council of ORAM, an LGBT focused organization for refugees, asylum, and migration. I was honored by the *Forward 50* as one of the top five most influential rabbis in 2017. I am the proud *Abba* of Alice, Ezra, and Charlotte-Hallel. *labshul.org; amichai.me*

Ebn Leader. Since 1999 I have been a student of Rabbi Art Green who at some point thought it was important that I connect with Reb Zalman. At our first meeting Reb Zalman asked me how old I was in terms of time spent consciously in God's presence, a question I have carried with me since. I help train rabbis at the rabbinical school of Hebrew College, and I have co-authored two books on Hassidism: *God in All Moments*, with Or Rose; and *Speaking Torah*, with my teacher Art Green and others. *hebrewcollege.edu/rabbinical*

Julie Leavitt. I am a dance movement psychotherapist and body-oriented spiritual director. I love bringing movement, dance, and body awareness to prayer and offering embodied ways to listen for Sacred Presence. This work was supported and guided by Reb Zalman and his holy teachings.

Michael Lerner. Reb Zalman headed my rabbinic ordination *beit din*. I have been the rabbi of Beyt Tikkun since 1996, editor of

TIKKUN Magazine: A Bimonthly Jewish Critique of Politics, Culture and Society, and co-chair of the interfaith Network of Spiritual Progressives. Among the eleven books I've written where Reb Zalman's influence can be deeply found are my national bestseller: *Jewish Renewal: A Path to Healing and Transformation, The Socialism of Fools: Anti-Semitism on the Left*, and *Embracing Israel/Palestine*. The University of California Press will publish my book, *Revolutionary Love*, by 2019. My wife Cat Zavis is in the ALEPH Rabbinic program, my son Akiba is a professor of Jewish Studies, and I have two amazing grandchildren, Ellie and Jeremiah. *tikkun.org; beyttikkun.org*

Herb Levine. I carry forward the radical theological agenda of Reb Zalman's paradigm shift thinking in my book *Words for Blessing the World: Poems in Hebrew and English*. Reb Zalman taught me that one has to learn to explode the forms of Jewish prayer in order to get at their inner essence. Like Reb Zalman, I understand that Jewish Renewal will better serve and endure when undertaken in both Hebrew and English.

Neshama (Rose) Lipari. Reb Zalman became an important person in my life. I studied with him at Friendship Farm and also during summers when he taught at Elat Chayyim. My personal life changed as we studied and made *Shabbos* together with other local Jewish spiritual seekers and teachers. He had a strong positive effect on my son. I always felt supported by him in my studies with spiritual teachers from different traditions. My given name was Rose and I was never happy with it. Reb Zalman opened my eyes to the possibility of taking a new name. He helped me shed there being a right and wrong way in terms of religious observance. Over time I began to use spiritual insights in both my life and my psychotherapy practice.

Prahaladan (Philip) Mandelkorn. I am a former U.S. Navy Seal Team Platoon Commander, *Time* magazine correspondent, and Senator Robert Kennedy's speechwriter. I served later as Director of Teacher Training at Satchidananda Ashram and collaborated with Sri Swami Satchidananda on the books *To Know Your Self* and

The Living Gita. I also collaborated with Reb Zalman on the book *Fragments of a Future Scroll.* Reb Zalman called me Pip. *yogakabbalahblogspot.com*

Neil Markowitz. Growing up in the spiritual desert that had become Conservative Judaism in 1960s America, I all but gave up on our tradition as a path to deeper spiritual insights. Along with a generation of "seekers," I looked longingly to the East for inspiration and answers. A class with Reb Marcia (Prager) at P'nai Or in the 1990s opened a door which was kicked off its hinges by subsequent study with Reb Arthur and Phyllis Berman, Reb Elliot, and especially Reb Miles Krassen, whose time in Tucson helped turn the wilderness into a garden. From there I was led to our beloved Reb Zalman, who replaced the door with a porthole to another dimension of experiencing Jewish consciousness. *eeexchange.org*

David Evan Markus. I was over ten years into a government career when Rachel Barenblat, then an ALEPH student, convinced me to attend a Jewish Renewal retreat at Elat Chayyim. Soon I was attending DLTI and decamping to Philadelphia's Mount Airy neighborhood. Before long, I was a student in the ALEPH rabbinic and Hashpa'ah (spiritual direction) programs, an intern in a Renewal *shul,* a member of the ALEPH Board and then co-chair of the ALEPH Board, a rabbi and spiritual director, pulpit leader and teacher in the ALEPH Ordination Program, and Founding Builder of Bayit: Your Jewish Home. I continue in my public service track as North America's only pulpit rabbi to also maintain a fulltime oath of office. *yourshulbythesea.org; yourbayit.org*

Melvin Metelits. I was ordained as a *Maggid,* a teller of sacred stories, by Maggid Yitzhak Buxbaum in 2006. This ordination was later confirmed by Reb Zalman. I have told stories and taught Torah at many synagogues and *havurot,* and I speak at special occasions such as weddings, bar mitzvahs, confirmations, and other simchas. Most recently I appeared with a panel of local rabbis on Shavuot teaching on the topic "Harvesting Revelation." An active member of P'nai Or Philadelphia. I have also organized several Torah study groups using a participatory, interactive model of approaching Torah by exploring and comparing ancient and contemporary ethics.

Goldie Milgram. Riveted during Reb Zalman's teaching at RRC, where I first became a rabbi (1993), I soon delighted in traveling worldwide on assignment for Reb Zalman with my *hubbatzin*, Barry Bub. While serving as co-dean at the Academy for Jewish Religion (ca. 1993), I founded and still direct Reclaiming Judaism (2000), adding Reclaiming Judaism Press as well as distance-learning for both Maggid-Educator and B-Mitzvah Educator training. Personal ordinations from Reb Zalman: *Rabbi, Maggid, Mashpi'ah, Shaliach.* Honored by the Council of Jewish Federations, Covenant Foundation, National Jewish Book Awards, and the Jewish Futures Conference. Recent books and resources: *Seeking and Soaring: Jewish Approaches to Jewish Spiritual Guidance and Development; Reclaiming Bar/Bat Mitzvah as a Spiritual Rite of Passage* (second edition), *Mitzvah Stories: Seeds for Inspiration and Learning, New Mitzvah Stories for the Whole Family, and MITZVAH CARD* decks in several languages; *ReclaimingJudaism.org*

Tamara Miller. I first met Reb Zalman at the National Havurah Institute and was intrigued by his unorthodox teachings. Fast forward ten years when I found myself in rabbinical school at the Academy for Jewish Religion in New York City. I became a member of Ohalah and had the privilege of hearing Reb Zalman many times and receiving his many blessings. My memoir, *You Are the Book: A Spiritual Memoir*, was published in 2017. Wisdom I learned from Reb Zalman is sprinkled throughout the book. I am presently a fellow with Rabbis Without Borders, a program initiated by CLAL. *rabbitamara.com*

Hal Miller-Jacobs. I rediscovered my Judaic essence in large measure while studying with Reb Zalman at Elat Chayyim. For example, the encouragement to *daven* the *Amida* with a *tallit* covering the head was profound. I went on to be a graduate of the Davvenen' Leadership Training Institute and become cofounder of the Community Hevra Kadisha of Greater Boston.

Yocheved Mintz. At a CAJE Conference in San Antonio I saw a gentleman in white, walking, guru-like, at the head of a line of what looked like disciples or ducklings. He proved to be Reb Zalman. When I needed to speak to a rebbe, it was suggested that I call Reb Zalman. He answered my phone call, never asked for my name, and engaged me in counsel for forty-five minutes. He ended with sage advice I've remembered the rest of my life: "Don't allow yourself to be a *shmatta*." Years passed, I became a rabbi, got involved in Ohalah, and eventually met Reb Zalman in person, telling him of our previous encounters, and becoming one of his loving and loved ducklings.

Reuben Modek. A secular Israeli spiritual seeker, a yogi meditator, and a newly minted social worker and curious about Judaism, I joined the Jewish Renewal Life Center in Philadelphia. There I studied and davened with Reb Zalman and the P'nai Or community during the year that led to rabbinical ordination studies and ordination through both the ALEPH Rabbinic Program and The Academy for Jewish Religion. I am currently the founder-director of Hebrew Learning Circles of Nyack, New York, a Renewal Synagogue, and Hebrew School Without Walls. *hebrewlearningcircles.org*

Sue Mauer Morningstar. Reb Zalman endearingly called me "Sue, *leibn,*" and I was honored with Reb Zalman's and ALEPH Ordination Program *smicha* in 2009. I live in Ashland, Oregon, and serve as the Associate Rabbi at Havurah Shir Hadash. I was raised in a loving modern Orthodox community on Long Island. I have been active with Rabbis for Women of the Wall and in reinterpreting and renewing ceremony and ritual. I am also a nurse practitioner and enjoy working together with my life partner Howard, an integrative family physician and herbalist, at our sacred healing center in southern Oregon. *morningstarhealingarts.net*

Eileen Nathanson. At age sixty, happy in my chosen career as a practicing physical therapist and Physical Therapy faculty member at NYU, the question spontaneously arose of what I should do with the last phase of my life. Inspired by Reb Zalman's Aging to Sage-ing work at age sixty-four, and later, his exhortation to go deeper into Judaism, I retired to Philadelphia, Pennsylvania, and immersed myself in Jewish life and study at The Jewish Renewal Life Center. Today I am an active member of P'nai Or Philadelphia and continue to participate in Torah and *mussar* study, create gardens for community members to enjoy, do watercolor painting, and help other elders do so.

Leah Novick. Until my forties, I was a progressive, social action Jew from an Orthodox background, with a strong Hebrew education and connection to Israel. Before connecting with Reb Zalman, I had been studying Goddess literature, and having mystical experiences and past life recall. Interaction with Reb Zalman and Kabbalah study solidified my relationship with *Shekhinah*, and I began experiencing myself as being "called" to the rabbinate. After receiving his rabbinic *smicha*, leading renewal groups and teaching, I consolidated my research and insights into *On the Wings of Shekhinah: Re-Discovering Judaism's Divine Feminine* and a CD of the same name, with music by Desert Wind and my own guided meditations. Presently I advise renewal groups, offer soul-memory counseling, and do interfaith work. *RabbiLeah.com*

Jackie and Leon Olenick. Our Jewish journeys took us through all the Jewish movements, including a three-year stint with Chabad until Reb Zalman woke up our *neshamot* and released our inner spirits. We created Jewish Renewal *havurot* in the Twin Cities and South Florida. Reb Zalman encouraged Leon to find a career that matched his soul, and he chose chaplaincy. He is now a Board Certified Chaplain and has been engaged in hospice work for over twenty years. Jackie incorporates Jewish thought, values, and feminism in art and jewelry design. Our greatest honor was when Reb Zalman ordained us each as *a Ba'al HaBrachot, Master of Blessings*. To sum it up, we were both "Zalmanized." *jackieolenickart.com*

Batya Podos. I am an ordained *Maggidah-Omanit*—educator, storyteller, and guide in the Jewish tradition, and Dean of the Reclaiming Judaism Maggid-Educator training and/or Ordination program, specializing in curriculum development. I teach across a broad spectrum of settings, denominations, and age groups in the roles of principal, teacher, *B'nei Mitzvah* educator, service leader and Torah teacher for Shabbat and holy days, and scholar-in-residencies for *shabbatonim*. I am one of the founders of Abraham's Tent, an interfaith summer camp. My recent publications are *Rebecca and the Talisman of Time* (Portal Center Press), a novel for middle school students, works in *New Mitzvah Stories for the Whole Family* (Reclaiming Judaism Press) and in *The Language of Life*, by Milt Markewitz, an exploration of the energetic patterns of the Hebrew letters. *ReclaimingJudaism.org*

Marcia Prager. I am a rabbinic graduate of the Reconstructionist Rabbinical College and also received personal *smicha* from Reb Zalman in 1990. I am the founding Dean of the ALEPH Ordination Program, appointed by Reb Zalman to develop this innovative seminary. I codirect the Davvenen' Leadership Training Institute, created with Rabbi Shawn Zevit to expand Reb Zalman's ground-breaking work on davenology. I serve as rabbi of P'nai Or Philadelphia, am the author of *The Path of Blessing*, a contemporary Hassidic text exploring the Jewish practice of blessing, and creator of the P'nai Or *siddurim* for *Shabbat* and other innovative compilations of prayer and liturgy. In 2010, I was selected by the *Jewish Daily Forward* as one of the Top Fifty American Female Rabbis. *aleph.org/ordinations; dlti.org; pnaior-phila.org*

David Rafsky. I am presently on three committees at our San Diego JCC, and am very involved with Adult Jewish Education, the Book Fair, and the Film Festival. The JCC, with some of my input, now has offered two more spiritual classes, and we have changed the meditation weekly class that my wife Rhonda Mason offers at no charge, to Jewish Meditation. I have also served on the board of our *havurah*, Shir HaYam, an ALEPH community.

Geela Rayzel Raphael. I am an "unorthodox rabbi," a wild woman Shechinah Priestess. I graduated as a rabbi from the Reconstructionist seminary, have been honored as an Eshet Hazon, and inducted as a *Kohenet*. I have served four congregations, and my path includes being an artist and ritual leader. Understanding the deep mythic structure of the heroine's journey, I bring skills of group work, song leading, and inspiration into creative ceremonies. I am the author of two children's books, *Angels for Dreamtime* and *New Moon*, as I seek to influence the next generation through my work. I also paint *tallitot*, offer Shechinah Oracle readings, and teach about spirituality and other Jewish mysteries that guide my path in service to the Divine Feminine. *shechinah.com; interfaithJewishweddings.com*

Simcha Paull Raphael. I first met Reb Zalman in Montreal in 1976 and have been a "Jewish Renewal Hassid" ever since. From 1980 to 1983, I served as the first Executive Director of B'nai Or Religious Fellowship (1980-1982), the organization that later became ALEPH. In 1979, upon Reb Zalman's encouragement, I first began studying little-known Jewish teachings on life after death, and later wrote the classical study, *Jewish Views of the Afterlife*—twenty-fifth anniversary edition to be published in 2019. I received my Ph.D. in Psychology from the California Institute of Integral studies (1986), and ordination from Reb Zalman as a Rabbinic Pastor (1990). I am the Founding Director of the DA'AT Institute for Death Awareness, Advocacy, and Training. I work as a psychotherapist, bereavement counselor, spiritual director, and Adjunct Professor in Philadelphia. *Daatinstitute.net*

Carol Rose. I met Reb Zalman when I was seventeen at a Hillel retreat in Winnipeg. After marrying my husband, Rabbi Neal Rose, we returned to Winnipeg where Neal accepted a position in the Department of Judaic Studies. We quickly became part of Reb Zalman's vision of an intentional Jewish spiritual community (B'nai Or). I worked as an educator and writer, receiving an M.A. in Theology, while we raised our five children. Ordained by Reb Zalman as a *Mashpi'ah*, (Jewish spiritual director), I began working as a spiritual counselor. My publications include *Behind the Blue*

Gate (Canadian National Jewish Book Award for Poetry), *From the Dream*, and *Path of the Mothers*. Neal and I received the 2015 Lieutenant Governor's Award for the Advancement of Inter-Religious Understanding (Manitoba). *ms.carolrose.blogspot.com*

Neal Rose. Directly after receiving Rabbinic ordination, I and my wife Carol moved to Winnipeg, where I joined Reb Zalman in the Department of Judaic Studies, specializing in *Hassidism*, Holocaust Literature, and Yiddish. After completing my doctorate, I developed an interest in healing and spirituality. This led to studies in Family Therapy and Spiritual Counseling. I began both practicing and teaching Family Therapy at the University of Winnipeg. I developed a specialty in counseling clergy of all faiths. I became Director of Spiritual Care for Winnipeg's Jewish Community long-term care facility (2000). In 2015 Carol and I received the Lieutenant Governor's Award for the Advancement of Inter-Religious Understanding (Manitoba). Currently I am a chaplain in St. Louis and Senior Rabbinic Scholar at Congregation B'nai Amoona.

Deliah Golda Rosel. Raised without any Jewish education, I looked to Nature as my spiritual connection. Reb Zalman offered the joy of Hassidism and the experience of YHVH as Divine Healing Energy in an egalitarian social setting, making the wisdom of my heritage accessible to me. I completed training in Davvenen' Leadership (DLTI), Shamanic Healing, and Spiritual Direction at Elat Chayyim. I created *L'Chaim Qigong*™ — *a Jewish Approach to Qigong Healing* as my dissertation for my Doctorate in Ministry. I now lead monthly Embodied Shabbat Prayer Services at my home, The Hidden Torah Healing Center in Western Massachusetts. Reb Zalman's wisdom infuses my life and my thirty-year private practice in the healing arts—combining medical massage, integrative acupressure, energy medicine, and spiritual direction. *Deliahrosel.com*

David G. Roskies. A native of Montreal, Canada, and a product of its Yiddish secular schools, my exposure to Reb Zalman in the 1970s was formative. Since 1975, I have been teaching Yiddish

literature and culture and Jewish literature at the Jewish Theological Seminary, and have served as a Visiting Professor of Yiddish Studies at the Hebrew University of Jerusalem. In addition to awards and nine published books, in 1981, Dr. Alan Mintz and I founded *Prooftexts: A Journal of Jewish Literary History*. I served for seventeen years as editor-in-chief of the New Yiddish Library series, published by Yale University Press.
JTSA.edu; https://library.osu.edu/projects/hebrew-lexicon/99995056.php

Janice Rubin. I am a Houston-based photographer, musician, and teacher. Since meeting Reb Zalman in 1993, I have been serving as a Jewish educator, facilitating classes in meditation, and Jewish music and chant. I graduated from the fourth Davvenen' Leadership Training Institute (DLTI) and have been creating musical services and organizing programs for ALEPH in Houston and other locations. I serve as a PRN hospital chaplain, sing with hospice patients, and serve as a *rosh* (head) for the *chevre kaddisha*. I am currently training as a *Mashpi'ah* in ALEPH's spiritual direction training program. An internationally published photographer, I am the creator of the touring exhibit and book *The Mikvah Project*, which explores the contemporary renaissance of ancient ritual.
janicerubin.com

Laurie Sanford. Feeling detached from Judaism, I met Reb Zalman and was able to unexpectedly attend his teaching of Kabbalah at a Buddhist Retreat Center. I went on to become a depth psycho-dynamic psychologist and continue to do meditations, visualizations, and gratitude practices that I learned from Reb Zalman to this day. I also learned to value my own connection to the Divine and to translate these gifts into my work as a psychologist, relationships, and in my work in the world. Finally, I am now, in addition, participating joyfully in both the ALEPH Hashpa'ah Training and the Wisdom School programs.

Steven Schatz. I met Reb Zalman while living at the Lama Foundation in 1972 and my life has never been the same. The numerous profound experiences with Reb Zalman at Lama Foundation touched my soul and awakened a connection with

Judaism as a spiritual practice, which has been lifelong.
brothingguru.com

Julie Schechter. After being influenced by my Orthodox paternal grandparents, in 1996 contact with Reb Zalman opened a door within me that led me to co-create Tampa's Renewal congregation, Or Ahavah. In 2007 I became a founding member of Kol HaNeshama's monthly Jewish meditation group in Sarasota, Florida. Over the years I have sponsored many alternative Pesach seders, Woman's Life Cycle celebrations and in April 2018, the first Kirtan Kabbalah open to all communities, a program co-sponsored by the Association of Professional Jewish Artists.
ReclaimingJudaism.org

Leslie Schotz. I learned with Marcia Prager in 1981 at a SUNY Stony Brook Jewish college group. In 1995, Rabbi Dr. Shohama Wiener welcomed me to the Academy for Jewish Religion where I was ordained as a rabbi in 2002. In 2011, I became the first Doctor of Ministry candidate of the Hashpa'ah Ordination Program through ALEPH and NYTS. My teachers/mentors became Rabbi Nadya Gross, Rabbi Steven Silvern, and Rabbi Shawn Zevit. After my Hashpa'ah ordination in January 2014, Reb Zalman approached me to bless my work on *Spiritual Direction for Jewish Children*. I published *Shalom: A Congregational Guide to Jewish Meditation; Spiritual Direction for Jewish Children*, and am included in *Ain't Gonna Let Nobody Turn Me Around: Stories of Contemplation and Justice*.

Howard Schwartz. I started writing poems in 1965, when I was twenty. Soon after, I began to write brief parables and published my first book, *A Blessing Over Ashes*, in 1974. In 1977 I took a year-long sabbatical in Israel, where I met my wife, Tsila. I also met Professor Dov Noy, the world's leading Jewish folklorist, who had created the Israel Folktale Archives and encouraged me to look into them. There I came across a story that inspired me to do *Elijah's Violin & Other Jewish Fairy Tales*, published in 1983. I published three more books in this series. My major work, *Tree of Souls: The Mythology of Judaism*, which took twelve years to

complete, was published in 2004. More recently, I finished *A Palace of Pearls: The Stories of Rabbi Nachman of Bratslav.*
howardschwartz.com

Arthur Segal. My love of Judaism and the Jewish people sent me on a personal quest for Jewish spiritual renewal after retirement from a successful oral medicine practice. I was ordained a rabbi after ten years of intensive study and have become a chaplain and author of many works, including *The Handbook to Jewish Spiritual Renewal.* My *bashert*, Ellen Freedman Segal and I, have traveled to over one hundred fifty countries, visiting and aiding Jewish communities where they exist. At home on Hilton Head Island, we enjoy a life of shalom, *shleimut*, and gratitude, with our parrot, Avivit Keter.
hiltonheadjewishweddings.com/about-rabbi-arthur-segal/

Audrey Seidman. Strong in Jewish tradition but uneducated, and after coming out as a lesbian, I felt disconnected from institutional religious life. In my forties, at Elat Chayyim, as my search for spiritual meaning unfolded, my hunger for Jewish learning was stoked and fed. After a Shavuot with Reb Zalman, I went on to celebrate my Bat Mitzvah. I then completed training in the Lev Shomea Institute for Spiritual Directors, earned three units in Clinical Pastoral Education at Albany Medical Center, and completed the Sage-ing® Mentorship Program. I presently serve part-time as outreach chaplain for the Jewish Federation of NENY, and I am privileged to companion and guide others on their spiritual and conscious aging journeys and to support interfaith connections.

Rami Shapiro. My spiritual life B.M.R.Z. (Before Meeting Reb Zalman) was a blend of conventional Judaism, Zen Buddhism, and Hinduism. My spiritual life A.M.R.Z. (After Meeting Reb Zalman) was a blend of conventional Judaism, Zen Buddhism, Hinduism, Sufism, Christian mysticism, and a postmodern neo-Hassidism that left me forever on the edge of ecstasy. Reb Zalman supported me when I created a *shul* in my own image, gave me his blessing for many of my books (especially my rendition of the Hebrew

Prophets, Hassidic tales, and *Tanya*) and congratulated me when I realized, after twenty years in the synagogue, that it was time to move on. "Enough with the Jews!" he told me. "Your mission is to bring a Perennial Judaism to the world." So I did. *rabbirami.com*

Ruth Broyde Sharone. A documentary filmmaker and journalist for many decades, I met Reb Zalman in 1992, while organizing "Festival of Freedom," a pioneering interfaith pilgrimage to Israel and Egypt. One of a few intrepid souls who engaged with Muslim leaders, he immediately became my interfaith mentor. I produced/directed the documentary "God and Allah Need to Talk" (2003), and in 2007 I was the first woman to receive Reb Zalman's title of *Rodephet Shalom* (Pursuer of Peace). My interfaith memoir *Minefields & Miracles* includes many anecdotes about Reb Zalman. The same week he died we were scheduled to have a Skype call to share news about my latest project, *Interfaith: The Musical*. He would have embraced its tagline: "Broadway-bound on the wings of peace." *interfaiththemusical.com; MinefieldsandMiracles.com*

Debrah Shenefelt. I was fortunate to meet Reb Zalman early in my search for spiritual meaning and fulfillment. He was a beacon of light that illuminated possible pathways for me to wander, and they ultimately led to me becoming a rabbi ordained through ALEPH in 2010. His firm belief that each of us has *rebbetude* (teachable wisdom), whether or not we are a rabbi, helped me find the courage to found a Jewish Renewal community called Or Ahavah ten years before becoming ordained. Influenced by Reb Zalman's creative approach to Jewish learning and practice, Or Ahavah now includes a teaching program called Mystic Torah through which I teach Jewish Meditation, Kabbalah, and *Mussar*. *orhahavah.org*

David Shneyer. I am a rabbi, cantor, singer-composer, guitarist, clarinetist, and leader of the Fabrangen Fiddlers band, a group engaged in the rediscovery of Jewish folk music and the development of new Jewish liturgical folk music. I helped to start the Fabrangen Jewish Free Culture Center. I am also the founder, executive director, and spiritual leader of Am Kolel and Kehila

Chadasha, two trans-denominational Jewish communities based in the Washington, D.C. area, and I direct the Am Kolel Sanctuary and Renewal Center, an ecumenical retreat near Poolesville, MD. A member of T'ruah: The Rabbinic Call for Human Rights and the Montgomery Countryside Alliance, I am devoted to social and environmental justice. *rsa.fau.edu/david-shneyer; am-kolel.org; e-kehila.org/*

Daniel Siegel. Despite my yeshiva background, I was unaware that Judaism was a spiritual practice whose purpose it is to bring the practitioner into a close relationship with God. Reb Zalman made that connection for me, one which changed the course of my life and allowed me to become fully "deployed" as Reb Zalman's first rabbinic ordinee and an agent for the spiritual renewal of Judaism in a universal and egalitarian context. *alephcanada.ca*

Shoshana Silberman. When Reb Zalman, and his then wife, Elana, moved around the corner from us, we became quite friendly, but not "followers." After my encounter with him, I began my career as principal of a Jewish school, workshop leader, and author. Although I rarely bought into his "whole package," I often came away with new ideas that I applied to educational experiences that I created for children and adults. Reb Zalman also taught me the importance of stretching in order to grow intellectually and spiritually. (And yes, we had our beloved third child. That adorable baby is now forty-three!) My last "baby," my tenth book, is called *The Rosenstein Haggadah.*

Naomi Steinberg. I met Reb Zalman in the early 1980s when he visited the Jewish community in our redwood region of northern California. I was enchanted by Reb Zalman's presence, but not interested in his topic: he was counseling the congregation on what they should look for when hiring a rabbi. I thought, "What does this matter to me?" Many years later, I became the rabbi of that community and have found great joy in serving Temple Beth El for nearly three decades. I also serve B'nai Ha-Aretz (Children of the Earth) and the Jewish community of Southern Humboldt County, and I can be heard monthly on KMUD radio's "Jewish Spiritual

Perspectives." My original songs are featured on *"A Child's Chanukah." templebetheleureka.org*

Ahouva Steinhaus. A Reform Jew and UCLA dropout, in 1967 I was living in the Haight Ashbury when Rabbi Natan Schafer took me to Winnipeg to meet Reb Zalman, his mentor and teacher. I spent time with Reb Zalman there, and in Philadelphia, Boulder, and the San Francisco Bay area, attending many retreats with him. I became the first Executive Director of B'nai Or (now ALEPH) and I was an ALEPH Board member in the nineties and early 2000s. Also in the nineties, I served as co-coordinator of the Network of Jewish Renewal Communities. Since 1996, I have been a lay leader of Shir HaYam, a *havurah* in San Diego, California. I was ordained a Reverend by Reb Zalman in the 2000s. Presently, I am working on a memoir of my life in Jewish Renewal.

Bahira Sugarman. Before meeting Reb Zalman, I was initiated into the Mysteries of the Goddess and was a student in The Arica School for clarifying consciousness. Through my renaming ceremony, Reb Zalman assisted in the reawakening of my Jewess soul. Shaya Isenberg's and my involvement with Jewish Renewal became central to our teachings of relationships as a spiritual path. In his paradigm shifting work with conscious aging, Reb Zalman asked us to develop and implement the Spiritual Eldering curriculum and Leadership Training Program, and then to develop the ALEPH Sage-ing® Mentorship Program, now The Sage-ing® Legacy Mentorship Program. Ordained as a Spiritual Guide by Reb Zalman in 1996, I've been celebrated as a Woman of Vision and Healer of Souls at an ALEPH Kallah. *yerusha.org/sageing*

Meira Bracha (Michele) Sumka. I was a semi-traditional feminist Conservative Jew until seeing Reb Zalman for the first time at the ALEPH ordination of Rabbi Yafa (Joanie) Chase. Realizing that he was an unusual teacher, not the guru I imagined, I wanted to study with him and was excited to attend his last Shavuot retreat in 2014 at Isabella Freedman. I am also a student at Reb Nadya Gross's Wisdom School, a Sage-ing Mentor, and an ALEPH *Mashpi'ah*. I have two wonderful daughters and sons-in-law, from whom I have learned much about life, plus two fantastic grandchildren. I presently live in Silver Spring, Maryland, with my husband of fifty-one years, who has given me the opportunity to live in Kenya, Bosnia, and Israel.

Bonita Nathan Sussman. It was the rabbinic *smicha* that I received from Reb Zalman that changed the course of many lives including my own. Because of this *smicha* I was invited to teach at the Academy for Jewish Religion, where, at a yearly retreat, I met a member of the Jewish community of Uganda. Thus began my journey with Kulanu, a group that supports the development of emerging Jewish communities around the globe. All the souls that I have touched — through encouraging people in their journeys toward Judaism by organizing conversions, distributing Torah scrolls, *siddurim,* and other books of Jewish learning — are a credit to Reb Zalman. *bonitasussman.weebly.com youtube.com/channel/UCezJM2DIEV_x4DJ19nyinbA*

Moshe Waldoks. I was ordained by Rabbis Zalman Schachter-Shalomi, Arthur Green, and Everett Gendler and presently serve as the Senior Rabbi of Temple Beth Zion (TBZ), an independent synagogue in Brookline, Massachusetts. I co-edited *The Big Book of Jewish Humor*, which is now in its thirty-sixth printing. Also, I earned a doctorate in Eastern European Jewish Intellectual History at Brandeis University. I am married to Anne Waldoks, a clinical psychologist. We are the proud father of three daughters, and we have been blessed with a grandson. *tbzbrookline.org*

Rivkah Walton. I joined Reb Zalman at B'nai Or in 1978, and his teachings have continuously informed my career as an artist and community-builder. My approach to Judaica design forefronts the spiritual dimensions of each piece. I work in diverse media, from silver *Kiddush* cups to fabric Jewish DreamPillows™, and from sculptural to midrashic portraits of Biblical women. I've brought my vision to the National Havurah Committee and Moving Traditions, and twice served as Associate Director of ALEPH: Alliance for Jewish Renewal. Most gratifyingly, I was the founding Director of the Institute for Contemporary Midrash and architect of ICM's Bibliodrama Training Program. I was also honored to serve as graphic designer and editor of Reb Zalman's last book, *Psalms: A Translation for Praying*. Aleph.org/psalms; *intuitivedesign.com; icmidrash.org*

Nahum Ward-Lev. I was a public high school teacher when I met Reb Zalman. Following a Four Worlds workshop with him, I began to seriously study Jewish texts. This interest in Jewish texts led me into rabbinical studies and ultimately to become ordained as a rabbi at the Hebrew Union College. Reb Zalman's teaching about the Four Worlds has stayed with me to this very day. I developed a learning process to explore each of the Four Worlds of a Jewish text using the four levels of rabbinical hermeneutics as a guide. I have led workshops using this process at synagogues, churches, retreat centers, and seminaries across the country and I am always moved by the camaraderie, aliveness, and wisdom that emerge from these workshops. *nahumwardlev.com*

Ellen Stein Weaver. I am a Rabbinic Pastor and Mashpi'ah Ruchanit ordained through ALEPH. My work is titled Weaving Wholeness and blends the Four Worlds in whatever way is useful in the moment. I'm a Licensed Clinical Social Worker, specializing in Internal Family Systems Therapy, trauma, and Interpersonal NeuroBiology. I am also a licensed massage therapist, and have trained in many modalities of intuitive body and energy therapies, as well as medical massage. I live in Philadelphia, and work by phone as well, holding sacred space for clients, students, and directees. A shaman for decades, I later studied Shamanic Jewish Healing with Rabbi Gershon Winkler. I have been blessed to participate in many classes and trainings with Reb Zalman for over twenty years, and I'm an active member of P'nai Or Philadelphia.

Rodney Weiss. Before I met Reb Zalman I was Jewish, and after I met him I was Jewish. I was given a book, *The Jew in the Lotus*, which led me to attend Naropa University where I met Reb Zalman. We developed a bond that allowed me to develop a more in-depth experience of my own Jewish journey. Through our conversations, I have been inspired to help and work with others as he worked with me. *rodneyweiss.com*

Bob Weissberg. I met Reb Zalman in the early nineties. I had become interested in Jewish meditation practices and Kabbalah, and in 1994, I took a class at Elat Chayyim with Reb Zalman, "The Next Rung," intending to learn about Kabbalah. He taught me about davening. Then, I went to Elat Chayyim in 1996 to learn more about davening, and Reb Zalman taught me more about Kabbalah. Over the years, I have participated in and sometimes led services and meditations from a Renewal perspective, which has been a great joy in my life.

Shohama Wiener. When I met Reb Zalman in 1983, I was a rabbinical student at the Academy for Jewish Religion (AJR). We formed an instant connection, and I began to study monthly with him. In 1986, after my ordination, he was my spiritual guide on a trip to Israel. When he ordained me as *Mashpi'ah Ruchanit*, I took this into AJR, first serving as Dean, then President. I also long-served as *Rosh Haspa'ah* for Reclaiming Judaism and the ALEPH Ordination Program, and as Founder and Director of ALEPH's training for Jewish spiritual directors. I currently serve Temple Beth-El of City Island. Major publications: *Seeking and Soaring: Jewish Approaches to Spiritual Guidance and Development; Worlds of Jewish Prayer: A Festschrift in Honor of Rabbi Zalman M. Schachter-Shalomi; The Fifty-Eighth Century: A Jewish Renewal Sourcebook.* Yourshulbythesea.org; *ReclaimingJudaism.org*

Ira Stewart Wiesner. At the onset of midlife, I confronted an urge, a questing, for deeper meaning and purpose in life. Through a series of synchronicities, I would find myself heading in one direction of inquiry when suddenly something — an article, a workshop, or such — highlighting Reb Zalman, would cross my path. Each time, my journey would be radically redirected elsewhere, but to where and why remained veiled but impelling. In retrospect, it reminded me of the movie scene where Reese's Pieces were dropped on the floor to entice ET out of hiding. After carefully guiding me to my current *makom* (place), I sense I was led to where Reb Zalman from the start wanted me to get to in order to find my Jewish self.

Gershon Winkler. Since meeting Reb Zalman, I served eleven years as a circuit-riding rabbi across the length and breadth of rural West Virginia as well as part-time Hillel Director for West Virginia University in Morgantown. I eventually relocated to the wilds of New Mexico where I founded the Walking Stick Foundation— now in its twenty-first year—dedicated to the research and dissemination of the more aboriginal wisdom of Judaism. I have also since published several works on ancient Jewish wisdom, including *Way of the Boundary Crosser* and *Magic of the Ordinary: Recovering the Shamanic in Judaism.* Currently, I serve as the Jewish Chaplain for a Forensic Hospital in Southern California and reside in the San Bernardino Mountains with my beloved, Rabbi Dr. Miriam Ashina Maron. *walkingstick.org*

Carlos Zarur. I was born in a Sephardic family (you may say "Orthodox," but that word doesn't apply for Sephardim even if we're labeled like that here in the United States). As I am a scholar in Sephardic Studies and Anthropology, Reb Zalman used to contact me to talk and clarify some doubts regarding Sephardim and their cultures. I never got that clear of a vision of my own folks until Reb Zalman opened my eyes to their beautiful and inspired words.

David Zaslow. I am the author of two interfaith books, *Jesus: First-Century Rabbi* and *Reimagining Exodus.* Together with my wife Debra I lead interfaith concerts and weekend retreats in synagogues around the country. I received my ordination as a rabbi from Reb Zalman in 1995. *rabbidavidzaslow.com*

Debra Gordon Zaslow. I was a teller of world folktales until I met Reb Zalman, who was my husband's teacher. I began my journey as a Jewish storyteller in 1988, and have never looked back. Reb Zalman encouraged me along the way and certified me as a *Maggidah* in 2000. I teach storytelling at Southern Oregon

University, and I am the author of the memoir, *Bringing Bubbe Home*, and a CD of Jewish stories, "Return Again." *debrazaslow.com*

Shawn Israel Zevit. I have served since 2013 as lead rabbi at Mishkan Shalom in Philadelphia, Pennsylvania, and have worked for decades with dozens of congregations, organizations, and social justice, artistic, and educational initiatives in the Jewish and larger world. I am cofounder/codirector with Rabbi Marcia Prager of the Davvenen' Leadership Training Institute and serve as the Associate Director for the ALEPH Hashpa'ah (spiritual direction) program. I am a liturgical recording and performing artist and one of the founders of an annual Jewish men's retreat and Menschwork, and author of *Offerings of the Heart: Money and Values in Faith Community*. A graduate of the Reconstructionist Rabbinical College, I also have rabbinic *smicha* from Reb Zalman and from ALEPH as a *Mashpia*. *menschwork.org; dlti.org; aleph.org/ordinations; store.cdbaby.com/Artist/ShawnZevit*

Jeremy Zorn. I met Reb Zalman in the summer of 2011, while living, farming, and learning with the Adamah Fellowship at the Isabella Freedman Jewish Retreat Center in Falls Village, Connecticut. Following this experience, I enrolled in graduate school at Florida State University, where I engaged in research comparing the language of renewal in the work of Reb Zalman and Martin Buber. My next adventure led me to Jerusalem, where I joined Achvat Amim—"Solidarity of Nations"—a wonderful volunteer and educational collective that supports human rights in Israel/Palestine. Currently, I teach middle school and enjoy making music in Orlando, Florida.

INDEX BY AUTHOR

Reb Zalman at a Spiritual Eldering retreat.
Photo by Justin Freed © 1990

GLOSSARY

The terms explained in this glossary are in Hebrew
and/or Yiddish, unless specified as another language.
Transliterations have been made as simple and
compact as possible, and are done by sound and not
specific Hebrew letter correlates. H, kh and ch are
used for gutturals *chaf* and *chet* according to the
preferences of each contributing author.

A

Adonai	Lord
Afikomen	Greek term adopted into Judaism for the ritual of breaking off a half-piece of matzah at the seder and hiding it for children to find at the end
Aish	Fire
Al tevilat gerim	Blessing component for someone immersing in a *mikveh* for conversion
Aliya	Going up to witness and bless the Torah reading; also means the mitzvah of moving to Israel
Allahu akbar	Arabic. God is great
Amei ha-aretz	Talmudic term for those who are unscholarly, uneducated every day folk
Amida	Standing individual prayer at the core of virtually every service
Aron kodesh	Holy ark, a beautiful cabinet where Torah scrolls are kept
Assiya	Physical World, a dimension of divine emanation in Kabbalah, Four Worlds model
Atara	Collar-like area on a *tallit*, prayer shawl, often embroidered with the blessing for donning it
Atzilut	Spiritual World, a dimension of divine emanation in Kabbalah, Four Worlds model
Avinu	Our father, a traditional metaphor for God
Avoda zara	Heresy, worship of non-Jewish gods or idols; can be a metaphor for over attachment to wealth, addictions, etc.
Axé Rabi	Portuguese term for "Power Rabbi" or "More power to you, Rabbi!"

B

Ba'al tefillah	Prayer leader
Ba'al ha-Bracha	Ordination title for one who is masterful at blessing others
Bahira	Effulgence, shining and bright
Banei Ishaq	Sons of Isaac
Banei Yaqub	Sons of Jacob
Baruch ata olam	Bless you, world
Baruch HaShem	Literally "Bless the Name," meaning "May God be blessed" or "Thank You, God"
Beis Hamikdash	Temple that stood in Jerusalem
Beit din	Jewish court
Beit midrash, bes midresh	House of study for Jewish learning
Bereishit	Genesis, first book of the Torah
Beynoni	In between, partially evolved ethically and spiritually
Bima	Stage, also platform where prayers are led and Torah is read
Bina	A *Sefira*, the divine quality of Understanding on the Tree of Life (Kabbalah)
Birkat Hamazon	Grace after meals
Bocharim	Young men
Bracha	Blessing
Bris milah, brit milah	Covenantal circumcision for a boy on the eighth day of life or a male convert
Briya	World of Intellect, a dimension of divine emanation in Kabbalah, Four Worlds model
Bubbe	Grandmother

C

Chabad	Hassidic movement associated with the Lubavitch dynasty. ChaBaD is an

	acronym for *Chochma* (wisdom), *Bina* (Understanding), and *Da'at* (Knowledge)
Chas v'chaleela	Heaven forefend
Chevra	Community of friends, students, colleagues, or those doing good
Chevra kadisha	Burial society
Cholent	Sabbath stew
Cohanim	Biblical priests and their descendants

D

Davenen, davvenen', davening	Yiddish and "Yinglish" for heartfelt prayer
Devarim	Book of Deuteronomy, fifth book of the Torah
Devekut	Spiritual state of cleaving to God
D'var Torah	A teaching, explanation, and interpretation of Torah verses

F

Festschrift	German. Compilation of scholarly articles honoring an individual
Frum	Religious, in an Orthodox sense

G

Gan Eden	Garden of Eden; metaphoric for paradise
Ger tzedek	A term for a person has converted to Judaism; literally, "righteous convert"
Get	Jewish divorce document and process

H

Haftorah	Reading from the Prophets
Hakafot	Circlings of the prayer space holding a Torah
Halachah	Jewish law; literally, "path" or "way"
Hallel	Specific selection of psalms sung on certain holidays
Hamotzi	Blessing over bread, to start a meal
Hasharat hanefesh	Concept of immortality of the soul

HaShem	The name; Biblical name for God that is also used, particularly in *frum* communities, as a respectful way of referring to God in conversation
Hashgacha pratit	Personal providence
Hashpa'ah	Spiritual guidance or spiritual direction
Hassid(im)	Disciples of a Hassidic Rebbe, also a metaphor for zealous follower(s), and may also be used outside of Orthodox contexts for those who study with, or support, a particular Jewish teacher
Hassidut, hassidus	The religious and cultural traditions of the movement that evolved from the life of Yisrael ben Eliezer, the Ba'al Shem Tov, an Eastern European rabbi and teacher (circa 1698-1760), credited with founding the Hassidic movement
Hatafat dam brit	Covenantal ritual of drawing a drop of blood from the penis of males converting to Judaism who was previously medically circumcised
Havdalah	Ritual of blessings over wine, spices, and candle flames for concluding Shabbat and holidays
Haver	Friend
Havurah	Community organized for Jewish prayer and/or study and caring that does not own a building and is most often lay led
Hergish	A feeling
Hesed	A *Sefira*, quality of divine lovingkindness on the Tree (Kabbalah)
Hiddur mitzvah	Making a mitzvah more beautiful for the recipient or participants; literally, "Embroidering a mitzvah"
Hochma	A *Sefira*, quality of divine wisdom of the Tree of Life (Kabbalah)

Huppah	Jewish wedding canopy symbolizing the Jewish home the couple will create together

I

Imahot	Biblical foremothers: Sarah, Rebecca, Rachel, and Leah

J

Jahiliya	Arabic. Into the unknowing

K

Kabbalah	Jewish mysticism
Kabbalat Shabbat	First part of the Friday evening service; welcomes the Sabbath using the metaphor of a bride
Kaddish	Memorial prayer
Kaddish d'Rabbanan	Special version of the Kaddish prayer that honors all teachers
Kadosh	Holy
Kapoteh	Hassidic robe for males
Karpas	Greens for the Passover *seder* plate
Kavanah, kavanot	Spiritual focus (foci) or intention(s)
Kavin	Units of fluid
Kavod hamet	Treating the corpse with respect
Keli	Vessel
Ken	Yes
Keter	The *Sefira* at the "crown," top of the Tree of Life, according to Kabbalah
Ketubah	Jewish marriage contract
Kiddush	Blessing of Sabbath and/or holidays over the wine or grape juice, which symbolizes the Life Force and joy
Kinyan	Symbolic ritual of acquisition done during a Jewish wedding
Kippa	Yarmulke, skullcap, symbol of living consciously in relationship to Source and mitzvot

Kisdeh de chayutah	Signs of life after death
Kishkas, kishkes	Literally, intestines. Inner or gut sense, as in "trust your gut feeling"
Klal Yisrael	All Jewish people everywhere
Koach	Strength
Kol ha-kavod	All honor/respect to you; colloquially, congratulations
Kol yoshvei teyvel	All that dwell on earth
Kosher v'yosher	Fully kosher or proper
Kriat shema al ha-meeta	Prayer practice for bedtime including the *Shema*
Kvetch	Complain
Kvitel	A written personal prayer or request for guidance and blessing

L

Lamed vavnikim	Thirty-six people in every generation for whose sake the world is sustained
Leibn	Heart-friend, dear one

M

Maariv	Evening service
Ma'aseh b'reisheet	Act of creation of the world
Machzor[im]	High Holiday prayer book[s]
Mae de Santo	A priestess of Umbanda, Candomblé, and Quimbanda, the Afro-Brazilian religions
Maidele	Young woman
Malchut	A *Sefira*, divine quality of the Tree of Life that is *Shechinah* releasing/birthing the world that is divinely manifested at all times
Mashiach, meshiach	Messiah
Mashpia('ah)	Ordination title for a spiritual director or guide
Megillat Rut	Book of Ruth
Meshugga	Crazy
Midrash	Commentary in the form of a story

Mikveh	Ritual bath in natural waters
Mincha	Afternoon prayer service
Minyan	Quorum of ten for prayer; colloquial for one's prayer or personal community
Mishebeirach	A personal blessing for physical, emotional, or spiritual healing
Mishkan	Tabernacle
Mishpacha	Family; as a metaphor, affinity group, or family of preference
Mitnagdim	Opponents to the Hassidim
Modeh[ah] Ani	Gratitude prayer
Moshe Rabeinu	Moses, our teacher
Musaf	Additional prayer service after the morning service on Shabbat and Holidays
Musmach[im]	Ordinee[s]
Mussar	Ethical and character development movement initiated by Rabbi Israel Salanter

N

Nefesh	A single soul
Neilah	The concluding service of Yom Kippur
Neshama	The soul within you
Nevi'im	Prophets within the Jewish Biblical canon
Niddah	Term for one who is menstruating or who has menstruated and not yet gone to mikveh (ritual immersion)
Niggun	Wordless melody
Nosh	Snack
Nu	So?

O

Olam	World or eternity
Olam ha-t'chi'ya	Resurrected world

P

P'nimiyut haTorah	Interpretation that reveals inner, mystical, and redemptive meanings of a verse or section of Torah
Parsha, parshiot	Torah portion(s)
Pareve	Neither dairy nor meat
Pasuk, p'sukim	Verse(s)
Peckel	Package; colloquial for burden
Pri ha-aretz	Tree fruits
Rachel imeynu	Rachel, our mother (one of the four Biblical matriarchs)

R

Rasuliyat	Arabic. Prophethood
Ribono shel Olam, Riboino Sheleilem	Literally, "Master of the Universe." A name for God.
Ro-eh v'eino ro'eh	Seeing while not being seen
Rosh Chodesh	Monthly new moon celebration
Rosh Yeshiva	Head of a yeshiva

S

Sabba	Grandfather
Savta	Grandmother
Salaam alaihu	Arabic. Peace be upon him
Sefer, sefarim	Book(s), in some contexts sacred texts
Sefira, sefirot	Quality(ies)/divine emanations that comprise the Tree of Life (Kabbalah)
Selah	Rest note for the Levitical choirs
Seudah Shlishit	Third Sabbath meal
Shabbat	Sabbath
Shabbaton	A full Sabbath gathering for prayer, study, and community-making
Shabbos	Shabbat, Sabbath
Shabbosdik	In a Shabbos mode or manner
Shacharit, Shachris	Morning prayer service

Shaddai	One of the Hebrew names for God, derived from the Hebrew root for breasts, and mountains
Shaliach	Emissary
Shalosh Seudos	Third meal of Shabbat, also *Seudah Shlishit*
Shamash, shames	A helper, and on the menorah, the ninth candle or flame which is used to light the others
Shana	Year
Shariyat	Arabic. Muslim code of religious law
Shechinah, Shekhinah	Presence of God; for some Divine Mother
Sheva Brachot	Seven Blessings recited during a Jewish wedding ceremony
Shir HaShirim	Song of Songs
Shir El	Song of God
Shiur(im)	A learning session(s)
Shiva	Initial week of mourning practices after the death of a first degree relative
Shlichut	Mission
Shloshim	Thirtieth day memorial ritual after burial
Shmira	Watching over a body until the funeral
Shmita	Biblical commandment to leave fields fallow on a seven- year cycle
Shoah	Holocaust
Shochet	One trained in Kosher slaughter ritual methods for animals and birds
Shofar	Ram's horn blown for New Moon and on High Holidays
Shtiebel(e)	Small prayer space
Shtreimel	Large fur-trimmed Hassidic hat
Shul	Synagogue
Shulchan Aruch	1565 codification of Jewish Law
Siddur(im)	Prayer book(s)
Smicha	Ordination ceremony or certificate
Sofer	Scribe

T

Tahara	State of being ritually pure for persons and objects
Tallit, tallis, talleisim, tallitot	Prayer shawl(s)
Talmid(im)	Student(s)
Talmidei chachamim	Extremely learned Talmud scholars
Talmud Torah	Hebrew School
Tamar	Biblical daughter-in-law of Judah; the fruit that is a date, or date palm tree
Tannaitic	From the era of the Tannaim, rabbinic scholars of the Mishna (200 CE)
Tanya	A collection of books to guide Jewish spiritual practice written by Shneur Zalman of Liadi, first published under this title in 1796
Tariqat	Arabic. Sufi path of spiritual learning
Tawhid	Arabic. The knowledge of the oneness of God
Tefillah, tefillot	Prayer(s)
Tefillin	Wearable prayer boxes containing Biblical verses; phylacteries
Tehillim	Psalms
Tekiah gedolah	Final long blast of shofar
Teshuva	A process of admitting wrong speech or wrong action—to self, another, the natural world, or God/Source—and renewing trust through a return to ethical/mitzvah-centered living
Tevila	Immersion
Tiferet	A *Sefira*, quality of divinely manifested compassion and beauty on the Tree of Life (Kabbalah)
Tikkun(im)	Repair(s)

Tikkun klali	Reb Nachman's prescription of ten psalms to study for complete renewal
Tikkun Leyl Shavuot	All night study to enhance ability to "stand at Sinai" and receive Torah on Shavuot
Tikkun olam	Principle of repairing and healing the world from inherent and subsequent problems
Tree of Life	A diagram of the flow of divine emanation that is eternally manifesting creation (Kabbalah)
Trope	Musical notation symbol symbols for chanting sacred texts
Tzadeket, tzaddik	Ethically and spiritually developed person
Tza'ra'at	Biblical term for traumatic stress manifested by skin symptoms; derived from Prophet Miriam's distress
Tzedaka	Giving money for charitable purposes
Tzitzit	Knotted fringes on a *tallit*; reminder of the commandments
Tzuris	Trouble, as in, "beset by troubles"

U

Upshirin	Ritual of giving a first haircut to a three-year-old boy

Y

Yah	God, as in "*Hallelu Yah*—praise God"
Yahrtzeit	Anniversary of a death
Yayin	Wine
Yedid Nefesh	"Dearest Soul," a mystical hymn
Yechidut, yechidus	Session of spiritual guidance; also, solitary prayer
Yesh me'ayin	Creation as something from no-thing (Kabbalah)
Yesod	A *Sefira*, quality of Foundation on the Tree of Life (Kabbalah)

Yetzer ha-ra	Evil inclination; concept found in Rabbinic Period and Mussar
Yetzira	World of Formation, a dimension of divine emanation, Four Worlds Model (Kabbalah)
Yiddin	Jews
Yiddishkeit	All things Jewish
Yisrael, Yisroel	Jewish people, country, land of Israel

Z

Zayde	Grandfather
Zikr	Arabic. Sufi-originated practice of repetitive movement with chanting of a verse or names of God

If you have new vignettes about
Reb Zalman for possible inclusion
in the next edition,
please see Calls for Submissions
at ReclaimingJudaism.org

Reb Zalman's archives and full bibliography
are available through the
Post-Holocaust American Judaism Collections
at the University of Colorado, Boulder

94938629R00152

Made in the USA
Middletown, DE
23 October 2018